Hiding With The Hooligans

By

Dave Radford

First published 2012 by Fast-Print Publishing of Peterborough, England.

www.fast-print.net/store.php

HIDING WITH THE HOOLIGANS
Copyright © Dave Radford 2012
ISBN: 978-178035-418-7

Cover design by Magnus Shaw at MAGNESIUM
Cover photography © Dave Radford at Bathtub Photography
Inner Photography © and courtesy of Alan Roe

Unfortunately, while every effort has been made to identify the photographer
responsible for taking the picture of the Sheffield Wednesday game in '77/'78,
I have so far been unable to do this."

An environmentally friendly book printed and bound in England by
www.printondemand-worldwide.com

Mixed Sources
Product group from well-managed
forests, and other controlled sources
www.fsc.org Cert no. TT-COC-002641
FSC © 1996 Forest Stewardship Council

PEFC Certified
This product is
from sustainably
managed forests
and controlled
sources
PEFC www.pefc.org
PEFC/16-33-415

This book is made entirely of chain-of-custody materials

Dedicated To:

My Father
Bill Radford – 1928 to 1996
who issued the immortal line,
"Eeeeeeeeee, Saltergate, 'ome o' good football!"

and

My Mother
June Radford – 1931 to 2008
who started the ball rolling by saying,
"Bill! Take him to a football match. I don't want him ending up like him next door!"

Thanks Folks!

As with anything, there are thousands of people I need to thank for getting this thing to the stage it's at. Me, for a start - I had to write the bloody thing! However, I would like to thank just a few people, so eyes down for a full house. Craig Thomas should begin proceedings – for a start he gave me bags of encouragement and it was he who thought the articles would be popular in the first place – so, if you're unhappy, blame him! I also couldn't have done this, or it would have been much harder, without recourse to Stuart Basson's *'Official History of Chesterfield FC.'* Top marks must also go to all round top cockney diamond geezer Richard Copcutt for being such an absolute gem and making some of the more miserable Chesterfield matches somewhat enjoyable. Thanks also to Jan Hutchings and Sandra Wood who typed out some of the original articles from the fanzines and into a more manageable system. Chris Hutchings for some excellent blurb. Denny for giving me regular kicks up the 'arris to get this finished. Alan Roe for managing to break up the prose with some excellent pictures. Pete Whiteley for sending through some great pictures which I sadly couldn't use, but thanks for trying Pete! Magnus Shaw for cover design, creativity and website. Tracey Townend for press releases and stuff. *Chesterfield Relate* for offering me a nice warm office in which to write, in exchange for a few hours of reception cover – ta, Lynn! My mentor and surrogate mother Elsie Bolton and my very dear friend Jeannie Hopper who has been, throughout my life, inspiring – a few words here will never convey my real gratitude. All my family: Jen, Chris, John et al. Most of all, thanks to *Chesterfield FC* and their supporters, without whom none of this would have been possible.

My final heartfelt dedication must go to the beautiful Keren Tregidgo for proof-reading the early part of the book (and falling asleep. Does wonders for your confidence that!). Keren was plagued by life and, sadly, walked away from it in March 2012. On that day a light in me went out. I will miss her more than anyone will ever know and now I can never tell her.

I am sure there are lots and lots of people I have missed, and if I have and you think you should have been mentioned...... Eeeeeeee, life's a bitch, ain't it?

How It All Began

This book, originally called *The Radfordgate Tapes*, starting life as an outstanding regular feature within the cut and pasted pages of the Chesterfield fanzine, *The Crooked Spireite*, is in danger of immortalising northern town football in the 1970s and 80s. It's also in danger of being misread as a work of fiction from a man who watched too much Monty Python and Father Ted. Hooligans of the time were supposed to be vicious, cynical thugs, capable of callous crimes. Here, Dave Radford has captured in a series of vivid literary snapshots a slice of social history that hasn't yet been forgotten because no-one bothered to preserve it in the first place. This is the story of a large group of young men expressing themselves in ways their grandparents were doubtless ashamed of, all in the cause of football supporting. To sum up their behaviour is hard: they went nuts so we wouldn't have to? They were very, very naughty so we could stay safely tucked up on Saturday winter afternoons watching Grandstand?

The pleasure is in the detail, and also in the insane, yet at the same time banal truth of hooliganism in the days of Wilson, Heath and Thatcher. The silliness of bad boy behaviour is here (where usually it's never spotted), and the swaying of its pendulum between pointlessness and deep meaning. There is a historical reality in this book that not even the most skilled sociologist could ever capture. This really was the 1970s and this was Britain. What this rule and law breaking says about those times is for us to figure out. Did they occur as an outcrop of the three-day week? A function of life chances for blokes where still little more than the factory floor and the dole queue beckoned? Is it down to remarkably unsophisticated working class parenting? With *Hiding With The Hooligans* in your hands you can have a very deep think or you can just sit back and enjoy (or better still, both). Whatever, thanks are sincerely worth conveying to Mr. Radford for being there and for being – almost – one of them.

Craig Thomas

Some Kind Of 'Foreword' Pass

As I was browsing through *Waterstone's* the other day, trying my best to make use of a £10 voucher and their '3 for the price of 2' offer, I stopped to glance idly at the sports section. It's not often I do this as the last thing I want to read is some drivel written by some overpaid, pampered, Premier League plonker – and, let's face it, that's all the sporting section usually contains. But on this day I stumbled across a book by TV presenter Adrian Chiles about his sentence as a West Bromwich Albion fan. As I normally do with books that elbow their way on to my 'Oh, I might like this' list, I read the opening pages and gradually came over all unnecessary, like some 50 year old father caught playing air guitar to *'Won't Get Fooled Again'* by his 20-year-old son.

I didn't really need to read on; in some ways I didn't want to read on because the truths inlaid in those pages might have been a little too close to home, and I must admit I had a fair idea of what Mr Chiles might be driving at. You see, I have looked, like many others, I assume, at my Chesterfield-supporting addiction and, like someone taking a lung-full of nicotine or a snort of cocaine, convinced myself that I could stop whenever I wanted. Really, I could. Easily. I've even said, *"I'm never going again!"* at the end of another disastrous season and looked at people's shocked expressions, and actually thought, at the time, that I wouldn't. While this might seem a fairly reasonable comment to make most of the time, where football is concerned it's just a knee-jerk reaction to make yourself feel good, to make it seem as if you have some control over this beast. But, come the following season, no doubt like me you'll be queuing with everyone else for that season ticket (okay, so queuing might be pushing it a bit at Chesterfield) and be filled with as much hope as one can possibly muster and, trust me, after 45 years this isn't really a great deal.

With these thoughts streaming through my head I pushed Adrian's book back onto the shelf, only to dislodge the book next to it onto my foot. I cursed, thinking that perhaps Wayne Rooney was getting his own back on me for saying he was a pampered plonker but, as I turned the book over in my hands, I noticed that it was a book on football violence.

As I pushed the other sports books aside, I found more of them. There were lots. In fact, it appeared as if every knuckle-dragging hooligan with enough brain cells to self-tattoo 'HATE' across his fingers had written a book about how his firm had terrorised most of the country during the 70's and 80's – the dark years when football violence roamed the terraces like some predatory animal, hungry for blood. They all seemed to be saying the same thing; they were all very boastful, perhaps with every right, but they did start me thinking.

Why would people want to go out on a Saturday afternoon and beat up a set of total strangers just because they happened to support a different team? And, why football? Why was that the perfect sporting vehicle for such lunacy? Perhaps it's because football evokes such powerful emotions in people. Admittedly, for most of us, they aren't necessarily violent emotions but the question remains: Why? What happens in our lives to make football so all-consuming? Perhaps it's some massive character flaw, some craving that has yet to be satiated. I will never know, and never answer it in this book, because this is just my tale: the story of the crazy things I saw during football's worst nightmare.

Hiding With The Hooligans
(or Diary of a Hooligan Hanger-on)

It was at 7.20am on Sunday, July 7th, 1957 that my mother gave birth to her first and eldest son: me. As with my sister before me, I was born at home and, apparently, I followed hard on the heels of an exceptionally violent thunderstorm during the night which shook my mother's bedroom. My mother has taken great delight in reminding me that I have been, "Nowt but trouble ever since."

The family home, then, was a Coal Board house in Stonebroom, a small mining village in the north east of Derbyshire. My father was a miner at Morton Colliery, while my mother worked the check-out of the Fine Fare supermarket in Alfreton. I suppose, in some ways, we were the archetypal working-class family. We ate coal, wore our best rags on a Sunday to church and wiped our noses on our sleeves. You know the sort of thing: the usual story from that historical period.

I think it's fair to say that my mum and dad expected nothing more from me than to make them proud, chest-puffed-out parents, which is something I've managed to avoid doing with spectacular ease. I suppose I could also add that they were relatively directionless when it came to my own career aspirations because, as far as my father was concerned, anything I did that didn't include following him down the pit would have been fine. He would probably have been ecstatic if I'd coupled 'anything' with cultivating prize-winning chrysanthemums. As I say, anything, as long as I didn't follow him down the pit, and that really was always the bottom line.

Mine was a very ordinary childhood. I played football on the street, had my best Dinky cars taken from me on the threat of a punching from Jimmy Clarke across the road (wonder if he's still got them?), and had my first sexual experience with the girl next door. It wasn't really a sexual experience – well, I was only 7 – but I did get to feel her developing bosom (she was my first older woman) as we played around under a mountain of coats in her back garden.

The Bennetts were our next-door neighbours throughout my nine years at Stonebroom. They were a big family consisting of five girls and one boy. They weren't an odd family but they were incredibly intense. I always felt sorry for Mr Bennett, Jack, who wore the expression of a man who'd had fun just six times in his life and regretted every minute of it. Joyce, his wife, was a woman of leisure – or, at least, she seemed to be. Ian was the eldest of the Bennett clan; a tall, lanky, bespectacled youth who had all the charm and charisma of a wet Sunday in Rhyl, and although he never actually threatened me, not like Jimmy Clarke at any rate, I was slightly afraid of him and I didn't particularly like him. So, it may come as something of a surprise to find that Ian was to play a huge part in my all-consuming passion with football and all things Chesterfield.

One of my earliest memories is standing just outside the kitchen door and listening to my mother issuing instructions to my dad. I remember the phrase so well that she might only have spoken it yesterday: "Take him to a football match or something. I don't want him ending up like him next door." 'Him next door' was, of course, Ian Bennett. My mother always thought him a slightly effeminate boy and, although some years older than me, she didn't want him turning out to be my role model. For some reason, my mother thought that taking me to a football match would plant my feet quite firmly in the heterosexual rose bed. Perhaps if she had known of my secret pre-pubescent fumblings of one of the Bennett women, then things might have turned out differently; but she didn't and the deciding moment in my football upbringing had been uttered. If my mother had known the effect that simple phrase was to have on my life, she might well have been happier had she insisted my father take me to the dogs. In retrospect, she probably thinks that is exactly where I've ended up.

The idea of me going to a football match had probably been discussed at length; not with me, of course – that would have been too much to ask for. But I had no real concept of football outside of playing it on the street and watching it on *Match of the Day*. However, this didn't stop my dad from whisking me off one dreary Saturday afternoon to watch non-league Alfreton Town.

I have absolutely no idea who Alfreton played or, indeed, what the score was that day; and I only vaguely remember the ground, surrounded by trees, muddy and pretty much empty. But I could hear the players talking to each other and the supporters holding conversations with the players as they passed. It was fun: people laughed a lot, so I guess it must have been. But, in my heart of hearts, I can't remember thinking that I'd like to go back for more. It didn't exactly set the pulse racing. I'm not laying the blame at Alfreton Town's door. I am sure it was all very good; it just wasn't for me – not at 7 years of age anyway.

To be fair to Alfreton, I remember just as little about my first visit to Saltergate; yet for some inexplicable reason this was a different experience altogether. I remember climbing aboard my dad's Honda 50 and being despatched there on that fateful day. Who played? Who scored? Who won? Who cared? This was the start of an all-consuming passion that very soon gripped me and has held me fast ever since. I doubt that I watched much of the football. In fact, I'm sure I spent the majority of the time watching the other spectators. I cheered when they cheered, laughed without understanding the jokes and loved every strange and wonderful minute of it.

Perhaps the most vivid memories from my first season as a Spireite can be whittled down to wet motorbike rides up the A61. Along the way were landmarks I associated with the journey. From Stonebroom we would travel through Morton, turn right onto the A61, race through Clay Cross and, then, when we passed *The Royal Oak* pub in Tupton, I knew we were almost there. Similarly, on the homeward journey, I always looked out for *The Royal Oak* landmark, knowing that, once we had passed it, we were as good as home. Which is madness really: Tupton may be 3½ miles from Chesterfield but it must be a good 7 miles from Stonebroom. I was totally oblivious then of how important this landmark would prove to be in future years and the changes it would make to my Chesterfield supporting habits.

I was turning into a fan. Not just an armchair fan like so many of my peers but an actual fan – and I was proud of it. To my knowledge, I was the only boy on our street that went to a football match on a regular basis. Every week some wag at the ground would mention the fact that I needed an orange box to stand on. Everyone would laugh and every week my dad would promise to make something we could bring with us – but he never did get round to it.

But then it happened, an event so awful it could have stopped my Chesterfield-supporting habit while still in its infancy; but, instead, it ended up determining my footballing future. While working a morning shift, my dad suffered a crushed ankle and broken leg in a bad pit accident. A coal wagon broke free and rolled back, pinning him to the wall. It could have been much worse, I suppose; it could have happened in the winter. However, it happened in the summer and the fact that my dad couldn't ride his motorbike meant very little. If it had been the football season, I don't know what I would have done. But it did cut short my dad's days as a miner. He was classed as unfit to go back down the pit and was offered light duties. I've no idea what 'light duties' meant except that he wasn't allowed underground and the money was a lot less – certainly nowhere near enough to keep a family of four, especially when one of them was forever tugging at his sleeve and asking when they were going to the football again. Because of that, he knew he had to look for other work.

At weekends my mother was working behind the bar of the *Duke of Wellington* at Shirland and the landlord there, Charlie, persuaded my dad to take a pub. He put in a good word for us with the *Home Ales Brewery* (sadly, no longer in existence) and we took over, yes you've guessed it, *The Royal Oak* at Tupton. I was now just 3½ miles from my favourite football team. I don't care what anyone says, broken legs aren't all bad – especially when they happen to someone else!

Once we were settled in the pub, my dad started selling some sort of lottery ticket for the club, behind the bar. For doing this, he received a couple of complimentary season tickets for the Cross Street wing stand, and jokes about the orange box were no longer relevant. I have no idea why seated areas are called 'stands;' it made no sense when I was 9 and makes even less now I'm 54. I did ask but the answer never came. At the time, I thought it was because my dad was too engrossed in the proceedings on the pitch. I think it's closer to the truth, though, to say that he didn't know either but didn't like to let on. What I did know was that at the age of 10 I was a one-club man, having by now firmly nailed my colours and allegiance to the mast of Chesterfield Football Club.

I did get to sample the so-called delights of First Division football (nowadays repackaged and renamed 'Premier League') on two occasions quite early into my passion, both at Hillsborough. The first time was to see Sheffield Wednesday take on the might of Manchester United who, at that time, boasted a powerful side equipped with footballers like Charlton, Best and Law, players I usually associated only with *Match of the Day*. If I had actually seen the game, well, who knows, my head could well have been turned by such talent; but so huge was the attendance that night that I saw very little indeed. A Manchester United supporter lifted me above his head and asked for a commentary but I didn't know enough about the teams in question, became heavy and was eventually plonked back down on the ground. My dad fared even worse: he saw nothing of the first half at all. At half-time he managed to negotiate a little space so he could jump up and see the pitch. But you can hardly spend the whole of the second half pogo-ing, so he made an executive decision, grabbed my hand and we trooped out to sample the best that Owlerton could offer in the way of fish and chips. It was fine by me. Two months later I was back again, watching Wednesday entertain Leicester City. I was not sufficiently moved to make a habit of it. A couple of years later, I skived a day off school to watch Santos play there but that was so I could say I had seen Pele. The next time I would darken their doors would be to watch my own dearly beloved Chesterfield.

As I've said, by the age of 10 I was verging on fanatical; I just couldn't get enough of Chesterfield FC. I knew the players and the people around me at the match and I was also beginning to understand the jokes. Each Saturday, as we walked up towards the ground, along Saltergate and past the Stalinesque statues outside the NUM building, my dad, on gaining sight of the stand roof, would look down at me and say, "Eeeee, Saltergate, 'ome o' good football." I believed him. I echoed his sentiments because even at the ripe old age of 10 I knew he wasn't speaking literally. I knew he meant Saltergate was home – the place for us. Over the years I have argued with my father about everything: politics; religion; who should open the batting for England. The list is endless – but at the end of any argument I'm sure Saltergate was, for both of us, the home of football.

Two years later, I was an old stager, a seasoned veteran with a season ticket in the Cross Street wing stand, and it was about this time that my sister decided she wanted in on the act. I hadn't realised that my sister, Jennifer, had been in any way envious of me nipping off to the football of a Saturday. It had never crossed my mind that she might like to go, too. But one day she asked if she could, was given the green light and it's been the same for her ever since. For my dad this was a blessing in disguise as he was beginning to tire of my footballing demands and so he quickly shelled out for season tickets for both of us and handed over my match day responsibility to my sister. He was always a Chesterfield supporter – just never quite as animated or as passionate as his son. In order for my sister and I to be nearer to the singing on the Kop end of the ground, my sister and I opted for tickets in the Saltergate wing stand because, by now, we were both punching the air in celebration of goals and shouting lightweight abuse at the opposition and short-sighted referees. It was good to be away from the disapproving looks my dad used to give me when I did this. We were devastated in defeat, ecstatic in victory and, together, shared a wonderful love. We did the whole number: autograph hunting, scrapbook making, programme-saving – there were no limits.

But as my sister got older, juggling both football and boyfriends became a precarious pastime. I waited in the wing stand for something to give. Boyfriends came and went with monotonous regularity, matched only by Chesterfield's performance on the pitch.

I can't say that I was particularly interested in whom my sister was or wasn't seeing but there have been times when the attentions of my sister's suitors have been particularly useful. I did, for example, become close friends with a lad called Dave Turner. Now, I liked Dave. He was a Sheffield United fan and it's not often I utter the words 'like' and 'Sheffield United' in the same sentence, I can tell you. But I was young, 12 or 13. My sister was just turning 18 and Dave Turner fancied her. I know he did, he told me. I also assumed that was why he spent so much time playing football with me, thrashing me at *Subbuteo* or taking me to Bramall Lane to watch his heroes. Presumably, Dave was working on the hopelessly inept philosophy that runs, *'The way to a girl's heart is through her younger brother.'* Not, perhaps, a philosophical piece of reasoning you might have come across all that often, which could have something to do with the fact that it's complete and utter rubbish.

As I've said, I liked Dave despite his Sheffield United shortcomings and, in retrospect, I wouldn't have minded one bit if he and my sister had gone on to make a happy couple. At the time, however, I gave all that very little thought. I just tagged along and sampled the delights of Alan Woodward, Tony Currie, Geoff Salmons and Len Badger; although, I have to say, I enjoyed the latter two much more when they moved the few miles down the road to Chesterfield and pulled on a blue shirt.

I probably spent a season going to watch Sheffield United – when Chesterfield were away, of course – and the thing I enjoyed most was the game of ten-pin bowling we always had before the game. That, perhaps, says more than all the anti-Sheff United ramblings I can come up with. But, despite Dave's enthusiastic encouragement, despite being just five seconds away from winning the Golden Goal[1] (if only Bill Dearden could have waited five more seconds!), despite the lure of ten-pin bowling, my head would not be turned. I was, even at that age, blue right through.

As for Dave Turner, well, perhaps he should have invited my sister along to Bramall Lane instead of me because, while he was trying to attract her attention through me, she was out cultivating relationships in other areas. I thought most of them were disastrous and, although he played a very small part in the equation, I cannot let this piece pass without mentioning John Plater – the bastard!

John Plater was the brother of my once best mate Colin and to this day I swear he only went out with my sister because, as they sat in the front room, my mother would walk through from the pub and keep him well supplied with free pints of Home Ales' best. I never really realised, until I started writing this, what a draw my sister must have been. Think about it: attractive, 18 years old, single, football fan, living in a pub. That must be as close to heaven as any bloke from the 1970's is going to get. The only reason I mention John Plater here is because the swine thumped me in the stomach one evening and, while I choked and sprottled on the hearth carpet, the pair of them sat back and watched me. There is a good chance that I was being a pain in the arse, because I'm pretty sure I could be (I was 13, you show me a 13-year-old that isn't), but I don't think I deserved a punching whatever I was doing, especially as he was in my house with a free pint in his hand. You could say this was my first introduction to mindless violence – and the tosser wasn't even a football fan! Fortunately, it didn't last long: my sister dumped him and was left the proud owner of his *'Sgt Pepper's Lonely Hearts Club Band'* LP. What a swap! The girl 'did good' and hopefully broke his heart.

Eventually, though, my sister settled for a sensible young man who had a leaning towards the club himself. I liked him: he had a car... Now I had a regular lift to away games.

---

[1] The 'Golden Goal' was a popular money-making scheme run by clubs at that time: you bought a ticket with a time on it and if the first goal coincided with the time on your ticket, you won a sum of money – probably about £20. I don't think it was ever used at Saltergate as the time would have read, "2 weeks on Tuesday!"

After 4 years in *The Royal Oak*, my dad decided he'd had enough of being a landlord and my mother had given birth to yet another football fan, so we quit the pub and moved to the semi-detached wonderland of middle-class Wingerworth. Even though the free pints of Home Ales Best had dried up, my sister's boyfriend remained loyal and, I can safely say, he was given the seal of approval – by me, at least.

But marriage must do something to you. After the initial burst of different away grounds they began, tediously, to choose the matches they would attend rather than storm along to every one. In fairness to my sister, I'm sure she missed the thrill of it all – in fact, I know she missed the thrill of it all – and I suppose paying a mortgage and a gas bill can't be half as much fun as screaming at crap refs and cheering like mad when Town scored.

My younger brother, Chris, had withstood the Chesterfield bombardment for some time but I was worried. I could see that peer pressure would eventually lead him to supporting one of the so-called 'big' clubs, so I seized the nettle and invited him to join me in dipping his damp toes into the electric atmosphere of, rather ironically, perhaps, Chesterfield away at Sheffield United on a Tuesday night – via special train, of course. I can still remember my mother's anxious face as we disappeared up the road. Football violence was rife at this time and while I had never been involved in anything remotely resembling hooliganism this was a local derby and even my mother, in all her footballing innocence, knew what that meant.

As we got off the train at Sheffield, the voices of around 1,000 Chesterfield fans were already joined as one. Stations provide excellent acoustics and I looked at my brother and he was smiling and singing before me. I knew from the glint in his eye that he was hooked and I had him. He had flirted briefly with Chesterfield, been to a couple of games without making comment and he thought he could handle it – but this was his biggest trip so far. His casual, small time affair was about to turn into his biggest romance, too.

My sister, by now, had given up the beautiful game in favour of childbirth. Not satisfied with one, however, she decided on a replay and has only just fully rediscovered Chesterfield FC as she educates her son (in particular) on the finer points of total commitment to football. Her daughter will be next, although, at the moment, she wants to be an archaeologist (many would argue she can see all the relics she needs to by watching Chesterfield) which is slightly disconcerting. But how lucky they both are to have two mad uncles to provide them with badges and scarves and any amount of paraphernalia.

As I have said, I have seen them all, from Bobby Charlton to Pele, but no matter how great the name, how wonderful the stadium, I am in love with Chesterfield Football Club and attached to it by an invisible umbilical cord. I have missed friends' weddings and parties, and come up with the most elaborate excuses imaginable, all because Chesterfield were playing. I remember missing the wedding of one of my close-ish friends because we were engaged in a friendly at home to Huddersfield, and as the bus I was travelling on passed the church he was getting married in, I bobbed down behind the level of the window so no one would see me. It would have been much easier to have simply gone to the wedding!

I have travelled thousands of miles and spent what must now be a small fortune on watching Chesterfield. I have been chased round cities, towns and motorway service station car parks. I have had my life threatened and my face ever so slightly damaged. But then, they do say love hurts.

It's difficult to put into words what it all actually means. This drug which sees me laughing one week, long face the next, who am I to explain it? My long-suffering parents were well aware of my Saturday moods. If we lost, then they disappeared upstairs, knowing rational conversation was impossible. This is not now the problem it used to be but I'm still hard work after defeat.

A few years ago, I was watching the Sunday highlights programme on my girlfriend's TV. Chesterfield had snatched an important victory in the final minute at Scunthorpe the previous day and as I watched the goal I noticed myself in the crowd, captured on national television for all to see. It was a strange experience: I didn't look like I knew I felt at the time. As you can imagine, a last minute goal is a wonderfully happy and jubilant affair, especially if it gives you a victory, but there was such an intensity to my expression that it silenced me. My girlfriend, who was watching the highlights with me, said I thought more of Chesterfield FC than I did of her. She said I was an embarrassment – but what did she know? What I felt for Town reached a depth of emotion she had never experienced or encompassed. Well, not from me, at least. To my now ex-girlfriend, this was just a game but, of course, she couldn't have been further from the truth.

So that was how I became a Spireite. Nothing miraculous really: just a few events which culminated in me following a football team from a lower league. I'm not unique, far from it – there are thousands more like me up and down the country who, week after week, are forced to listen to the bleating of the pampered in the Premier League. No, I'm certainly not unique.

Perhaps what is interesting – to me, at any rate – is where, when and how I became aware of football violence. If I'm being totally honest, I'd have to say that I haven't got the foggiest idea. My earliest recollection of being uncomfortable with a particular situation was during the 1971/72 season. We were living at *The Royal Oak* public house in Tupton, and Chesterfield were due to play Aston Villa, recently relegated to Division 3 (League 1 in the latest money) in the Football League Cup. I had my ticket and was excited by the prospect of watching my team play a side like Villa. After school, I sat on the wall outside the pub watching the stream of claret and blue coaches go past and waving my blue and white scarf at the supporters inside. Most of them, it has to be said, gave a cheery wave to the young, naive 14-year-old who didn't know any better, but one coach slowed as it approached the roundabout and all I could see were 50 slavering faces pressed against the window. They gesticulated, cursed and were basically not very cheery at all. I stopped waving my scarf and watched in disbelief as they went past. On the back seat, one lad was proudly showing off his knife to me through the window. At that moment, I think I would have readily given up my ticket for the wing stand. Instead, as there were no takers, I just went back inside and pretended to be excited about the game but all the time worried that I might bump into the lad with the knife again. I didn't – he was probably busy showing it to other Chesterfield fans – and we lost a good game 2–3 in front of a crowd of 13,572 supporters.

There was a lot of trouble that night. In fact, I don't think I have ever seen the Chesterfield Kop taken in quite such a manner. Later on that season, Aston Villa came again and beat us 4–0 in the league in front of 12,510. They were as good as promoted, as good as champions really and, once again, their travelling support made it a very difficult night for everyone boasting a blue and white Chesterfield scarf. However, Villa were one-offs – they didn't come around that often in our division – but just to give you some idea of how huge their following was, when we played at Villa Park on the penultimate game of the season, the attendance was a massive 45,714. Our gates were good –between 8 and 10,000 for every home game – but *that* was silly.

I remember very little about the following season, but come the 1973/74 season I was working, had money in my pocket and was eager to watch the Blues away from Saltergate – and with that year being relatively successful, it made it all the more enticing.

As It Was In The Beginning...

Despite being a never-miss-a-home-match man, I never truly took up being on the road with Chesterfield in earnest until the 1973/74 season. I was 17 and had been working for the last two years. I did occasionally grace away grounds with my presence before this but I usually travelled in the all-too-safe company of my dad, or my sister and her boyfriend, and usually in the relaxed atmosphere of a car. Even then, however, there were moments that led me to believe that all was not well on the terraces. Perhaps my earliest recollection of any disturbance came as early as the 1970/71 season – November 10th, 1970 to be exact – when my dad decided to take me and a friend of mine, Chris Malton, to the midweek fixture at Doncaster. He paid for us all to sit in the stand and we watched Town ease to a 2–1 victory. During the game, there was a running battle around the ground as Chesterfield hoodlums chased Donny supporters. I was somewhat disturbed by what was happening, when Chris Malton turned to me and said, "I wish we were down there with them, don't you?"

I smiled a smile that was supposed to convey something like, *"Of course, Chris, I like nothing better than getting my head broken. What a bummer my dad is such a Tory and made us sit down."* But it probably expressed what I was actually thinking: *"Are you fuckin' mad! They're fighting, you know – that means pain, physical pain!"*

That's something I have to say I have never been very keen on. I should have expected nothing else from the boy Malton: he was well-known for his short temper and right hook – something I had the dubious benefit of feeling one day when he smacked me in the mouth for disallowing a goal that he scored during a game of 'Wembley' on the playing fields. I was the goalkeeper and the keeper was always the ref in 'Wembley,' and I have to say I never disallowed another one of his goals. Fortunately, though, my dad *was* a Tory. And, also fortunately, I left with nothing more than a cold backside from the hard Doncaster seating.

My next encounter with violence came just a few weeks later when thousands of Chesterfield supporters descended on Millmoor for the Boxing Day fixture. A large crowd of over 14,000 swelled the Rotherham terraces. I travelled to the match with my sister (Jennifer) and her boyfriend (John) and felt nothing but safe all the way through. After the game, which we won comfortably 2–1, thousands of Spireites spilled haphazardly onto the pitch, imbued with a sense of celebration more than anything malicious, and there was a general feeling of pure Christmas spirit. I also remember – rather vividly, as it happens – a Chesterfield supporter running onto the pitch, snatching the corner flag out of the ground and hurling it, javelin-like, among the departing Rotherham fans. I also have a very clear and comical memory of a Rotherham fan being carried out on a stretcher with the corner flag sticking bolt upright from his chest. I hasten to add that the latter is only a comical memory because I'm more than positive that I never actually witnessed such an event. It was merely the thought process of a busy 13-year-old mind. The 'what ifs' that surged through my mind were always very quickly answered by a stream of possible scenarios – most of which wouldn't have been out of place in a Spike Milligan show.

However, after that brief dalliance with the comic possibilities, I was confronted with the ugly reality of football hooliganism the following season. It was January 1972 and we had drawn Stoke City in the third round of the FA Cup – a glamour tie and no mistake. I was sure I would be there, convinced that my dad would not miss the chance to see his current Town hero, Kevin Randall, against his former one, Gordon Banks. I was convinced that, for all his gathering lack of interest over the last few seasons, he was sure to want to go to this one. But, no! Disaster struck just seven days before the game when he finally gave in to my pestering with a resounding, "No! I don't have time."

Didn't have time? Didn't have time!? This was the FA Cup! It was Stoke! It was Gordon Banks! For God's sake, man, make time! These were the things running through my head, all of which I was too young and too scared to say. I was completely distraught. How could this be? How could the man who looked upon Saltergate as 'the home of Good Football' not have time? I really didn't know what to do and so I did what any self-respecting 14-year-old would do: I sulked. In fact, I put on the sulking performance of the year! In an attempt to lighten my load, my sister put an arm around me and explained that I could actually have gone with her and John... "if you had a ticket," she added, as a cruel rider. I continued to sulk. This was turning out to be one of the events of the year. Eventually, my mother, worn down by my masterful performance, caved in. Three days of a moping, sullen 14-year-old proved just too much. It would have been too much for anyone, to be fair, I'd put in such an awesome performance. (In fact, the sulk got such critical acclaim I was actually nominated for BBC Sports Personality of The Year!)

Right, so I had the promise of a lift, the go-ahead from one of the head honchos in the house; all I needed now was a ticket. This would be especially difficult as I had school all week. But, fortunately, school and I didn't get on. Tupton Hall had long since given up caring about me and I had long since given up caring about it, so wagging the afternoon off to go into town to get a ticket wasn't a big deal. However, my mother pre-empted my afternoon school strike and came up with a note confirming a bogus dental appointment. A note was really the least of my problems; I was a fourth year leaver and I could more or less do as I pleased, as long as it fell short of pulling down my trousers and peeing in the headmaster's desk flower arrangement... errrrr, hang on a minute, I did that... well, you get the picture. Let's just say, school was fairly lax about our comings and goings.

Originally, I was just going to get my registration and walk out of school but, now I had the note, I could leave whenever I wanted; I could walk out in the middle of a lesson, if I desired! You may think my mother was soft in providing me with the excuse but I don't think so; she was actually quite cunning as she didn't provide me with the bus fare to get into town. And so, that Thursday afternoon, I walked out of school and tramped the 3 miles from Tupton to Chesterfield and purchased my ticket for the game. The excitement was huge. Although I was travelling with my sister and her husband-to-be, I would be sitting alone – and it was all new and a little bit scary. That night, the *Derbyshire Times* boasted that around 5,000 Chesterfield fans were expected to make the journey. There was a special train and everything. I could hardly sleep the night before the game and the journey down on the day was brilliant. We passed countless buses and cars, blue and white scarves streaming from the windows, and we were all hooting and waving to each other. Suddenly, you had more friends than you realised.

The game itself was brilliant; we pulverised them. Randall ran Mike Pejic (later of Everton and England) ragged and, although we were 1–0 down early on, we continued to play them off the park. Eventually, our future manager waltzed round Gordon Banks and notched the equaliser. Randall also managed to hit a post and head one over the bar, while Ernie Moss missed his trademark sitter. In the end, Stoke snatched an undeserved victory with a deflected shot; but it was a great game – thoroughly enjoyed. As we walked back to the car, replaying various moments from the game, I heard a loud roar from behind. It wasn't the kind of roar that goes up when a team scores; it was different somehow, and it made me feel uncomfortable. I had no idea why I felt this, as I had no idea what was happening, but the following day I heard a rather grizzly tale, told to me by a friend who'd been there and had been standing behind the goal with the massed army of Chesterfield fans. Apparently, there had been some fighting behind the goal before the game but things had escalated when the game ended and the Town contingent were making their way out of the ground. A brawl had broken out at the bottom of the steps to the exit gate. This quickly escalated and was the cause of the roar I had heard. It was simply two sets of fans charging towards each other. I never knew that running could sound so frightening.

The experience was strange, surreal almost. It's like the idea that if a tree falls in a forest and no one sees it, does it make a sound? Well, I hadn't seen this, so could it actually be true? The following few days answered my enquiring mind quite categorically since I had the story returned to me from several people and each time I heard it I felt more unsettled by it. I don't know why hearing my first football violence should be more troubling than seeing the stuff I had seen previously at Rotherham and Doncaster – but it was.

If I thought this sort of behaviour was going to go away, then I was very much mistaken. Two weeks on from the Stoke City match – on February 5th to be precise – violence came home to roost at Saltergate before my very eyes. This was just a 'friendly' (if it is possible to have such a fixture with our dear, dear neighbours, Sheffield Wednesday) and it was one of those occasions when the violence on the terraces took your attention from the action on the pitch. I watched open-mouthed from my regular seat in the wing stand as gangs of rival fans stood and momentarily traded insults. But, then, the bad-natured badinage rapidly disintegrated into rival fans hurling lumps of rock and stone at each other. Some of the police on duty inside the ground were hit by stray missiles. Or, perhaps, they weren't so stray after all. Several people were arrested and the *Derbyshire Times* made interesting reading that week – especially the section on local court hearings. It told how one Wednesday fan, on being told to control himself by a policeman, had suggested that he take the said officer of the law round the back and sort him out. He was arrested. It is interesting that in the midst of rock-chucking hooligans, a copper should calmly suggest to one of them that he simply 'controls himself.' A Town fan from Brimington, arrested for his part in the missile-lobbing, summed the whole thing up very nicely. According to the newspaper article, he said: *"I didn't like the Chesterfield Kop being taken over."* I think that's a fair point and I, for one, would have let him off!

Over the next few games, things seemed to go back to normal – right up until March 11th when we played Barnsley at home. The following week's *Derbyshire Times* led with the headline: **"ARRESTS FOLLOW ROWDYISM AT SOCCER MATCH."** Need I say more? I will, anyway. Basically, Barnsley fans had been set upon in the Cross Street end of the ground – the open-ended terrace, traditionally reserved for travelling supporters – and, despite appeals over the public address system for fans to behave themselves, both before the game and again at half-time, the trouble continued. Up in the Saltergate wing stand it was difficult to make much out or, indeed, feel threatened by it. Nevertheless, eight people were arrested: seven of them juveniles. A sign of things to come? This incredibly dull game was, in fact, only livened up by what happened off the pitch. Perhaps even the players were more interested in the trouble; they certainly played as if they were! The only fan arrested that was old enough to get his name in the paper was a Barnsley hooligan who apologised to the court and swore he would never attend another football game again. The newspaper reported that he told the magistrate: *"I've certainly learned my lesson,"* and the rather 'matter-of-fact' postscript read: *"Bill Smith* [name changed to prevent me getting a beating from an irate and reformed

Barnsley fan] *who has 15 other convictions for football violence was fined £15."*

According to the press, Saltergate was now one of the Football League's 'trouble' grounds, and the question of what to do about soccer hooliganism was high on the agenda of every club.

In the April of 1972 it moved a little further up the agenda at Chesterfield FC. Following unruly behaviour at several games, the FA hit the club with a warning. The local headline made grim reading: **"'CURB VIOLENCE OR ELSE,' FA WARNS SALTERGATE FANS."** Unless the club's supporters began to behave responsibly, the FA would take further action. They warned that if there was any repetition of the behaviour seen in the home game with Rochdale then action would be taken. Now, I can't remember any trouble, ever, with Rochdale at Saltergate. I can recall some at their ground, Spotland, but never in our own back yard. Neither can I find mention of it in any newspaper. Nonetheless, Chesterfield were ordered by the FA to display notices around the ground warning spectators that, in the event of further misbehaviour, "further action" would be taken. I'm not sure what they meant by 'further action' but I assume it was closing a part, or all of, the ground.

Arthur Sutherland, chairman at the time, went on to say: *"I only hope that the unruly element – who can usually be identified by their stupid way of dressing in odd, self-style uniforms – stay away."* Describing your average Chesterfield thug as having an "odd, self-styled uniform" makes him sound more like a graduate from Chesterfield Art College than a hooligan. I hardly think that 'Gessler,' the self-styled leader of the Chesterfield Kop, spent much time worrying what he would be wearing come the weekend. And I doubt Mrs Gessler ever grabbed him on a Saturday morning and said, *"If you think you're going out to kick someone's head in dressed like that, our Gessler, then you can think again!"* It's difficult to imagine that she spent her mid-week hours designing loose fitting jeans that would allow the man in her life more freedom should he wish to kick someone in the groin, or designing him a little pocket where he could safely stash his cosh. I doubt if Chesterfield's 'ooligan element were ever going to meet up the night before a big game and decide what tomorrow's ensemble might be. It just didn't happen. And I find it strange that men who dressed in their own 'self-styled uniform' (a suit) and spent their time ruining (and that isn't a typing error) football clubs up and down the country would think they had any right whatsoever to say who was and who wasn't fit to come into the ground.

After the brief flirtation with the top end of Division 3, the following season, 1972/73, was a much more sedate affair. The club found itself languishing in the lower half of the league for most of the season and there was precious little for your law-abiding Town fans, let alone the hooligans, to get excited about.

Occasionally, bored through poor football and suffering badly from the lack of numbers to warrant getting physical with anyone, the members of the Kop would perform the Saltergate shuffle. This rather strange ritual would see them stamp and scuff their platform-soled feet on the cinder bedding between the concrete terrace steps, their massive Oxford bags billowing out like sails, and wafting a dark, unhealthy and incredibly dirty, dust-filled cloud that, to the untrained eye, could easily have been mistaken for a fire. The absence of flames and heat of any kind were a bit of a giveaway but, working on the premise that there is no smoke without fire, the Old Bill would readily dive in and try to ignite some. I was always very surprised by the action of the law: rather than leave them to it – which is what I would have done – they insisted on pushing their way to the centre in order to inhale as much toxic cinder dust as humanly possible. Five minutes later, after a small skirmish, a blue helmet would invariably bounce onto the pitch and, two minutes after that, two grubby and probably innocent supporters would be escorted to the policeman's ball below the main stand.

I made a couple of away trips this season: they were both in the company of my sister and brother-in-law and there was nothing particularly notable about either trip – not even the score. However, there were two incidents of note. On September 23rd we played Blackburn at home – always a side willing to bring its fair share of travellers. There were minor fights in the street as I walked up to the ground, and an even bigger one inside. Hostilities on the Kop were soon brought under control but they kicked off again towards half-time as the Chesterfield supporters made their way round to the half-way line. I'm not sure what happened after the game – I wasn't hanging around to find out – but I did hear that the windows on some of the travelling supporters' coaches had done a disappearing act. This kind of story had usually been embellished by the time I got to hear it, and so a tale about broken windows may well have begun life as "someone threw a stone."

However, in this instance, it would appear that no one needed to embellish anything as two juvenile fans ended up in court after smashing windows on a Blackburn coach.

The only other notable event that season was in the return fixture with Blackburn at Ewood Park in March when goalkeeper, Jim Brown, was hit by a dart thrown by a Rovers fan. It stuck in his leg and I can recall quite vividly the picture in the *Daily Express* the next morning. For Chesterfield to get a mention in the national press was something of a minor miracle but to get a mention AND a picture, well, you just knew it was serious. This was a major story. Thugs beating one another senseless was one thing; injuring the players of the opposing side was new territory for most football hooligans of the time. Whether the dart incident was retribution for the smashed coach windows it's hard to say and I have to add that I don't much care – although I bet Jim Brown did and my bet is he probably still does. Because of the serious nature of the crime, the Football Association swung into action and did absolutely nothing. The local paper did run the obligatory letter from *'Disgusted of Blackburn'* and it was a good one too, although he did let himself down slightly by penning the line: *"You mustn't blame the actions of one or two stupid people on the vast majority of sensible fans whose only desire is to see a good match."* They are fine sentiments indeed and ones I wholeheartedly supported. Unfortunately, though, from my position on the terraces I got the feeling that the "one or two stupid people" were growing in number by the week. Only time would tell...

Mists, Mellow Fruitfulness And Wynnie's Tours
SEASON 73/74

The hooligan season kicked off in fine style at the Baseball Ground in Derby on August 31st when around 3,000 assorted Derby and Chelsea fans battled it out on the pitch. It was, quite simply, nothing short of a riot. The press, as one would expect, had a field day. An article I read whilst researching this book had the fabulous line: *"There was a vile eruption of a horde of senseless thugs."* It does sound as if it was written more for the *Viking Times* than the *Derbyshire Times*, but it made me laugh.

Because of this mindless outbreak of thuggery, Derby County led the modern world into erecting barriers around the pitch. The club itself went to great lengths to point out that these were, in fact, just barriers and not cages as certain journalists had described them. Unfortunately, after the opening day scrap, many thought 'cage' was a more than suitable description considering the animals they contained. The Derby PR machine, however, was still eager at this stage not to upset the supporters that didn't get involved in violence.

On the home front, things were slightly more peaceful. Rather than try to upstage Derby the Chesterfield hooligans went for a more subtle and low key approach during the home game with Grimsby on September 7th. It started when a Town hooligan jumped over the wall at the Kop end, dummied his way past two coppers and bolted for the Grimsby fans. It was a great move, leaving the police bewildered and flat-footed. I imagine the Grimsby fans were delighted to see this idiot running towards them – and you could almost see them polishing their boots in readiness. The Old Bill, obviously embarrassed, gave chase and they, in turn, were chased by a more menacing and larger group of Town thugs who, I imagine, the Grimsby fans were not so delighted to see. The whole thing resembled a 'Keystone Kops' routine more than a serious attempt at football violence. The leader had made it as far as the half-way line when he realised the police were closing in fast, so he headed for the Compton Street end, threw himself over the wall and into the forgiving arms of the public (who had very little say in it, to be fair.) The ones that didn't make it to the safety of the terraces were escorted, jostled and generally given a helping hand out of the ground by the out-of-breath police. Just three Town fans were arrested and were each fined £30 for threatening behaviour and possession of crap haircuts!

While football violence was on the increase, fashion was definitely on the decline. There were two distinctive dress codes in the early days. First up, you had the platform-soled shoes, the Oxford Bags and the awful feather-cut which always looked as if it had been done by a barber suffering from Parkinson's disease who was reading the instructions on how to make this cut from a step-by-step guide. Second, you had the more menacing Doctor Marten Boots (ox-blooded), turned up Levis, denim jacket and short hair. Of course, there were always variations on these two distinctive themes. I myself admit to being a Doc Marten man. I'd worn them for ages and, for me, it was a comfort thing. But with my Doc Marts I wore flares; I wore them for as long as was humanly possible. (Always been a hippy at heart, I guess.)

Anyway, in this season of power cuts, early kick-offs and early finishes, Chesterfield, on the playing front, were starting to flatter. It was probably meant to deceive as we never showed the consistency of a team destined for promotion but when we were good we were very good indeed and watching us play at home just wasn't enough anymore. Unfortunately, the hooligan problem was a very real problem and the papers were full of games being held up as fans battled it out pitch-side. It wasn't confined to the big clubs either; this was happening at every league club in the country. So, what my friends and I wanted more than anything was a safe and relatively cheap way of getting to away games. Supporters' Club Travel had been suggested but dismissed on the grounds of expense and the fact that they were probable targets for hooligans. The *East Midlands* bus company also used to run special buses to away games. (This was before they became victims of corporate hooliganism in the form of Stagecoach takeovers.) Once again, this received the vote of no confidence on account of the fact that their buses were notorious for being full of absolute nutcases and Chesterfield's most wanted. Being the soft, yellow-livered girlies that we were, we couldn't possibly mix with youths like that. Well, we could; we just didn't want to.

I remember very clearly the day Dave Wynne walked up onto Wingerworth Lido (a patch of scrubland that doubled as a football pitch). He ambled through the bushes, hands pushed deep into his pockets and, in a voice that said, *"Look I don't care one way or the other but...,"* he asked if anyone was interested in going on his coach to watch Chesterfield at Cambridge. We were speechless. I mean, we all knew that Wynnie didn't particularly like football. We looked at each other, perhaps each waiting for the other to commit first, but before long Wynnie had a definite five bookings and, after telling us to be outside Queen's Park swimming baths Saturday morning, he left. We shouted after him, asking him the cost, but he simply shrugged his shoulders and disappeared back through the bushes.

Dave Wynne was a strange character. I'd known him for years and yet didn't really know him at all. He was younger than me and attended grammar school, so perhaps we didn't mix in the same circles. Having said that, I knew other people from his school and we were really close friends. The one thing about Wynnie was that if he said he was going to do something, then you knew damn well he'd do it. Although I was looking forward to the game on the Saturday, being a natural-born coward and worrier to boot, I couldn't help but be concerned. It bothered me who was taking up the other 45 places on the bus and it bothered me that some bus company had hired out a bus to a schoolboy! But there was little I could do about any of it now, so I trusted to luck, waited for Saturday and the birth of Wynnie's Tours...

A Cambridge Degree

February 2nd, 1974 Cambridge 1 v 2 Chesterfield

It was with a mixture of trepidation and excitement that I caught the bus into Chesterfield that morning. I can't speak for my friends that day but I'm sure similar thoughts had crossed all our minds. Thoughts about who will make up the numbers, will we like them, will there be any trouble, all flitted, I'm sure, around our heads. Football hooliganism had hit the headlines big style and the media made it sound as if every football supporter in the country was hell-bent on kicking seven shades of shite out of each other. (It could be argued that the media were making a three course meal out of what was no more than a snack.) Trouble is, if that argument had held any merit then I wouldn't have had enough stories to write this tome in the first place!

Many people have questioned me over the years concerning the hooliganistic qualities of your average Chesterfield supporter, and I can understand their doubts. Chesterfield would not be the first name to spring to your lips when discussing football violence. But these were the early days for hooligans, the days before the police really knew how to handle mobs of thugs hell-bent on dismantling teeth and rearranging someone's wedding tackle, and, like everyone else during the 70's, Chesterfield sported a hooligan element that was, at times, downright vicious.

So, is it any wonder that I stood outside the Queen's Park swimming baths that morning with a certain amount of trepidation? As I looked around me at the people waiting for the coach, I knew exactly how Wynnie had filled the bus. For some reason he knew a hard core of thugs that would travel on his buses; he just needed the rest of us to make up the numbers and keep the costs down. Apart from my five mates who had travelled in on the bus with me that morning, I knew very few of the rest. I knew their faces, I'd even heard what they were capable of – and that was frightening enough – so to be travelling with them was just a little scary.

As this had now turned into an official promotion-chasing season, there was always going to be a large away following; I just didn't expect to be travelling with the bulk of the Chesterfield hooligans! I suppose my concern was slightly eased when one of the lads accosted me as we started to climb onto the bus and pointed out that there wouldn't be any trouble on this trip as, "Cambridge don't have any lads, do they?" Just how he actually knew about the state of Cambridge's lads I don't know as this was, to my knowledge, our first visit to the ground. Anyway, if he thought it was going to be an easy day out then that was good enough for me. I was more than happy for him to take a day off, as it were, and let me get on with actually watching football.

The journey down was really quite peaceful. The wintry sun was shining and God was in his footballing heaven. Well, he was until we passed the sign telling us we had entered Cambridge.

Now, the one thing that coaches had in 1974, which they don't have now, is windows that open: long oblongs that slid back and forth enabling you to give the person three seats back frostbite. More importantly, they also enabled you to shout obscenities at passing supporters/people (something sadly lacking from the game today). I was soon to discover that these windows were also incredibly handy for slinging objects out of – and at. Sounds terrible but in 1974 it was an absolute must. And so, as we lumbered on into Cambridge, every time we passed someone, oblong-shaped heads would appear at the windows to deliver a volley of abuse. Gems like, *"You fuckin' old wanker,"* and the equally favourite, *"Oi, you... fuck off!"* stung the peace and tranquillity of this beautiful city. It didn't matter who it was – old-aged pensioner, housewife, student, dog – they all received the same treatment. We were nothing if not fair; Chesterfield fans really didn't discriminate.

The prophecy that Cambridge might not have any lads seemed a reasonable one until a motorcyclist, equipped with flowing Cambridge scarf, appeared behind the bus and started to deliver the occasional two-fingered gesture to the Chesterfield supporters snarling on the back seat. This was, perhaps, his worst move of the day, for Dylan, a rotund and very witty Town fan who was sitting just behind me, downed what was left in his half bottle of whisky and gave me a nudge: "Ere, watch this," he said. He stuck his arm out of the window and gesticulated at the Cambridge fan. The guy on the motorbike echoed Dylan's sentiments and stuck up two very positive fingers in response. I'm not quite sure how much enjoyment he gained from it but I am sure that all of it disappeared when an empty half-bottle of whisky zipped from Dylan's side window and cannoned off his crash helmet, much to the delight of everyone on board. For a moment, I thought he was going to fall off. His bike wobbled alarmingly but he managed to regain control. He may well have been sporting a full-face helmet but I swear you could see the shock register in his eyes. Panic and self-preservation took over and the motorcyclist quickly decreased speed, dropped out of bottle range and buggered off round the nearest available roundabout. His parting 'V' sign was not half as confident as the one he'd given on arrival!

But he was only a momentary deflection and it was soon back to hurling insults. As I have said, Cambridge is a beautiful city and some of the university buildings were really quite splendid. So, shouting, *"Fuck off, you Cambridge bastards,"* at four students, who were very possibly from everywhere but Cambridge, did seem rather strange. It also seemed unfair that these colleges, which devoted their time to teaching English to pimply youths who would one day go on and make a living out of the use of this language, should have these obscenities echoing through their hallowed halls. It was a naive view, perhaps, but it was well meant at the time.

My friend, whose nickname I promised I would not mention for the sake of embarrassment, Morph, and whose real name was Neil Richards, turned to me and said, "This doesn't seem right, does it?" He had been thinking along the same lines as I had but neither of us knew quite how to make obscene remarks out of the windows without actually being obscene. However, Morph was nothing if not resourceful. "I know!" he said, with a gusto similar to that attached to all great thinkers, and, upon passing the next group of innocent people, he shoved his oblong-shaped head through the window and screamed, "ABUSE!!" It caught on like the plague and it wasn't long before hardened nutcases were shoving their faces to the window gaps and screaming "Abuse!" at everyone they saw. Admittedly, some were obviously not acquainted with the word for they took it one stage further and screamed, "Fuckin' abuse," but most, it has to be said, were more than happy with the rib-tickling idea.

Even now, all these years on, I still smile at the thought of a bus-load of football supporters all shouting, "Abuse!" at everyone they passed. The looks on people's faces just had to be seen to be believed. There they stood, ready for a bus-load of insults which would surely come their way, and what did they get? "Abuse!" That's what. It still makes me giggle when I think of the possible conversations that went on when these people got home:

"Tarquin, a bus-load of football supporters just shouted 'Abuse' at me."

"Huh, bloody hooligans. They should be locked up; shouldn't go around swearing at people like that."

"No, no, Tarquin, they didn't swear."

"But I thought you said..."

"'Abuse,' Tarquin. They shouted, 'Abuse!'"

"But...?????? What the bloody hell are you on about, woman?"

Etc, etc.

What would Brian Rix have paid for a farce like that? It was one of those gems that only ever happens the once. No matter how hard people tried to resurrect it in other cities, it never really had the same effect or caught on quite as well as it did in Cambridge.

Eventually, after much pestering from the passengers on board, the driver slowed down and, about a mile from the ground, unloaded his motley crew. And there we were – nowhere – standing on the side of the road, small estate on one side and a park on the other. In the distance, over the other side of the park, the floodlight pylons showed the way but it was much too early for the match. Someone decided his first priority was to have a wee. Now, me, I would have waited until I found a public convenience or until I was inside the ground, but this particular supporter marched smartly across the road, walked down the steep incline of someone's front lawn, unzipped his flies and delivered all over their front room window. Bad enough, you might think, but if you consider that the family were all sitting comfortably watching *Grandstand*, well, it makes your average piss look very poor indeed. The family didn't do anything; they just sat there amazed, bottom lips dropped to trough-like proportions. Frank Bough had just lost an audience of four. It wasn't as if the lad made a big deal about it. I mean, he wasn't showing off – well, not to the point where he was shouting, *"Hey, lads, look at what I can do."* He just did it, minimum of fuss, as if the family were not there, as if he was doing it against the wall. (I know it was wrong but it amazed me; well, could you do that in those circumstances? I find it hard enough if someone else is in the same toilet!) I looked back to the family; they hadn't moved. They just sat there, frozen to the spot. They're probably in the same position even now!

Some of the older members of the bus mob were now eagerly searching for a pub and I was eagerly hoping they wouldn't find one but, although we were just one bus-load, there seemed to be Chesterfield fans everywhere, doing anything and everything they could. Some were playing on the park, having a lovely time on the swings and slide, while others just rushed up and down in a headless chicken sort of way. Amid this confusion, I watched as a girl walked towards a Town fan who seemed to be taking control of events, and he stopped her and very politely asked if she knew the way to the ground. It was a stupid question; you would have had to be very short-sighted indeed not to have seen the floodlights but, as she pointed toward the ground, this youth, oaf, prat (delete as you feel necessary) leaned forward and groped her. It was quite sickening and if I had been anything other than a complete coward then I might have said something. As it was, I just felt sick and wanted desperately to chase after her and apologise, to explain that we weren't really all like that, but as she was now screaming, "Fuck off, you dirty Chesterfield bastard," it probably wouldn't have been a wise move.

When someone suddenly noticed the pub I was half-glad, as the girl would be forgotten, but equally worried that, with drink inside them, this mob would become completely out of control. I now realised how out of my depth I was. Shouting *"Abuse"* or even *"Fuck off"* out of a window was the absolute limit to my hooligan credentials. I have never had any desire to be one, you understand, but it isn't until you get in a situation like this that you realise you really don't have what it takes to cause mayhem and destruction wherever you tread. With that thought in mind, I walked very slowly towards the pub and, yet, still managed to reach it before the majority of the Town thugs did. I found myself in a really awkward position where one half of me hoped we would get served so that, at least, everyone was kept under the same roof rather than out causing trouble, and the other half of me hoped we'd be turned away so that no one would get drunk and the situation get more out of control than it already was. (What you might call a lose/lose situation.) Perhaps I worried too much? I suppose it didn't really matter one way or the other because the outcome would be the same, regardless of the landlord's decision. As I stood on the threshold of the pub, I heard the landlord carry out his rights. "I'm not serving you. Clear off!" he said.

I was just clear of the door when the first table went over. The others stayed in the pub until every table was in a similar position. The landlord was not amused. Neither was the old bloke in the corner who was just about to six it up and win yet another free pint (although I dare say his fellow dominoers were mightily relieved). Fortunately, we were well clear of the pub by the time the police turned up. You may wonder why I didn't walk away and relieve myself of all the stress and strain that I was placing upon my young shoulders. The answer is simple: this bunch of thugs was my safety blanket. Walking to the ground alone would have been asking for trouble – even I knew that – and if it came down to a bunch of Chesterfield nutcases getting into a fight that saved my yellow skin, then so be it.

After the pub it all got completely silly and could possibly have got out of hand had it not been for the kids' play-park. Now, the sight of 50 hooligans seeing how high they can get on the swings is another of those rare moments that one can only really appreciate by being there – but so much of this trip was turning out that way. Those who couldn't get a swing played on the slide. I had a go on one of those roundabout things and, thankfully, this stupidity kept everyone quiet until we eventually trooped off to the ground.

Football violence was a problem in those days but, then, I have to say that dim police were an even bigger problem. At Cambridge, though, I thought I saw a slight spark of intelligence, a glimmer of hope, from an overworked police sergeant. The first novelty was the smile; I didn't expect it and I don't think I was ever greeted by a policeman in such a warm and friendly manner in all my ensuing away trips. I think it took everyone aback. I mean, I almost trusted him as he gathered us together and told us, politely, that we could go anywhere in the ground bar the Cambridge kop; if we tried that we would be thrown out. If we invaded the pitch we would be similarly dealt with. At the end of the match we were to wait five minutes for the ground to clear and would then be escorted back to the coaches. It was for our own safety. The last comment brought a deluge of laughter but it was all well received. It was probably the first time I'd ever seen football supporters being treated as human beings – and was probably the last for many years to come. I was somewhat aghast at these modern policing methods.

Obviously, you don't need me to tell you that the first thing some of the Chesterfield contingent did on entering the ground was to try and infiltrate the home end. I was more than happy observing this from the side and some of it was hilarious. Some of the conversations between the hooligans and the police were unreal:

Police: "Where are you from, son?"

Hooligan: "Chesterfield." (Such honesty!)

Police: "Well, you can't come on here. Go and stand over there."

Hooligan: "Can't see over there."

Police: "Well, go over there, then."

Hooligan: "Tell me, constable, is your head really that shape under your hat?"

Police: "No."

Hooligan: "Bet it is. Bet that's why they call you tit head."

Police: "Go away, son."

'Go away, son!' Blimey, talk about restraint. I can't believe how an arrest wasn't made. Was this policeman on Mogadon? Two Chesterfield supporters did actually make it onto the Cambridge kop – not enough to cause any trouble but enough to be able to say, *"We did it."* Perhaps, more importantly, enough for the rest of the Chesterfield fans to point at and sing, *"One John Carter, there's only one John Carter,"* etc (you know the tune). Obviously, an alias has been used for two reasons: one, the usual one, he might seek me out and hit me; and, two, he is now married with two children and a very successful plumbing firm.

One minute you're dealing with a mindless moron who simply wants to beat someone's head in and the next minute you're with someone with a sharp sense of irony and an almost warm sense of humour. I might make comments about mindless morons and so on but, in actual fact, most of the hardened hooligans were really quite intelligent; enough so that they were seldom outwitted by the police.

As far as the football was concerned, well, it was a good game. Chesterfield took the lead after 29 minutes when Ernie Moss rifled in an unstoppable volley. The delight was uncontrolled; even the lads in the kop jumped up and down, which led to them being removed by the police. We were singing about promotion now and a win here would go a long way towards that. The lead, alas, was short-lived – around nine minutes, to be exact – when the referee awarded Cambridge a penalty. Jim Brown set himself in the centre of the goal and guessed correctly, saving it superbly. Cue more scenes of jubilation. However, these were even shorter-lived as the referee said Brown had dived too soon and he made Cambridge take the penalty again. This time they equalised. Despite controlling the second half and exerting tremendous pressure on their goal, we couldn't seem to break them down and we looked like we were heading for a 1–1 draw; not a disaster but not what we deserved. With Chesterfield pressing forward and the Cambridge fans trying hard to remind the referee that he really ought to end the game, Dave Thompson controlled the ball just outside the penalty area and, spotting the keeper off his line, arched a delicate chip into the back of the net. It was an important goal: it kept our promotion chances alive. It was the sort of goal that makes you run on the pitch in delight – no more than that, just delight – and several Chesterfield supporters did just that! It was an odd situation. It was almost as if they ran on, got so far and then remembered the warning of the police, *"Anyone running on the pitch will be thrown out,"* so ran off again. I'm sure none of them were doing it for any other reason than pure unbridled delight. One lad, who had burst onto the pitch, had slipped as he turned to make his way off and dropped his Union Jack flag. Morph (being the decent Town fan that he is) stepped over the fence onto the running track and retrieved it for him. As he handed it over, both of them were grabbed by the police, their arms thrust up their back and marched out of the ground. I was amazed. It wasn't so much an invasion; more like five lads jumping onto the running track with delight – and I thought that was what football was all about. Considering that this was the last minute of the game, it made it appear to be a pretty pointless exercise, and it became ridiculously pointless when Morph appeared at my side some 30 seconds later. He had merely followed the constable back into the ground through the open gates. It was at this point that I realised it was not a spark of intelligence I'd seen upon entering the ground, it was just the sun shining off of a truncheon. These police were as brain dead as the rest, but patronising with it.

The police did keep us in the ground for the promised five minutes and were very insistent that we walk with them to the waiting coaches. We did as asked and, in full triumphant voice, we stepped out of the ground and down the road, escorted on each side by policemen holding back snarling Alsatians. I was in the middle of this mass of fans when someone at the front started to jog. Gradually, everyone followed suit. You could see the policemen looking at each other. They had not reckoned on this but, so as not to appear non-conformist, they jogged with us. The beat of the songs increased along with the pace of the supporters. It wasn't long before *jog* became *steady run*, and the baffled policemen ran with us. After about 100 yards, someone sounded the charge and we were off, sprinting down the road. The policemen attempted it for a few strides but soon gave in. If I could have heard them I'm sure I would have heard the words, *"Oh, fuck 'em!"*

It wasn't the first time this particular stunt would be pulled and it usually worked. In essence, we were now free to roam the streets of Cambridge and cause untold amounts of trouble. But it was as if the point had been made, so we made our way to the coach park, pointed ourselves in the direction of Chesterfield and headed home. I was quite pleased really: after the pre-match entertainment, it had all gone off without too much of a fuss and, if this was going to be the usual trip with Wynnie's Tours, then he could count on me every week.

The journey home, however, has probably never been bettered in all my travels. It was one of the funniest I have ever encountered. Cambridge might not be a lengthy trip but, back then, there was always an obligatory pit stop to empty bladders and refuel on chocolate and crisps. The service station we pulled into was hardly your five star convenience; in fact, the only thing open – apart from the toilet, that is – was a small newsagent's counter which had been added to the main building. It sold papers and quite a large selection of chocolate bars and pornographic literature. Fifty youths cramming up to the front of this counter must have been quite alarming for the lady who was manning/ladying it and, for some reason, she just turned round and walked away. There was a pause and a moment of quiet as supporters looked at each other in amazement. It was just a few seconds... and then it was pandemonium as people realised everything was free. Being only 5ft-4ins and about as aggressive as a field mouse, getting to the counter was a problem – well, it was an impossibility, actually – but I have to say here and now that I wouldn't have missed the opportunity of a free Mars bar. No way! Coward I may be but, in this instance, who wouldn't have helped themselves?

The woman was only gone a minute but when she returned there were rows of innocent, smiling, chocolate-filled faces looking at her. She looked disgusted and could tell a certain amount of her stock had been pilfered. To stop any similar action, she pulled down a metal grille. We watched her tidy a few things before she walked away again. I started to walk away myself.

"Sod it," I thought.

"Lift it up," someone else thought, because she hadn't locked it.

Suddenly, *"Oh, I'll nick a chocolate bar,"* had turned into, *"Oh, I'll nick this **box** of chocolate bars."* People were ferrying the bloody stuff onto the bus and then coming back for more!

Amid this grab-anything-that-isn't-nailed-down time, someone made a play for the heap of nude books pinned to the glass countertop by a large metal ashtray. The ashtray went skywards, the dirty mags went floorwards and then the ashtray dropped, shattering the glass countertop.

"OOOOPS!" someone said – probably someone who had been eyeing up the glass counter for his dad's greenhouse!

If the woman hadn't returned, I'm quite sure the whole building would have been dismantled and taken away on the bus. She would have returned to an empty space and a squashed Mars bar. As it was, she did return and, once again, pulled down the grille, this time locking it. One youth, who had been desperately trying to get hold of that month's copy of *Penthouse*, actually ended up paying through the grille for it (I suppose it makes a change from 'paying through the nose') and one or two other evening papers were bought by lesser hooligans – perhaps through guilt, although I very much doubt it.

I felt terrible; it had been like walking into an empty supermarket only to find that everything was stacked on shelves out of my reach. I had really fancied a bar of chocolate and I must have been the only person on the bloody bus who came away empty-mouthed. It still annoys me – it shouldn't, but it does.

Now, the amount of confectionery stolen could never be consumed by even 50 of the hungriest hooligans and, so, someone hit upon the idea of chocolate as a weapon. Before long, half-eaten chocolate bars were winging their way from one end of the bus to the other. The people on the back seat were trying to sell what they had pinched (remember, we did virtually have the contents of a medium-sized newsagent's on board). The trouble was it cost more from them than it did in the shop! When they couldn't sell it, they simply took a bite out of it and slung it at someone. It might not sound much like fun but, if you kept your head down, then watching a squidgy chocolate bar thump into some unsuspecting lug'ole really was quite entertaining. Perhaps I would have thought differently if one of the unsuspecting lug'oles had been mine – but it wasn't.

I cannot paint an adequate picture of the goings-on at this time on the bus but everyone was finding it funny to some degree... or they were until the police car pulled alongside and signalled for the bus driver to stop. Everyone immediately thought the same thing and we executed the emptying of the bus with commando-like precision and efficiency. Everything that had been pinched was lying on the grass verge at the side of the road before the driver had even opened the bus door. The police boarded and saw this spotless bus. It looked as if someone had been round with a Hoover! And these smiling, cherub-like faces couldn't possibly have committed such a dastardly act as pinching from a newsagent's, could they?

"Have you got room for these two? Their car's broken down," boomed this 8ft police sergeant.

Naturally, being good Chesterfield supporters, we embraced them fully. (Hooligans, maybe, but they wouldn't have seen you stuck. Makes you think...)

As we pulled away, 50 faces were glued to the windows as they waved goodbye to their plunder.

"Where's me *Penthouse*?" someone shrieked.

"It's out there," came the stony reply.

"Bastard, I paid for that," were the last words I can remember, as we laughed the rest of the way back into town.

The Chesterfield Brick

February 16th, 1974 Watford 2 v 1 Chesterfield

After the Cambridge game Wynnie had very little to do to coax us into attending the following fixture at Vicarage Road, Watford, and it was made even easier for him as we'd managed to stuff Charlton at home in between times. So we travelled south again in the hope of strengthening our position at the top end of the league. Watford had promotion aspirations themselves and were close to the top of the league. Having said that, we'd beaten them comfortably at home by three goals to one in the October and were looking for a similar scoreline today. Well, the supporters were, at least.

Standing outside Queen's Park Leisure Centre I didn't feel the pressing anxiety that I'd felt before the last trip. This might only have been my second outing with this particular bunch of hooligans but I was as ready as one could possibly be for anything that might happen. Hey, if it was as much fun as Cambridge then I would be more than happy. I was also slightly spurred on by the fact that Wynnie, flushed with the success of his Cambridge venture and, no doubt, now held in high esteem among hooligan circles, had decided to push the boat out and take two coaches! Wow, one schoolboy was taking two coach-loads of hooligans to a football match – what a terrifying thought – although, on that grey February day, the idea of being protected by twice as many hooligans was something of a comfort. Another large following of Chesterfield fans was expected as at least six other coaches were making the journey. It was an encouraging sign. One thing I feel the club has always been blessed with has been its away support – particularly when doing well, obviously.

Now, the journey to Watford is incredibly dull and on a wet Saturday in February, with just the motorway as scenery, that's about as dull as it gets. Most people were asleep – or at least attempting to reach that state – and it was with some relief that we pulled into a motorway service station. We dragged our weary bodies from the bus and started to make our way across the bridge to the other side of the M1 where all the interesting buildings were housed, such as toilets and catering. Half-way across, someone drew our attention to several coach-loads of football supporters – blue and white scarves streaming from the windows of the buses – pulling into the car park we had just left. Without giving it any thought at all, someone screamed, "Town fans!" and everyone turned round and ran back to greet what turned out to be 14 coaches of Leicester City fans! I've said 14 because that's what I remember it to be, and yet, even now, I'm thinking, *"No, that can't be right. That's a ludicrous number."* A part of me thinks I must have embellished the thought over the years but, having said that, I do remember standing on the bridge and counting them in while everyone was running back down to the car park. I was gullible but I wasn't stupid and, whilst I would have loved Chesterfield to have taken that many supporters to an 'ordinary' away game, I just couldn't see it. Needless to say, whether it was fourteen or seven, we were terrifyingly outnumbered and I feared the worst. (Leicester, if my memory serves me right, were on their way to an FA Cup quarter final. Could it have been against Luton? Wherever they were going, I'm pretty sure they won 2–0.)

Once the realisation of the mistake hit home, most of the Chesterfield hooligan contingent stood there, weighing up the situation. Me? Well, I leaned against the wall and looked for somewhere to hide when the shit hit the fan, as I was sure it most certainly would, and I had absolutely no intentions of letting any of that shit hit this particular fan! A lad I mentioned earlier, Chris Malton, leaned against the wall with me and watched as the first few Leicester fans made their way from the coaches. Now, I knew Chris well. I wouldn't have had him down as a hooligan – well, not till now at any rate – but there was certainly something amiss with him. I was well aware that he could handle himself and, as I pointed out in the Introduction, I'd felt his right hand when he punched me while we were playing football one night after school. I suppose that should have told me something: anyone who was prepared to hit a friend during a football kick-about has to have something a little bit loose.

We watched together as the first few Leicester fans single-filed towards the snack bar and toilets. Amongst this first bunch was a massive youth: tall, wide, long hair and long, black leather coat. He strode past us with what I thought was a justified air of confidence. He certainly looked far more at ease than the other Leicester fans, who all looked a little bit like I was feeling: scared shitless. My ex-near neighbour, with seemingly no thought whatsoever, ran after this big, tall, confident Leicester fan, spun him round and had to literally jump to make sure his fist hit the youth flush on the jaw. I've never believed in the saying: *'The bigger they are, the harder they fall.'* Usually, I've found that my own, far more credible version of that particular chestnut, *'The bigger they are, the harder they hit,'* is much nearer the mark. But this youth just crumpled. He fell in a heap and my neighbour ran back to me shouting, "See that? See that?" like a 10-year-old who has just discovered that Santa has been. See it? Christ, I almost felt it.

And then it happened. It kicked off, to use football parlance. All it had needed to ignite the masses was one little spark. This may sound really cruel but, leaning against the wall, it was all really quite funny, in a scary kind of way. I was amazed at the suddenness of it all. One minute it was quiet contemplation as the two sets of supporters weighed up the pros and cons; but one punch changed all that and put us in the ascendancy. It was crazy, really. If the Leicester fans had decided to get off their coaches, they could easily have slaughtered us – or so I thought from my relative point of safety. The Chesterfield thugs, who must all have breakfasted on three Weetabix that morning before loading their pockets with kryptonite, now thought that being outnumbered four to one was pretty good odds.

It was difficult to take it all in. The first few Leicester fans were running like headless chickens all over the place, trying desperately to get back on board one of the coaches. But watching them became boring, so I turned my attention to a Town fan who had walked down to the back of the coaches and started kicking the back lights in. The drivers, who were off the coaches and standing in a little group having a fag, did protest, which stopped the youth for all of 15 seconds – probably the amount of time it took for his brain to process the information received.

"Oi, you! You can stop that fucker right now!"

"Eh? ...... Bollocks!"

And he continued on down the line of buses. No one was going to stop him. The bus drivers had done their bit by protesting, although this probably acted more as an incentive than a deterrent, and now they moved back out of the way. I knew how they felt.

The only response from the City fans at this stage was to throw empty beer bottles from the windows of their coaches. When they'd run out of empty bottles, they started to throw full ones! I know this because one exploded at my feet as I cowered behind the bins at the back of the building. I did contemplate trying to catch one but that would have meant leaving the relative safety of the bins and heading out into hooligan country – and I wasn't about to do that. I must admit, I did find it slightly annoying to have to keep dodging bottles when the only part I was playing in this game was to keep out of the way. It was the injustice of it all. I wanted to explain to the thrower that the battle was nothing to do with me and perhaps he would like to take his aim at particular protagonists rather than someone pretending to be Switzerland. But I was there and I guess that was reason enough in those days.

The whole event was a kaleidoscope of motion, with things going off all over the place. If you wanted an artistic replication of the event, then just hang a Jackson-Pollock on the wall and stare at that for a few minutes. One of the best(?) stunts came from this lanky Chesterfield fan who picked up a 6ft-long iron bar that had been discarded behind the bins at the back of the snack bar – well, it wasn't the sort of thing you slipped into your pocket, not even in those days – and, armed with said bar, our conquering hero, who had appeared, thus far at least, to have all the ferocity of Lofty out of Eastenders on Diazepam, climbed up onto the wheel arch of one of the coaches, slid bar and arm through an open slit window and began to thresh. That's about the only way I can describe it: a backwards and forwards mowing action that, if you had been standing on the bus within its arc, would have taken your fuckin' head from your shoulders. From my vantage point, I watched through the back window as people dived for cover, desperately trying to get out of the way of this lunatic's assault. Nostalgically, and in the knowledge that no one was seriously injured by this action, it was funny. It certainly remains one of the most incredulous things I have ever seen and, although starting the day in good spirits, I was now starting to wonder if I might have to reappraise my thoughts on travelling by Wynnie's Tours.

While the maniac with the bar kept everyone busy at one end of the coach, a Town fan was desperately trying to clamber aboard via the front door. This was now beginning to take on a form of piracy. Why he thought that boarding a coach full of Leicester fans was a good way to start your day, I can't say. He fought like hell to get up the three steps and board the coach but was beaten back each time. I still can't understand why they didn't just let him get on and then beat the living daylights out of him. I mean, what chance would he have had against 50-odd rival supporters? Mind you, it wouldn't have been 50 because 30 of them were still trying to get out of the way of the iron bar. Unfortunately – or fortunately, depending on which way you look at it and which team you support – he never did make it.

At one point a Town fan struggled the length of the car park with this huge great boulder that he could hardly carry. I swear you could see his legs buckling under the weight of it. He reached the coaches and, with all his might, threw it at the nearest back window. If he'd thrown a normal-sized brick as hard as he could he would have taken out the whole of the back window. As it was, he threw the biggest boulder he could find as hard as he could – which wasn't very hard – and it simply hit the back window with what can only be described as a tap and fell to the floor. Everyone laughed, including the guy who had lugged it the length of the car park!

This intense fighting did ease and there was a sort of amnesty where everyone took a breather; they'd call it "Time out" in America, I guess. The trouble with this lull was that no one had arranged it and so anyone could break it at any time. And they did and, yes, it was a Chesterfield fan. There followed a few fights as people ran around trying to get back on the coaches, and taking a hiding in the process, but nothing compared to what had gone on before. There were no missiles being thrown now – probably because the Leicester fans had run out of bottles.

However, I felt the relative calm was still quite uneasy, although one lone ranger of a Leicester fan obviously thought differently. With one small step for mankind and one foolish step for a Leicester fan, he decided to get off his coach. I couldn't believe it. This had already been tried once and failed miserably, so why he thought people who would have killed him with an iron bar 15 minutes ago were going to be much friendlier now was completely beyond me. I think he made it about 10 yards. At that point there was a roar and the next thing I saw he was legging it across the car park with five Town fans hard on his heels. In the ensuing chase he lost his shoe, which was immediately sprayed blue (spray-paint, remember that? – no self-respecting 70's football hooligan was without the stuff) and thrown into some dirty allotment which backed onto the car park. The lad took a few smacks but the arrival of the police saved him from serious punishment, and my final memory is of him being helped to his feet, rubbing his head and pointing to his shoeless foot. The policeman was all heart and sent someone to retrieve the missing footwear for him. They ordered our coaches to load up and leave and, despite some arguments from Chesterfield hooligans, we did just that.

As we started to pull out of the car park, City's equivalent to Wynnie's Tours turned up. You could say we were lucky as I'm certain we wouldn't have fared so well against them. We were nowhere near Watford and, already, I'd had enough excitement to last me for a month of Saturdays and seen enough football violence to last me a lifetime!

I said at the beginning that the trip down to Watford is dull – but the trip down isn't half as dull as the place itself. My memory of it isn't helped by the fact that it was now raining and we were standing on an uncovered terrace. We were in the ground quite early, which I was really pleased about because I figured that we couldn't really get into any trouble inside the ground. If we had walked around the town I feel sure we would have been asking for it – and more than likely got it! But, once again, I was naïve and gullible to think that coming into the ground had anything to do with safety – far from it.

The lads now wanted to take the Watford kop. My heart sank. We walked round to the fence separating us from the home end and several Town fans started to scale it. There was a mixed reaction from the handful of Watford fans already standing on their kop: some just ran off without a second thought; others walked cautiously away towards an exit, waiting to see what would happen; and others just continued to read their programmes. It was a fruitless exercise in some respects and one that was bound to fail but, had the police not intervened, then these Town fans wouldn't have turned back. They would have run on and gone onto the kop, even if it meant taking a kicking. I suppose that's the thing I've never really understood, the willingness to get beaten up in the name of football, but at the time I was just grateful for the police intervention.

The game seemed to replicate the trip down; and the weather, it was dull. This was turning into a poor day all round. Chesterfield adopted a very negative approach against a Watford side that weren't really that brilliant. Having a negative approach to a game is one thing but it doesn't help when you fall behind in the first minute, which is exactly what happened. We should have upped the ante but we didn't. We continued to contain, perhaps hoping for a point or something. In the 24th minute it looked like we might just get that when Eric Winstanly equalised. It wasn't to be, though; we still continued to let them push and eventually they scored – as we all knew they would. It was a very depressing scoreline for two reasons: one, it didn't help our push for promotion; and two, we always looked a much better side when forcing the pace. My Chesterfield hero at the time, Albert Holmes, made his 421st appearance – and that was about as positive as the day got.

So, with nothing to cheer, feeling thoroughly miserable and completely soaked, we made our way out of the ground. I had to smile at Watford Constabulary's idea of post-match supporter segregation. While we had to walk down a narrow walkway to where the coaches were parked, the Watford fans had to walk up the same walkway in order to get to the public transport and into the town itself. A single blue line of police were all that separated the two factions. Insults were the obvious thing to hurl – and many did just that – but, then, why throw an insult when you can throw a punch? Philosophy obviously majored in the Chesterfield ranks and a punch *was* thrown. In fact, several were thrown, by both sides, to the point where the police had all on controlling the rival fans and keeping them moving. I just kept my head down and walked but you couldn't help but notice what was going on. Lots of stray punches actually hit the police who were in the line trying to keep the fans apart and I don't think that many of the police realised that a lot of these 'stray' punches were actually very much on target indeed! Eventually, we were guided back to the bus and escorted out of town.

In keeping with the rest of the day, the journey back was also dull. It wasn't helped by the fact that the coach driver got hopelessly lost. With everyone wet and the coach stinking of wet clothes drying on sweaty bodies, we journeyed fruitlessly around parts of England I care not to recall as the coach driver attempted to find the right road for the motorway and, as we journeyed, someone told the tale of 'The Millwall Brick.' He went on to explain how fans from that particular club had devised a way of folding a newspaper so that, when thrown, it would actually penetrate glass. He wasn't sure if this was common house glass or if it would actually go through a windscreen – all he knew was that it was possible. (Wynnie's tours were nothing if not educational.) The next hour of origami came up with nothing more than a piece of paper crumpled into a tight ball and the only chance it had of breaking glass was if it was followed hard on the heels by a brick!

When you are wet, when you have lost and are lost, when the bus driver won't stop and let you off to wreck a pub, the concentration span begins to shorten.

"Oh, fuck this!" someone shouted from the back, and he took his front page of *The Sun*, wrapped it around a lump of concrete and hurled it out of the window at a parked car. "There," he said with pride, "the fuckin' Chesterfield Brick!"

You would have thought the back of the bus had invented penicillin. The rest of the armoury was wrapped in paper and hurled at anything that stood still long enough. We were treated to other inventions, such as 'The Chesterfield Bottle,' 'The Chesterfield Stone' and even, would you believe, 'The Pair of Chesterfield Wet Socks.' This last item came about because the driver refused to stop at a skip to allow them to reload.

You may be questioning why we were travelling with an array of bricks and assorted masonry on board. All I can say is, it was, more often than not, the norm. If you passed a brick on the street, you put it on the bus because you never knew when you might need it. Most people picked up stones that they could hurl long distances with a certain degree of force. Others elected for the safety and comfort that came with a house brick. It was personal choice, really. Buses always looked as if they had just come from a quarry rather than a football match.

After the merriment of 'The Millwall Brick,' everyone on the bus settled down into some sort of order and relative silence. The driver found the right road and it wasn't long before we were heading towards the service station we had visited earlier that day. You know how it is when you realise something and you hope that no one else will notice? Well, I was like that: praying that no one would say anything and that we would just sail past and there would be no chance of a repeat performance of that morning's episode. But life, as I am sure you are aware, is often a bitch. Someone did notice and, as soon as the words left his mouth, the hooligans that had been so peaceful for the last hour suddenly wanted action. They were standing on the front steps, urging the driver to pull in. I'm not normally that fond of the police but I was bloody glad to see them barring the entrance to the service station to football traffic. The hooligans on board welcomed the police with their usual gesticulations but I breathed a deep sigh of relief and hoped that the day's events were now over.

That, perhaps, would have been asking slightly too much. Being deprived of stopping at the service station meant that the burst of adrenaline now needed to be released elsewhere. It was decided, by whom I neither know nor care, that it might be a good idea to strip certain people on the bus and throw their clothes out of the window. It was only done in fun but it didn't look like anything I'd ever associated with fun before, and I must admit to being slightly afraid they might pick on me. They didn't, thankfully, and I walked home fully clad. Some poor sod went home minus his shirt, I think. He had actually been stripped bollock-naked and his jeans were hung out of the window. But they took pity on him – well, I'll give them the benefit of the doubt. This stripping ritual was quite odd for a bunch of thugs but, gradually, this too died down and I was, for a short time at least, able to lie back, smile and think of Chesterfield. I could rest – but I knew that in a fortnight's time it would be a very similar story once again.

Mrs Jones And The German Shepherd

March 2nd, 1974 Rochdale 1 v 2 Chesterfield

My first two excursions with Wynnie's Tours were to the soft Tory underbelly that is the south, but this week we were travelling north; not very far north but it was north, nonetheless – Rochdale, to be precise. This was turning into a habit and was my sixth Town game on the bounce. Now, while I didn't mind following Chesterfield all over the country, I knew my employers were getting a little tired of my Saturday morning excuses. I was working, at the time, at *James Smith Nurseries Ltd* at Tansley and I was supposed to work a 44 hour week which included four hours on a Saturday morning. This was about the fifth Saturday morning I had missed in succession. To be fair to me, the difference in pay for doing 44 hours as opposed to 40 was minimal and that was the main reason I decided to lie in bed on a Saturday morning or nip off and watch Town away. I can't imagine that my employers actually missed me on those Saturdays – and I know I certainly didn't miss them – but I'm pretty sure if I behaved that way now I would soon find myself out of work! (Perhaps that's one reason why I found a job that was Monday to Friday.)

Now, it has to be said, with all due respect to Rochdale, that this was not the most glamorous of fixtures. For some reason the words 'Rochdale' and 'glamour' don't sit too well in the same sentence. Back then, Spotland, Rochdale's home ground, was a bit of a dive, certainly nothing like the revamped place I've visited since. I suppose we were expecting to win (but, then, I suppose we always did) and despite the thought that this might be like Cambridge, what with Rochdale apparently having no lads, Wynnie still managed to fill out the bus with the usual assortment of thugs and fans. It didn't go unnoticed that many of the usual crew that had been present for the other trips were now missing and Wynnie had drafted in what I thought were a few more supporters than thugs. I even considered that this might make us slightly more vulnerable in terms of being a target but with six other coaches of

Town fans heading in the direction of Manchester, even I felt we were relatively safe.

I'm not quite sure how Wynnie used to persuade people to travel on his coach but he always seemed to have a fairly casual approach to enlistment. Yes, he was guaranteed the likes of me and a couple of others from Wingerworth – and I dare say he roped a few in from school, too – but how he managed to get hold of your everyday football hooligan was completely beyond me. In many respects, I didn't care. As long as I could get there and back and stay safe in the process, I was happy.

Our route to Rochdale was straightforward: up the M1 to Leeds and then down the M62. Not the most scenic route but by far the quickest. We had left Chesterfield early as this was an early kick-off because of the miners' strike and power cuts. (For the younger members reading this, a miner was someone who dug coal from down a large hole in the ground and that coal was used for the production of electricity. For the middle-aged reader, this was the first miners' strike against Heath's government, which the miners actually won and which eventually drove Margaret Thatcher *(spit)* into culling them all.)

Despite the early kick-off, the supporters on this coach had managed to consume copious amounts of beer before we set off and were chugging it back with no thought whatsoever of the consequences. There was very little singing or talking as all you could hear was the fizz as another ring-pull unleashed yet more alcohol into someone's blood stream. The driver seemed oblivious to it all. He had probably driven one of Wynnie's mobs before and so knew what to expect – and it wasn't long before the first cry to stop for a toilet break was heard. As usual, it was ignored, not just by the driver but by everyone. The problem is, the moment someone mentions it is the moment you become aware of just how much you could use a toilet break yourself, and pretty soon damn near the whole coach was screaming for him to stop to ease the pain. The driver, however, remained impervious, despite the desperate pleas for him to stop so we could ease the pressure on our heavy bladders. I cannot, for one minute, imagine why he wouldn't stop because, for those in need, anywhere would do.

One could say it was the driver's own fault that the back seats of the bus were lifted to form a urinal. After all, needs must, as they say. One could also say that it was his fault that every possible vessel that could carry urine was being employed for that purpose; in fact, the driver was extremely lucky he didn't possess a hat! With the back seats down, one would never have guessed that underneath lay 4 inches of piss and vomit. Yes, not every one of the fans aboard that bus could drink 15 cans of beer without putting some of it back into the community, as it were. Mind you, you might not have known what lay beneath by *looking* at it but the disgusting smell might just have given it away!

And then, suddenly, without warning, after all the cries to stop had abated and probably about half an hour too late, the driver pulled into a motorway service station. If I'd known the driver's half-hour stop was going to turn into a two hour nightmare, I think I might just have pleaded for him to keep going. Come to think of it, if the driver had known that his half-hour stop was going to turn out the way it did, he might have decided to carry on, without any encouragement from anyone. But no one knew what lay ahead, and with the air now rancid and the bus smelling more like a 200-year-old, never-been-cleaned, outside toilet than a coach, I think we were more than grateful for the fresh air!

At first, all was well. We got off the bus and entered what passed as a motorway service station. It was only a small place; you ordered and ate your meals at the front of the building and browsed round the swivelling racks of cassettes and books at the back. No one, except for the driver, was eating and so, for us, it was a half-hour browse. Now, one of these swivelling things contained those huge eight-track cartridges which some idiot had invented as 'in-car' entertainment, feeling sure it would catch on. It's bad enough watching ordinary cassettes go sliding across the dashboard when you swerve to hit a Blades fan but brake sharply with three of these mothers on your dashboard and they'd go clean through the windscreen!

But I digress. Certain of those among our number decided that having one of these massive devices would be an asset; and, yet, apart from selling them on or, perhaps, even using them as a brick substitute, I couldn't understand why anyone would want one. I suppose one could relate it to the question of, why do men climb Everest? The same thing applied here and I was still contemplating this matter when a loud crunch alerted me to the fact that someone had broken the lock which sealed them in. To be fair, it hadn't just alerted me, it had alerted every Town fan; and anyone who dared gathered around the stand like flies round a dung heap, all hoping they didn't end up with Joe Loss or Mantovani – just try flogging them on a Saturday night in Chesterfield! I had been making my way outside at the time and, to be honest, I wasn't sure what happened next but, suddenly, people were running in all directions, mostly away from the building. Rather than run in that direction myself – which would have been the sensible thing to do – I walked back towards the café area to see why everyone was running? (Foolish me? I'll say so!)

As I arrived at the entrance, I was faced with a rather irate gentleman brandishing a rather vicious German Shepherd (dog, that is – let's face it, what use would a shepherd have been... of any language?) Suddenly, I was questioning why I hadn't run and, yet, I couldn't think properly because this bloke with the dog was screaming so loudly: **"CALL THE POLICE, MRS JONES!"**

I thought it was time we were on our way.

"YOU'RE NOT GOING ANYWHERE, YOU BARSTUDS! MRS JONES... THE POLICE!!"

(Jesus, he could read my mind.)

"YOU ARE GOING NOWHERE, NONE OF YOU, NOT TILL I GET MY GOODS BACK!"

For those who had gathered at the door with the intention of beating the bloke with the dog to death, freeing our bus driver from his bacon and eggs and making off into the afternoon, Fido did his party piece. He growled menacingly, slobbered alarmingly and then barked three times, pulling forward with each bark and taking himself a little nearer someone's leg. The dog had a quietening effect on everyone. Even the ordinary travellers, who had stopped for dinner and wanted to leave, thought it best to have another cup of tea first. No one was going to pass that dog – not and live!

No one wanted to be eaten and no one wanted to get nicked for pinching cassettes either but without our driver we were forced to stay. Mrs Jones had done her job well and several squad cars duly arrived. I had a feeling it might be a rather long afternoon and, so, I turned away and walked back to the bus. This was my statement, my way of saying, *"Nothing to do with me, I have a match to go to!"* Several others joined me and it worked a treat for at least two minutes until we were jostled from the bus by a burly copper and made to huddle in the car park with everyone else.

The police were from Wakefield (and right swines they were, too) but it might give you a rough idea of where we were when all this took place. The first thing the police did was tell us a whopping great fib: "Give us the tapes back, lads, and you can go."

Well, that did seem fairly simple and, as there had only been four taken and these had already been handed back before the arrival of the police, I thought, perhaps rather naïvely, that it had all been sorted out. A few of us even started to head back to the coach. Oh, if only life were that simple. The police, now in possession of the stolen goods, suddenly decided that they wanted the culprits as well.

SHIT! Who was going to own up to that? I couldn't see any way that anyone would possibly own up to the crime and all I could see was a long afternoon in Wakefield nick stretching ahead of me. And so, we stood there; a gaggle of Town fans wanting to be anywhere but a service station car park. We did look a motley crew, I suppose, but then it's difficult for 50 youths in jeans and denim jackets to look anything other than motley.

The police, perhaps wary that we outnumbered them and also conscious that in Wakefield their dinner would be going cold, decided to act. They told us all to line up so they could search us to see if we had any more cassettes hidden about our person. Eventually, we sorted ourselves into some sort of line. I was near the end and I took a look back along the line of thugs, semi-thugs, vandals and supporters that had been created and saw every conceivable and concealable weapon hit the floor before being trodden on and covered by the loose gravel we were standing on. I couldn't believe it! I was so shocked. When we boarded the bus in Chesterfield, I thought we were a little short on the heavies but it appeared that what these hooligans lacked in physical presence, they more than made up for in hardwear. The lad next to me dropped a knife that would have taken your leg off. I'm sure it was some sort of First World War field amputation instrument and it took a hell of a lot of covering, I can tell you.

The lad looked at me as he kicked the last few bits of pea gravel over the handle. "Cost me a fuckin' fortune that did," he said.

Stanley knives, darts, metal combs with handles sharpened to points all went the same way. I doubt if anyone would have used them but the fact that they thought to carry them was mind-blowing enough. In the end, the most dangerous thing found in anyone's pocket was a box of matches.

Then they searched the bus. The thought that some copper was going to ferret around in the squalid mixture lying under the back seat did make me smile and it was a little victory in what was turning out to be a horrid defeat.

"Right, then, who nicked 'em?" some power-crazed copper asked. "If we don't find out who did it we'll take you all down Wakefield and nick the lot of you."

Quite what he would have 'nicked the lot of us' for I don't know but I have seen enough cop shows to know that he would have thought of something. The idea of having no evidence might work on Perry Mason – but this was Wakefield, and we were football supporters. Who the hell was going to believe us? And, as no one owned up, we remained there, a neat line of football supporters standing on enough armoury to have started a war. But we were not moving; we were going nowhere.

I must admit to feeling a little scared as I watched a policeman walk from the bus towards us, brandishing a pickaxe handle. *'Jesus,'* I thought, *'surely he won't lay into us with that?'*

"OK, and who does this belong to?" he demanded.

There was a long silence before a hand waved submissively in the air.

"What are you doing with this, then?" the copper said to a young lad who was only half the size of the handle.

"Well," the excuse began, "I was walking through Queen's Park this morning and I found it and I thought, 'Oh, my dad needs a new pickaxe handle. I'll take it him,' so I just put it on the bus."

The grin that was breaking out on the constable's face matched the ones that had already broken out on the faces of the supporters. Personally, I would have let him off for being able to come up with any excuse other than, *'I want to hit someone with it,'* but the policeman opened the door of the Range Rover and suggested that the lad get in the back seat. The young lad climbed in, slightly dejected that his excuse had been so misinterpreted.

Now, remember, all along the police had said they wanted whoever nicked the *four* cassettes but when someone eventually stepped forward and owned up to it, they decided that *six* had been pinched. This was a crushing blow for everyone – and especially for the lad who had made the supreme sacrifice of owning up to nicking all four after only taking one! He thought that he may as well get done for the lot and then we would all be able to sod off. However, with him seated in the back seat of the Range Rover, as well as the other young lad, the police had shifted the goal posts once again and were now in search of another thief.

So there we were, standing in line, being searched and re-searched and searched once again for good measure – but we still weren't going anywhere. I had this awful feeling that if someone owned up to pinching the other two cassettes, the police might then decide that ten had been stolen and we would continue on like this all afternoon.

The sergeant looked at us closely; he was enjoying every minute. "Now, if anyone saw someone pinch a tape, then he could save himself and his friends a lot of trouble," he said, as if we were children likely to fall for such a lame comment. "Who knows, you might even get to the ground in time for kick-off."

This really was plucking at straws. I mean, who in their right mind would walk out in front of an assembled bunch of football hooligans and say they thought they knew who the culprit was? I was still trying to figure out the odds I would have given the policeman against anyone coming forward when someone did just that!

"I think I saw someone," he said. The rest of the line reeled a little from the shock. "He was small."

"Oh, fucking brilliant," I thought. *"All I need now is for you to say he had a denim jacket on and fair hair and I'm going to be doing time!"*

"He had a denim jacket on and fair hair."

The words just sort of echoed in my head. Surely he'd not said that. Surely this was just my vivid and rather over-active imagination playing tricks on me? Oh, how I wish it had been! Alas, he *had* said it. I stayed calm – through fear, I think – but I wanted to swear at him.

The sergeant coaxed the lad along the line of football supporters and asked him to pick out who he thought it was. The lad wandered slowly in front of us and eventually picked out about five supporters and, thankfully, I was not among them. The police chatted individually with the five and they all had friends who could swear to them being in other places at other times and, so, we were right back to square one.

How long we actually stood there I cannot say but it did seem like hours and the police were not going to budge until they had someone else. In the end, their patience paid off as two lads came forward and owned up; they were tall, dark and not a denim jacket in sight. Thankfully, the police were happy with this particular haul and they put us back on the coach and waved us goodbye. The guilty went to Wakefield nick and were charged, while the rest of us headed off to Spotland and what was left of the game.

Once on the road, a lot of attention turned towards the lad who had falsely picked out five very annoyed, and very innocent, Chesterfield fans! He was sitting on the seat in front of me. I tried to feel sorry for him but if he didn't see anything, then why open his mouth? Why try and get five perfectly innocent people into trouble? Did he say the culprit was a small person because he thought the attention from someone smaller than himself might not be so physical? I've no idea, and to this day I will never understand his actions. If I had seen something, I wouldn't have said. I mean, you knew who you were dealing with. He might have picked out a guilty party but that guilty party would have murdered him back in Chesterfield. This wasn't school where you could go to a teacher if a big lad was going to hit you. As it happened, he had picked out a friend of mine, Andy, who I knew had nothing to do with it and whose older and bigger friends also knew had nothing to do with it. So, I was in full agreement when Andy turned on him on the bus and gave him such a tongue-lashing that it frightened *me* – but the guy was angry and he had every right to be. So, when one of the other innocents walked over and smacked him in the mouth, I couldn't help but think he deserved it. He received a second smack in the gob from another 'annoyed of Chesterfield' and then it seemed as if everyone wanted to hit him. I had no intention of helping him (self-preservation) but I did think we were starting to overreact slightly. Fortunately, one or two bigger, stronger, more right-minded fans managed to stop the in-house brawling, although the lad was threatened as to what would happen to him once we were back in Chesterfield.

We made Rochdale with about ten minutes, perhaps less, of the first half remaining. As we pulled up towards the ground, the driver slowed at a junction and several supporters started to jump off in order to get into the ground. When my turn to jump off arrived, the driver had turned the corner and was doing about 30mph towards the coach park. I wasn't exactly pushed off; it was more that I was coaxed off. People behind me were shouting, "Come on! Come on!" as they were all eager to get off and get in. So I jumped! It was probably one of the most stupid things I've ever done and, believe me, I've quite a collection of those.

I hit the road and started to run but my little legs couldn't run as fast as my body wanted them to. It was one of those awful events that was over in a flash but you remember it in slow motion. I can vividly remember thinking that I needed to stay upright or I'd look like a right twat. I remember being aware that I was actually ahead of the bus. I was struggling desperately to stay upright and, yet, I was horribly aware that I was going to fall – eventually and embarrassingly! And, boy, did I fall! When my legs could no longer keep up with my jet-propelled trunk, I fell forward and slid. You have, no doubt, all seen the film of someone going down the cresta run on the Luge. Well, if you picture someone going down it in denim jeans and jacket with his arms outstretched, then you have the perfect picture of me. I thought I was going to slide right out of Rochdale – and I'll bet you can still see the skid patch of denim and skin to this very day! Not only did I look an idiot, I felt like one too, and it was a question of which hurt more: my burning, tarmac-pitted hands, knees and elbows or my severely dented ego. I was hurt physically and mentally but, despite the howls of laughter from those who stopped to witness the event, I strode back up the road with as much purpose and dignity as I could muster – and, believe me, it wasn't much.

I hurt so much I wanted desperately to cry but, instead, I turned my pain into anger. As I walked back towards the ground, I passed a van at the side of the road, the driver sitting quietly in his seat eating a bag of chips. I had been nothing more than a blur when I passed him the first time but I could see his face through the windscreen. I'm sure it carried a smug grin.

"Don't you dare say anything," I thought, and for a moment I almost got away with it.

He very nearly let me just walk past and lick my wounds as gracefully as possible. But I couldn't be that lucky and, at the very last minute, the guy looked up from his chips and said, "That was a stupid thing to do, wasn't it?"

Ha!! As if I needed reminding. I wanted to walk on – and perhaps I should have done – but in the end I couldn't resist some witty repost to the Lancastrian: "And you can just fuck off!" I screamed. That was about as witty as I was going to get after that fall. Poor bloke never said a word back but I wasn't going to give him the chance.

Once inside the ground the news that greeted us was that we were losing 1–0. As I picked the grit from my hands I wondered if this day could get any worse. There wasn't any serious trouble in the ground but it was mildly entertaining watching Chesterfield fans chase Rochdale fans around the ground and, to be honest, I was long past caring what might or might not happen to anyone else. I had enough to contend with; I was still in shock from my free-fall from the bus.

In the second half Town played much the same as they had in the last ten minutes of the first half and, although an equaliser always looked likely, we desperately needed to win. On 62 minutes Burton crossed and good old Ernie headed the ball back to Bellamy who rifled the ball home from the edge of the area. This was it; we were on our way. I was really jubilant but, then, it all seemed a bit strange. To me, we *were* winning as I'd missed Rochdale's goal and, so, I had to keep reminding myself that we needed another. Ten minutes later, Ernie bagged his second assist of the game; this time for Wilson to hammer the winner hard and low into the left-hand side of the net. Our jubilation was unfettered and suddenly my burning hands and knees were nothing more than a slight irritation. What incredible healing powers an away win has – someone should bottle it!

On the way home, we stopped at the same service station as we did on the way up – only on the other side of the road, obviously. Unfortunately, there was no connecting bridge and, although several of the lads were prepared to brave running across the motorway in order to retrieve their assorted scud missiles and armourlite rifles from the flimsy topping of pea gravel, no one actually did. As far as I know, the stuff is still there today.

So, if you trip over a rusty commando knife in a shitty service station going north on the M1, keep it – there is no forwarding address!

The Seaside Waltz

March 9th, 1974 Southport 1 v 1 Chesterfield

If I were to write, *'Travelled to Southport, got off bus, loads of fighting, got back on bus, came home,'* that would pretty much sum this trip up. Unlike the other games I'd been to this season, I can't really say there was anything that made the Southport trip stand out. There was no hilarious moment or odd quirky happening but, having said that, it still managed to be quite a scary episode, not because I ever thought I was going to get caught up in the trouble but because it all seemed to be happening that much closer to me. It was also the first time I realised that simply being in close proximity to football violence was enough to get you arrested. The police were rapidly losing patience with football supporters and they certainly viewed every away fan as a potential troublemaker. I suppose the police in Chesterfield were acting in exactly the same way with the supporters of clubs who visited us. It's just that I didn't see or care how they were treated by the police; I only cared about what happened to me (a theme that tends to run through all of these stories).

At Southport, the police were completely overwhelmed and looked unprepared for the scenes which confronted them. It was no surprise, therefore, that they were outwitted by the hooligans and went on to mismanage the event so spectacularly it was untrue. Once again, Wynnie had assembled a motley crew and one could have been forgiven for lapsing into thinking that this was going to be an easy day out as the journey itself was relatively tame. No service station was turned over and there wasn't a single fight with a supporter from another club before we arrived in Southport itself. This bout of non-activity pleased me immensely but my experiences to date had taught me not to take anything for granted. The incumbents on Wynnie's Tours had this knack of producing a violent situation where none really existed. I'm sure if Dave Wynne had run a coach to *Disney Land*, the chances are that Mickie, Minnie and Goofy would be on the receiving end of a real good kicking before we left!

Any dreams of a trouble-free trip were quickly and cruelly shattered as we pulled into the town. You could already see supporters fighting in the street and, while my stomach churned at the possible two hour nightmare that was in front of me, some of the Chesterfield fans were licking their lips, polishing their toe caps and insisting that the driver stop the coach so they could get to work. Don't get me wrong, this wasn't a full-blown riot – not yet – but one could see that it clearly had the potential. When football fans start scrapping *before* a ball has been kicked, I suppose you could say it does set the tone for the day, somewhat. While many on my bus were smiling as they jumped down from the coach, before running off to look for someone or something to hit, I stepped down gingerly and I remember thinking that getting into the ground and finding a nice quiet place to hide might be the best thing on the day's menu.

Unfortunately, once inside the ground, I realised that it was possible for football violence to coexist in two places at the same time. The thought that being in the ground would afford me a little more safety from the rough and tumble that was happening outside was cruelly shattered as my eyes fell upon the mass brawls in front of me. In fact, the trouble inside the ground was so bad that some supporters had taken to climbing the floodlight pylons in their desperate bid to escape the fighting. (Well, I assume that's what they were doing; they certainly didn't look like they were on their way to change a light bulb.) It's strange: despite the trouble, I never once questioned if I might have been better off staying at home – which is odd, really, because, being a coward of the highest order, one would have thought that would have been the easiest thing to do. And this was the crazy thing; this is something I will never be able to reconcile: if going to an away match was so tortuous, then one has to ask the very simple question, "Why go?" I wish I had an answer – I really do.

The whole day at Southport has become a bit of a blur. I seem to remember it did quieten down shortly after we scored and that probably had something to do with the fact that we were happy with the proceedings on the pitch. Equally, it could be that it was all so horrible I've blotted the event out of my mind.

When Southport equalised, my heart did sink for two reasons: one, we might not get the 2 points we actually needed to keep our promotion push alive; and two, the Chesterfield hoodlums might just get agitated and start causing a little trouble again. I shouldn't have worried, really: there was no chance of them causing a 'little' trouble because they all seemed hell-bent on causing loads of it. In fact, scuffles broke out almost immediately. It was as if the ball touching the back of the Chesterfield goal was enough to light the blue touch paper underneath the massed ranks of CFC nasties. To say they had short fuses is something of an understatement. The next 20 minutes or so were awful. Town fans would rush at the Southport mob and they, in turn, would run back, gesticulating all the time, encouraging Chesterfield fans to come that bit closer. I suppose it doesn't look like you're running away if you're inviting the opposition fans to come after you. However, asking the Chesterfield mob to "Come on, then" wasn't an invitation they were likely to turn down!

There is a lot of to-ing and fro-ing in football violence. It's a very energetic activity; a bit like dancing, really. You run three steps forward, screaming and waving your arms around, and then bounce three steps back, inviting the opposition to join you. But this definitely isn't the 'do-se-do' and, as if to amplify that message, the two sets of supporters always end up as one in their attempt to kick what is left of the living daylights out of each other. Twenty seconds later and they do it all again – in reverse. This frenetic activity usually sorted out those who were there to boast and run away and those who were there to kick someone's teeth in. Once you got down to the teeth dismantlers it usually got a bit ugly.

The coppers in the ground were hopeless, and helpless, in averting the trouble and I don't think I witnessed much of the second half at all. It was one of those days when you spend 45 minutes with one eye on the crowd's movements whilst trying to follow the football with your other eye and, then, in between times, you have to somehow look at your watch to see how long is left. I have no idea how I coped with the stress but making sure I was safe was always my number one priority. I was now beginning to think that a draw might be a decent result as this would give neither side a reason to start fighting again – although, so far, both had shown a willingness to battle it out regardless of the score.

As the end approached, the police managed to corral the Chesterfield supporters into one corner of the ground, which didn't please anyone very much and I felt less safe than at any other time in the match. There was nowhere to run to now. The brassed-off police were not treating the Chesterfield supporters with any sort of compassion whatsoever – and I suppose one can't blame them – but, suddenly, the police were more of a threat than the Southport fans! To me, it seemed as if this was as much a game for the boys in blue as it was for the fans and I got the distinct impression that Southport Constabulary were only interested in finding a decent reason to unsheathe their truncheons. I could be wrong, they may just have been fed up, but they did seem to relish their duties somewhat.

When the final whistle blew, I ran out onto the street looking for the bus while the majority of the Town fans ran out looking to give the police a reason to arrest them! And, to be fair, I think most of them complied. It was a bit like laying down the gauntlet. The police had slapped the Chesterfield fans across the face with their gloves and, come the final whistle, the honourable Chesterfield hooligans did what they had to do and readily accepted the duel. The streets of Southport rapidly resembled a scene from a Western. People were just running wild and hitting anything that moved. All it needed was a couple of cows to come running down the road and it would have looked more like an episode of *Bonanza* than it did a football match!

When we did eventually leave Southport, there were a couple of empty seats on the bus which indicated that the police had been slightly successful and had managed some notches on their truncheons that day. Someone suggested pulling up and going back into Southport to look for a couple of Southport thugs they wanted to say a special thank-you to. I banged my head against the window and hoped like hell that no one would listen. While most people on the bus did listen, the one person who mattered, the bus driver, just wanted to get home. I could have kissed him.

There were six Chesterfield fans arrested that day and they were all fined £20. Each one had previous football-related crimes against their names. In the press the week after, Southport police stated: *"We have never had to deal with football violence before."* Apparently, everyone in Southport was so really well-behaved – all of the time! Mmmmm, not quite sure I can agree with that one. I admit that I think we started it, and probably finished it, but their lot seemed more than eager to comply.

At half-time, during our match with Oldham at Saltergate the following Saturday, the Club, eager to dissociate itself with the fans who had caused such a rumpus the previous week, made an announcement over the PA system stating that it didn't want to be associated with the actions of the supporters who, and I quote, "were involved in unseemly incidents during the game." It went on to say that the Club could do without these supporters but, by now, no one could hear the rest of the announcement as the Town fans were joining together in songs of praise concerning their efforts the week before.

Boy, if the trouble experienced on Wynnie's tours was to continue at this rate, then I was going to end up with an early ulcer.

The Easter Brummie

April 15th, 1974 Walsall 2 v 0 Chesterfield

I remember the first time I visited the clean, white, architectural lines of that prefabricated biscuit tin, the Bescott Stadium. I hated it: mostly because Walsall played there but also because it had very little soul. In fairness, I suppose it's hard to build a brand new stadium and expect it to inherit character; that can only come with time. However, if anyone needed a new stadium, then it was Walsall. Their old tip, Fellows Park, was reason enough to redevelop or relocate. We all hoped they would relocate to somewhere nice but, sadly, they decided to stick around in Walsall, which was a shame. I suppose most of the older Chesterfield supporters will have visited the old Fellows Park. It was a ground that had everything – and most of it was falling down. It made Saltergate look like Wembley. So wonderful was its awfulness that I still swear it had been put together using the remnants of a 1914 *Meccano* set and a half-empty box of 'Beta Builder' remnants. It was shocking but it did hold memories and, until we played them in the breeze-block arena, I wasn't aware of just how strong they were.

Walsall is one of those trips that we all make. It isn't that far and you can rest assured that you will be home in time for a pint. And, with that as the basis of any argument, it always guaranteed a bigger than average following. Although it isn't what one would class as a local Derby, there has always been a sense of animosity between the two sets of fans – and back in 1974 it was probably at its peak!

Now, as I have said before, football violence is incredibly frightening and I make no apologies for this reiteration. It is, therefore, quite ironic that, while I hated being a part of it and around it, it was something strangely hypnotic to watch – providing, of course, that some degree of safety had been assured. For instance, if your side are dishing it out, then there is always a little bit of you, a slight thought process, that doesn't really care. In fact, it is even fair to say that you get ever-so-slightly smug about it. You might not want to get involved necessarily but it does no harm to watch, does it? If, on the other hand, your supporters are on the receiving end, it's one of the most awful feelings you can ever experience. It's very hard to describe that mixture of pure fear and self-preservation which courses through the veins faster than a flash-flood through Devon. Suddenly, everything else is insignificant – even the football. When, for example, a good thumping is a distinct possibility, then it's very easy not to care about your team's performance on the pitch and, indeed, the scoreline. In fact, there have been times when I've hoped, wished, even prayed that we wouldn't equalise or even win as I've been so afraid of what might happen if we did. Who in their right mind would put themselves through such purgatory just for a football match? Well, me, for a start! I loved going away to watch Town. I wished it had been safer, though, and yet, as a supporter, what do you do? Chesterfield were doing well; I couldn't just sit at home! So that was why I was here at Fellows Park.

For the benefit of those who have never visited Fellows Park, the away supporters were stuck behind a goal in a narrow, uncovered enclosure. A ridiculous brick wall at the back separated them from a shitty piece of ground and then the rail tracks. The portacabin toilets were always blocked, dark and ankle-deep in piss, while female supporters had to get down behind the bushes at the side of the railway lines, I think. When the police eventually figured out how to combat violence, the away supporters were kept in this tiny enclosure; but, before that, they were allowed to go up one side of the right-hand terracing. There was a fence about half-way along to stop people from negotiating a path directly onto the Walsall kop.

Now, this particular Wynnie's tour started like any other. Well, almost – the only difference being that this was Easter Monday. The coach driver had dropped us off outside the ground and then sped to the coach park to have his fortnightly, three hour nervous breakdown.

Once in the ground, there was a very half-hearted attempt at scaling the fence to try and get onto the Walsall kop and, once that had been quashed by the police, we all settled down to some proper football singing. I had, as normal, checked my immediate surroundings and all looked well. There was a large police presence, more than capable of putting down any supporter problems, and so, naturally, I thought that everything was going to be just fine. I had a good view, there was a good-sized crowd and the atmosphere was excellent. Everything you wanted for a football match, really; in fact, who could wish for more?

The game was, perhaps, ten minutes old when a gang of Walsall hooligans began singing at the back of the terrace, behind the Chesterfield contingent, and I got this awful, sickening, sinking feeling inside. Then, a few more Walsall thugs to my left started to sing and the sickening feeling intensified. Then, the nose next to mine exploded! I wasn't really watching and, yet, I saw what happened so clearly. The youth in front of me spun round and punched the youth next to me in the face. Blood shot everywhere and, then, this Walsall thug made his way into the crowd, punching and kicking out at everyone and everything in front of him.

Funny things, noses. After showering half the crowd in blood and snot, I thought the Town fan would be in need of major surgery, a blood transfusion or, at the very least, a lie down. (I think I would have required all three.) I was quite surprised by how much blood came from such a little organ. Cut someone's leg off, nothing; hit them in the nose and they bleed like the proverbial stuck pig. However, despite looking like a victim of a chain saw massacre, he simply wiped his nose on his hanky or sleeve (forget which) and he was well again. In fact, he was so well that all he could think of doing was to turn around and chase the lad who had smacked him and extract a little revenge. Quite the opposite from what my reactions would have been: if I had been hit that hard, I'd probably only just be regaining consciousness and I certainly wouldn't be thinking about any kind of retribution. In no time at all, I had weighed up the situation, realised the pitch battle going on behind me might actually engulf me at some point and decided that the best thing to do was simply remove myself as quickly as possible.

Now, all that is easily thought but running wasn't really an option, although my legs were insisting that it might be. A quick look at my surroundings told me that I was hemmed in at one side by warring factions and on the other side by the fence. So, in order to evade detection by either set of supporters, I pushed my way to the front of the crowd and stood against the wall. I couldn't see much but, then again, that had more to do with the fact that I had turned my back on play and was watching the crowd with more interest than I was watching the game. However, for the time being I did appear to be safe.

Two police officers were standing on the running track behind me and they watched as the fighting continued, with little sign of abating. They stood there, silent and immobile, watching something akin to a re-enactment of the D-Day landings being carried out by two sets of football supporters. Eventually, some high-ranking official (and, yes, that is an 'r' and, no, I'm not short-tongued), who had obviously seen this sort of mêlée before, came charging up the running track, screaming at the statuesque constables, "What did I tell you? Don't just stand there; get in and fuckin' sort it out!!!" And, with that, all three jumped into the hot, violent broth. I couldn't help but think that the acting officer jumped in with a little more relish than I thought healthy; he actually seemed to be enjoying himself!

At this point, more police flooded the terrace from the back and, then, things really did get chaotic. Some of the thugs, eager to avoid detection by the long, and now strong, arm of the law – and, consequently, avoid arrest or eviction from the ground – moved to the front and joined those of us who were standing around trying to avoid getting beaten up in the first place. Those hooligans who had already been walloped, and who were now looking for someone they considered deserving of a walloping back, also started to push towards the front as this was where all the action appeared to be. They obviously didn't care about detection, arrest or eviction because they simply waded in. Fists and feet were flying everywhere. Not literally, of course; they were still attached to their limbs although, given the ferocity of the punch-up, it did make you wonder how much longer it would be before I couldn't use that particular expression. The police, during all this, were grabbing anyone who had a collar they could hold on to for long enough and hauling them out.

One might argue that it was a fair response to a major disturbance but (and there is always a but) being accused of something I haven't done has to be my pet hate. I can deal with most things in life – just – but I can't handle that at all. So, now, I had another dilemma: not only did I have to find a way of keeping some aggravated, pretend brummie from giving me a punch in the mush, I also had to make sure the police didn't mistake me for one of the troublemakers. As I didn't want to get nicked for something I hadn't done or smacked for simply supporting Chesterfield, I took the only possible route out: I jumped onto the wall and got onto the side of the pitch – and I wasn't the only one, either!

Eventually, about 50 to 75 Town fans were lining the side of Fellows Park as the hooligans continued to battle it out on the terraces. I actually managed to sneak a look at what was happening on the pitch for the first time in what seemed like ages. So, for now, I was out of it – although how long I could remain on the side of a football pitch remained to be seen.

The only problem with being pitch-side is that you are instantly recognisable, mostly to the police, and, as I was doing my best to avoid being arrested, you might conclude that this wasn't the smartest move in the world. But I guess the thought of being arrested was a lot less worrying than the one of being thumped so, for now, I was quite content to stay pitch-side. I just hoped that the boys in blue would understand my dilemma. I think they did – or, at least, no one came up to me to tell me to get back into the crowd.

The Walsall kop thought this was really great and told us, in no uncertain terms, what a load of shit-bags we were, and if I'd have cared I might have agreed but I didn't care because I was safe, so they could sing what the hell they liked. They also told us how impressively violent they were and, once again, because I was safe I really didn't give a monkey's.

The game was stopped temporarily but it started again quickly as the police managed to heave most of the supporters back into the melting pot. A mass brawl erupted almost immediately. Well, it isn't rocket science, is it? What did they think was going to happen: the two sets of fans sit down and sign a peace treaty? I think not! Those still left on the running track, including me, questioned the police on the safety of the terrace environment – and with good reason, too, I thought. But, gradually, the police, through encouragement, the promise of eternal safety, tickets to the policeman's ball and, finally, threat of eviction from the ground, managed to lure every Chesterfield fan from the safety of the running track and back onto the terrace. Well, nearly all. There was just one rather stubborn individual who wasn't moving until he was sure it was safe to do so... ME!

I don't remember feeling particularly frightened at this stage – not while I was on the running track, at least – and perhaps that's why I decided to stay there. I wanted to continue to feel not particularly frightened. As far as I was concerned, nothing had changed. The fans were still fighting on the terrace; they were just fighting on a different bit of the terrace to where they had started but it still made it a fight in my eyes and no one was going to convince me otherwise.

Some pimply-faced copper grabbed me by the shoulder and told me to get back onto the terrace but, taking one look at the supporters still sprawling and brawling beneath me, I turned to him and said, as politely as possible, "No." I pointed to the maelstrom of bodies below me and put it to him that if he were able to sort out that particular problem, then I would gladly entertain the notion of life back on the terrace. He gave me an odd kind of stare; he wasn't sure whether to arrest me, punch my head in or simply chuck me out. Let's face it, he could have done any of them as they were all in the 'Coppers' Guide on How to Deal with Football Supporters' manual issued to each policeman at the start of basic training. But in the end he did nothing. He just looked around to make sure no one was watching, sniffed, put his hands behind his back and slouched off towards the safety of the kop. I don't blame him; I'd have done exactly the same thing.

Whilst I may not have been the first supporter to have braved climbing onto the pitch at Walsall, I was, quite definitely, the very last person to come down from it! That in itself, I feel, is something of an achievement and one I am justly proud of. It was an odd feeling being up there on my own. I wanted to get down and back onto the terrace because I've never been an exhibitionist but I was playing against raw, unbridled fear and I was about 16–0 down!

I did no more than stroll along the running track, stopping occasionally to watch the match. In my head I had decided that if things were settled by the time I got to the corner flag, then I would rejoin the supporters on the terrace. All I could do was hope we didn't score before then; I'm pretty sure jumping up and down at the side of the pitch would have been a throwing out offence! So, I sauntered down the running track; my body language suggesting that I did this kind of thing on a regular basis and that I was in total control of the situation. The reality, of course, was quite different. The reality was that, although I was staring at the pitch, I had absolutely no idea what was happening on it and a voice inside of me was screaming *'HEEEEEELLLLLPPPP!!!!!!'* for all it was worth.

At one point, the ball went out for a throw-in to Chesterfield and Ernie Moss came over to take it – or to pick the ball up, at least. As he did so, I patted him on the back and said, "Come on, Ernie," (probably the three most used words in the Chesterfield vocabulary at the time). I doubt if anyone ever said anything else to the man throughout his career. But the look he gave me back wasn't one of, *'Oh thank you, mate. That's really nice. Me and the lads really appreciate your support!'* It was more a look of, *'Why don't you fuck off, you hooligan, and let us play football.'* And I suppose I realised at that moment that I had absolutely no idea how the players viewed the supporters. Did they see us all as hooligans? Did we annoy them? I guess I'll never know. What is strange is that I can remember a two second encounter with Ernie Moss at the side of the pitch and, yet, had I not been through back copies of the *Derbyshire Times*, I couldn't have told you the score or anything else about this game!

Things had quietened down considerably on the terrace. The police had managed to part the two sets of supporters and I was beginning to think that my original goal to reach the corner flag might not be necessary after all. But you no sooner think that than some nutter breaks ranks and goes for it, and the whole thing kicks off all over again. I was asked once more to remove myself from the side of the pitch; this time by a more experienced officer. Rather than ignore him I told him what I intended to do – make the corner flag and rejoin the supporters – and he seemed to think this was a reasonably decent idea and let me pass.

I'd started my jaunt along the pitch side, around the half-way line and, eventually, when I reached the corner, I was finally persuaded to get back onto the terrace. The distance was no more than 40 yards but it might have been 40 miles as that was how long it seemed to take me to cover the distance. I remember very little else about the game, to be fair, and think the rest of the 90 minutes passed in relative quiet.

After the game, there was an eagerness present among the Chesterfield fans that I hadn't witnessed before. For some, like myself, it was an eagerness to get out of the ground and get to the bus in one piece but for the majority it was an eagerness to get outside and explode a few noses for themselves. Somehow, on my exit, I managed to get sucked into the middle of the crowd of Chesterfield fans eager for revenge. That may be a safe place to be whilst walking out but, once on the street, I knew I was little more than hooligan fodder. Fortunately, just as I'd been sucked into the middle of the crowd, as we pushed for the exit I was flung to the outskirts of it once that exit had been made. The roar from the Walsall fans running down the road towards us was almost as sickening as the roar from the Chesterfield fans running to meet them. I jumped over the railings and legged it across the road and down towards the buses. I could hear the battle raging behind me. It wasn't getting any closer but it was still raging.

Eventually, people did start to filter back towards the bus. Some of them were bleeding, some smiling with the obvious delight of having smacked some brummie and, once again, I was just glad to be in one piece. I was safe. I didn't care who had been hit or who had been doing the hitting.

On the way home the atmosphere on the bus was good and rowdy, to say the least. Bottles, which had been loaded on at Chesterfield, had to be despatched. The favourite method for this was to wait until the bus was going round a corner and then hurl them out of the windows. It had to be a long corner, though – the sort that made you sway visibly in your seat. It always appeared as if these corners gave you far more to aim at. Someone would stand at the front of the bus as a kind of look-out and every time a corner came up with a pub on it, or a car park of some description, the call to the back was made. As the bus slewed its way around the corner, about 20 arms would each sling a bottle just at the correct moment. The bottles would do a passable impression of a Barnes-Wallace bouncing bomb, skip along the pavement and then smash into a million fragments against the front grille of the car of whichever unfortunate had parked it in the pub car park that night. Some bottles would actually bounce up and smash on the bonnet. This bottle-skimming malarkey was quite a skill, I can tell you, and, while the unfortunate owners of the targeted cars might not have thought so, it was incredibly funny. I should point out that, once away from the town, they did only aim these missiles at inanimate objects and what always amazed me was that if the guy at the front, shouting instructions about approaching corners and cars, ever saw someone on the pavement, he would lean back and shout, "Hold it, lads. Someone's on the pavement," and no one would throw. I couldn't help but be impressed by that; 20

minutes earlier they had thought nothing of kicking seven bells out of a stranger but, once away from the ground, they were almost normal. Made no sense at all but, then, football violence never did.

As I say, the bottle skimming was a great pastime and it was usually used just as a bit of light entertainment against inanimate objects. However, I did see it used more than once against opposing supporters and, to be honest, I thought that was even funnier!

Not Exactly Safe Hands

April 20th, 1974 Hereford 2 v 1 Chesterfield

This was our last away game of the season and, for some reason, Wynnie wasn't taking a bus. Whether this was because he had been invited to his Aunty Mabel's wedding or little Billy's christening, I really cannot say. What I do know is that, although Wynnie wasn't attending, he did want to be there in spirit and, so, he somehow managed to coax me into being the organiser for this one. After all, Wynnie had a reputation to uphold. I'm not sure why he asked me to organise the trip. Perhaps it was because he realised immediately that I had the entrepreneurial skills needed to organise a 52-seater coach to Hereford. Perhaps it was because, as a long-standing Town fan, I had the kudos to carry this off? If I'm being brutally honest, I think it was because I was the only one soft enough to attempt such a thing, and when I eventually agreed Wynnie smiled and left. It was as if his footballing travelling dynasty remained intact, albeit ridiculously perched upon my not-so-strong shoulders.

The first bit was easy: I booked the bus. I couldn't believe how simple it was. I phoned *Slack's* of Tansley and booked a bus to Hereford, told them what time we wanted to be there and they gave me a price and departure time. I think the cost of the coach was £90, which seems incredibly cheap for a bus, but I suppose the average wage back then was about a fiver, so perhaps it wasn't so cheap after all. I remember quite clearly sitting in my bedroom wondering how much to charge. Dare I charge a little extra and try and make a little something for myself? But, then again, perhaps I should make it as cheap as possible to make sure the bus was filled. I worked out prices for just about every possible scenario and I think it's fair to say that I was shitting rather large bricks at the whole prospect. I couldn't believe how I'd got roped into this. I'd never done this before and wasn't the confident, self-assured individual that I would *still* like to be!

I remember going to the home game before the Hereford match and talking to my mate Rob. I expressed my doubts over who might or might not turn up. Even if everyone from Wingerworth turned up, I would still be a long way short on numbers. In fact, even some of those who had encouraged me to take this venture on had still to nail their colours to the mast and say they were actually coming. But Rob was adamant that everything would be alright and, if anything, we would be turning people away. *'Oh thanks, mate,'* I thought. *'I really needed to hear that. Now there'll be a pitched battle in Queen's Park as people try and fight to get on the bloody bus.'* It was one of those 'damned-if-you-do-and-damned-if-you-don't' moments. Despite Rob's assurances, I wasn't so sure. I didn't have the contacts that Dave Wynne had and, as far as I knew, he hadn't let anyone know that this particular bus was running.

Saturday morning I was up bright and early, mostly because I hadn't slept through the night. I just wanted to get this out of the way. I was very quiet on my way into Chesterfield and even quieter when I reached Queen's Park, which was more or less deserted. I swore – several times, actually. I cursed everyone I could think to possibly curse and then, suddenly, out of the bright morning mist, a few figures came slouching towards us.

"See!" Rob said. "I told you people would come."

Well, he had a point. People *had* come but it was going to take more than these five extra people to get this bus to Hereford. By the time the coach actually turned up I had less than 20 people standing around. I can't remember the exact number. I know that I'd worked out my worst case scenario but even that was better than the one which now presented itself. I told everyone that this was going to be an expensive trip and we had to dig deep and, eventually, after several whip-rounds, I had accumulated about £35. I told the driver my predicament and he said, "Just a minute. I'll go and see if I can take you for that."

I was absolutely flabbergasted. I thought he'd just laugh at me and drive away but to say he would actually find out if he could run the trip... well, that was something I wasn't expecting. The coach disappeared and ten minutes later it reappeared. We were all convinced that we were on our way to Hereford; a feeling that lasted as long as it took for the driver to open the door and say, "Sorry, mate. Gaffer says I can't take you for that." And, with that, he closed the coach doors, sped off up the road and left us standing there like idiots – none more so than me.

I knew it was a bad idea: me organising a coach! I knew it all along but these nincompoops would insist. I really did feel like shouting at Rob that it was all his fault. He was the one who was so sure people would turn up but it was too late now; the bus had disappeared over the horizon and so had our chances of attending the game... or had they?

I leaned towards my mate and whispered, "The supporters' club coaches leave from the bottom of Foljambe Road – let's see if they have any places."

With that, we hurtled off in the direction of West Bars. We were followed about ten seconds later by everyone else who wanted to go and had suddenly realised where Rob and I were running to. We arrived as Howard Borrell was counting up the numbers. True to form, there were three or four spare seats and Howard was good enough to let us on. Well, it made his life easier, I'm sure.

Okay, so it wasn't Wynnie's Tours. Okay, so I had been a huge flop – and it was doubtful if there was a career as a travel agent waiting for me – but I was on my way to Hereford so, in some respects, it had worked out just fine.

The journey down was exceptionally uneventful and I only then realised just how entertaining Wynnie's tours were: there was always something happening; they were colourful and vibrant and ever so slightly risky. Travelling by supporters' club coaches was like wearing a dull, brown hat in comparison.

Hereford itself seemed a fairly dull town but, then, to be fair, everywhere does when you're going to a football match. The one thing you aren't doing is taking in any architectural splendour, so perhaps I'm doing the place a disservice? I must admit, I remember very little about the game. I know the weather was fine and I know we lost 2–1, with Jim Kabia scoring for Town. What I do remember, however, is 'offering out' a young Hereford fan on the other side of a couple of fences from me. He stood there, just smiling at me, for some time and then started saying things along the lines of how he was going to get me. But he didn't just say it; he said it in a very creepy, 'Gollum-like' voice. The youth was a complete weirdo. In the end, after listening to his southern inbred drawl about how he was going to get me outside, I launched into a tirade of abuse that was a mixture of annoyance at this runt and also at myself for having fucked up the bus thing.

"Listen, twat," I said in a good, proper, no–nonsense, Derbyshire accent. "Why don't you just fuck off and die? If I see you outside I'm going to smash your fuckin' head in, you knob."

Gollum looked at me as if he'd already won. He smiled in a very creepy way and said, "I'll be seeing you outside, then," and, with that, he scurried back under the rock he'd crawled from.

It goes without saying that he was nowhere to be seen after the game – and for that I was truly grateful. I really shouldn't be getting into fights with fictional characters anyway!

The Final Fling...

As for promotion... well, we didn't quite make it. We finished fifth. We were 5 points behind the promotion spot. These days we would have been comfortably in the play-offs but, back then, it was close – but no cigar.

Apart from a minor incident where Bristol Rovers fans were given a running tour of the town before being smacked for not taking enough interest, the season ended poorly; not only did we lose at Hereford but we also lost our last home game, too.

It was a tame end to an interesting season but, surely, we could do it next year... couldn't we?

That Sinking Feeling
SEASON 74/75

After the violence of the previous season, Arthur Sutherland, Chesterfield's genial chairman and self-appointed righter of wrongs, went in the press demanding stiffer penalties for football hooligans. He was among many, at the time, who were suggesting stiffer penalties for these hoodlums. The right-wing press, as one would expect, harped back to the glory days when people were birched for less – and it might be fair to say that, in most people's eyes, birching was too good for most of these rowdy thugs. Despite having the full backing of the press (and every right-minded football fan), Mr Sutherland would not be placated. As far as he was concerned, these were serious offences, no doubt worthy of the death penalty! He ranted on, blaming parents, school teachers, the lack of conscription, the fact that kids get too much chocolate – in fact, everything – for the so-called lack of discipline. I dare say it wasn't like this in his day! And, because of that, Arthur wanted none of it; he didn't want to see Chesterfield fans carrying out random acts of violence at Saltergate – or any other grounds.

Well, he needn't have worried. Through the usual penny-pinching tactics of the directors and the fact that this board of men all seemed to have arms shorter than their exceedingly deep pockets, they managed to turn a side that had finished fifth in the league into one that struggled and, at Christmas, looked odds-on favourites to go down. This financial tight-fistedness, which has been something all Chesterfield fans have become accustomed to over the years, meant that we simply were not worth travelling to watch. In all honesty, we were hardly worth the bus fare into Chesterfield to watch the home games! However, if the chairman had thought a few words in the local paper were going to dissuade fans from dishing out the occasional knuckle sandwich, then he was very much mistaken.

The first of such fracas happened fairly early on in the season at a home game with Watford on October 26th. (Remember: this was in the days when the season actually started in late August, rather than late July as it does now.) It was an entertaining game which finished 4–4. (I suppose a 4–4 draw can't be anything but entertaining.) Both sides were languishing near the bottom of the table but these were early days and no one was taking too much notice of league positions at this stage. Before the game, teams from the two supporters' clubs had met for a friendly game of football. This was starting to happen more and more: supporters' clubs trying to show the general public that two sets of opposing fans could actually meet together and get on without resorting to beating each other up in massed riots along the high street.

Unfortunately, in the evening, after the main game, the Watford fans – no doubt extremely happy with the point their team had managed to get – decided to go into town for a quiet drink. I suppose a quiet drink in Chesterfield on a Saturday night is asking for an awful lot. But what they didn't expect was to be set upon by about a dozen deranged Town fans. They were chased through the town centre and all but one of them ran off. One Watford fan was hit by a dustbin that had been ripped from a signpost and, then, after dishing out a severe hammering to the rest of the Watford contingent, the group turned their attentions to the guy who didn't run away. In fact, their attentions were turned so much that they punched and kicked him until he lost consciousness. The guy was in hospital for three days. I heard the story the following day and, as with all good rumours, by the time it reached my ears the Watford fan had been killed! Two days later, he wasn't dead at all; he was in a coma. And then, finally, the truth emerged that he'd left hospital after three days. Even though the guy made a full recovery, it was still the worst football violence I'd heard of in Chesterfield. I'd seen a fair amount of it by now but this was indiscriminate, ugly and frightening. The violence I'd witnessed up until this point had been between rival supporters who *wanted* to get involved but this was against supporters who, well, to be honest, were like me; they wanted to watch their team, have a pint and then go home. Six of the Chesterfield fans involved in the attack were sentenced to six months in a detention centre; four of them were just 17 years old. Four more fans were sentenced to three months in a detention centre and one of those was just 15. It was reported in the *Derbyshire Times* that the prosecuting barrister, in his summing up, said: *"Visiting supporters appeared in the streets of Chesterfield in the evening at their peril."* Now, I know what he meant but, as a quote in a paper, it did look as if the prosecuting barrister was a Chesterfield fan issuing a warning!

He was right, though; it *was* true. And I hadn't realised, until starting to write this, just how rough Chesterfield was. I can always remember a retired police inspector telling me that, back then, square mile for square mile, there was more violence in Chesterfield than in Glasgow. I know you can make statistics say anything you want and I have no way of checking whether this particular pearl of wisdom is true or a complete load of codswallop. What I can be sure of, though, is that, at the time, the *Derbyshire Times* was packed with cases of violence – not all of them football-related, I hasten to add, but violence nonetheless – and one does forget just how bad things actually were in those days.

The Roker Roar

FA Cup Third Round

January 4th, 1975 Sunderland 2 v 0 Chesterfield

With little happening on the league front, the FA Cup was a welcome relief for everyone. Somehow we had managed to see off Boston (3–1) in the first round and Doncaster (1–0) in the second before landing a plum third round tie with Sunderland away. Everyone was going to go – third round ties don't come around that often for Chesterfield fans. In fact, I think they are so rare that Sotheby's could auction them off for a fortune! Wynnie had intended running a bus but the moment he heard there would be a special train he decided against it. Even a schoolboy entrepreneur of Dave Wynne's magnitude knew he couldn't compete with the might of *British Rail*.[2]

Two years earlier, in 1973, Sunderland, from Division 2, had pulled off a momentous FA Cup win by beating the might of First Division Leeds United 1–0 at Wembley. Although still stranded in the Second Division, their supporters always expected more from them; they finally managed to get back to the top flight the following season. There was the usual hype that surrounds such a fixture – what with us being the Third Division underdog and Sunderland being recent winners of the cup – but there was also a scary undercurrent, which must have had something to do with Sunderland being a regular set of thugs. I'd heard quite a few rumours suggesting your average Sunderland fan was harder than

---

[2] For the younger reader British Rail was a national company, run and owned by the government, and it made for exceptionally cheap public transport. It was later sold off to any old urchin so the public had to pay through the nose to travel by train.

granite and would bash your granny if he/she got half a chance. They certainly had a reputation; one I'm sure they were proud of and I'm sure others feared. We did know something about it because Sunderland fans, along with any other bus-load of muppets that fancied a ruck on a Saturday night, had taken to stopping off in Chesterfield to see what was on offer. Apparently, they weren't often disappointed.

I was booked on the special train with three of my usual travelling companions; although 'special' and 'train' were not two words that immediately sprung to mind when the thing rolled into the station! The train was full, as they always seemed to be, and *British Rail* had offered us the last line in supporter comfort – and I mean the *last* line. I've never been over-keen on a selection of converted cattle trucks (they're certainly not the images I conjure up when I think of travelling by rail) and, so, it was with some disappointment that I watched this thing hobble into the station. This train was so bad it was almost derailed! The transport (for it pains me to call it a 'train') consisted of occasionally-lit carriages with facing seats (no tables in between). Once again, 'seats' is probably over-egging the pudding a little as I seem to remember my 'seat' offering my backside very little padding before hitting the hard board on which it was mounted. Also, not all the toilets were fully functional. All of this made for an extremely uncomfortable and smelly journey. It was an exceptionally bleak picture and, had this train been a building, then it would have been earmarked for demolition!

British Rail had taken to putting on these carriages for football specials because they presented the vandal with very little opportunity to practise their vandalising skills. In fact, come to think of it, they might well have been expecting us to put this poor, wretched creature out of its misery. In some respects, it's hard to blame them. Why put on your best carriages when you know the chances are they'll come back looking like this one did when it started out and only fit for carrying football supporters at the very best? So this was it; this was how I was to spend the next few hours. If you were looking for a nice comfy ride to Geordieland, this was certainly not the mode of transport to be using.

We probably hadn't gone more than 10 miles before even more of the toilets packed in; they just weren't equipped for handling that amount of supporter waste. Toilet paper may well dissolve quite easily in water but the back page of *The Sun* is a different beast altogether – and that does tend to hang around a little longer, too. It was a truly

Dickensian scene: more supporters on the train than they had seats for; dark, dank and smelly; enough beer for everyone to get well and truly drunk and still have some left over for coming home; and a toilet-to-person ratio that meant continual queueing. In effect, a nightmare, a complete and utter nightmare. It has to be one of the worst train journeys ever. It's certainly not something you'll see Michael Palin making a documentary about on the *BBC*, that's for sure. It was uncomfortable, it was cold, and rivers of piss just made their way up and down the aisles. (If *British Rail* were 'getting there,' as they boasted on their advertisements, then they certainly weren't doing it on this trip!) As I say, I don't really blame *British Rail*; I blame the countless vandals up and down the country who had torn apart decent rail carriages in the past – but then, having said that, you really wouldn't treat a dog like we were being treated.

Eventually, after miles and seemingly endless miles of jarring train journey, we arrived in Seaham. Where? Yes, Seaham (or, at least, I think it was Seaham). It was a station not unlike Chesterfield's, only more remote; a station in which, I hasten to add, our train looked perfectly at home! There were two narrow platforms and two narrow exits/entrances, both out onto the road. Most of us had expected to be dumped on Sunderland Central. In fact, on the way into the main station most of us stood up and started to put on our coats. Then, some wise old hooligan screamed, "Sit down, ya twats. Bricks'll be coming through in a minute."

With my arm half-way up a sleeve hole, I tried to hurl myself into the seat, only to find that everyone else who thought we were getting off at Sunderland Central had hurled themselves into *my* seat. So, I just stood there, trying to look calm as I completed the coat manoeuvre. To my knowledge, nothing hit the train. Indeed, some fans were openly hanging out of the windows hurling obscenities as we raced on through the station. But the wise old hooligan (hereinafter known as 'git') looked at the sheep who had followed his nose below the window-line and said, "Best not get seen; they might recognise ya."

Yeah, like someone's going to stand on Sunderland Central and then report back to Roker Park, saying to his mates, "Right lads, we're looking for a Chesterfield fan, blue denim jacket and blue jeans. He's 5ft-9ins tall, brown hair, big nose, scar on his cheek; his friends call him 'Shit-for-brains.'" I mean, honestly, I admit to being naïve but that's not naïve, that's bordering on paranoia. I thought his point about a brick coming through was well made, though, but he had to go and spoil it by opening his mouth again.

Anyway, ten minutes later the cattle are driven off at Seaham and the eager cargo troop up the road towards Roker Park, a walk of about a mile. There was a heavy police presence – which was nice – and everything felt okay. We weren't followed by scores of Sunderland fans nor were we running away under a hail of bricks; it was just an ordinary walk on a very dull day. I suppose I was somewhat surprised. I expected to at least be taunted from the other side of the road – but, no, there was nothing.

Like Hillsborough, Roker Park had no segregated away end. There was an end opposite the kop which away supporters were supposed to use and, again like Hillsborough, that was also occupied by Sunderland's finest/hardest. I have to say, I was most impressed by Roker Park: it looked enormous. I'd heard many stories about the mythical beast they called the 'Roker Roar' and from the size of the kop I could understand why it had such an impact on those who'd heard it. By the time quarter-to-three arrived, the ground was filling up nicely, and it filled up to the tune of thirty-four thousand two hundred and sixty-eight, eventually. (I wonder why that doesn't look as impressive as 34,268?)

The away end was big and open and, as I've said already, it allowed fans to mix without the intervention of the police. When Sunderland ran out, I heard for myself the famous Roker Roar. I haven't heard anything like it since. People go on about the kop at Anfield but that's nothing in comparison. In fact, it's like trying to compare an episode of *Playschool* with *Die Hard 3*... Can't be done; just can't be done.

The roar from the away end was bad enough and, as always happens, four of us managed to get segregated from the main bulk of Town fans. For once, I was pleased: if there was any argy-bargy, then we were far enough away not to get caught up in it. We seemed to be surrounded by middle-aged blokes, which I also thought was a good thing because it meant I could cheer (a little) when Town ran out and try my best to encourage the side in a non-verbal way. On the way up to the ground, it had all seemed so ordinary; I could have been going to watch Town at Matlock, it was so quiet. But suddenly I was pushing my way into this huge crowd which was so much more intimidating than anything I'd experienced so far. I wanted us to win, obviously, and our position in the ground meant that we might just about enjoy that if it happened. However, such was the crowd that day that I couldn't see us getting out of the ground alive if such a miracle was to occur. Watching football was really difficult back then. It was hard to enjoy an away victory or a major cup upset to its fullest when you spent most of the game worrying about all the possible repercussions. Thankfully, we don't have any of that now. We can stand and shout, regardless of the score, because *they* are over there, and *you* are over here, and never the twain shall meet.

As for the game itself, well, there was nothing much to remember about it, really. Ernie missed a sitter – but, then, he usually did, bless him – and we were content to keep it at a very respectable 2–0 defeat. We couldn't even manage a goal when their keeper, Jim Montgomery, was stretchered off with a badly gashed knee. Their supporters seemed happy and, although I wasn't happy, I could see us getting back home alive, so maybe it wasn't so bad after all. And just as I'm thinking all this rubbish (ten minutes to go), the guy in front of me looks at his watch and turns to me and says, "I'd fuck off now if I were you."

Stunned doesn't really sum it up. I wasn't quite sure if it was a friendly piece of advice or a veiled threat. The man hadn't spoken to me all the game and, yet, here he is telling me to 'fuck off.' After picking my chin up off the floor, I looked at him and asked why.

"They'll fuckin' murder you, this lot, at the end of the match. Murder you!"

Hey, I only need that kind of information once. My friends had heard Confucius deliver this hammer blow and were in the same frame of mind as me.

"Shall we go?" one of them said, as if it was his own original thought, and we all eagerly agreed.

What a top idea it was, we conceded, and so we pushed our way through to the exit and walked down the steps that led to the tunnel under the terracing. Off these tunnels were exits out onto the street. We walked round the concourse, hastily shoving scarves up jumpers and inside jackets. About six skinheads in the fashion of the day – that being Doc Marts, turned up jeans and scarves hanging from wrists and belt loops – guarded the first exit. (It seems strange to think that men who'd kick your head in rather than look at you would stoop to putting a scarf around their wrist – a silk one at that! If they did it now they'd be called everything from a 'Jessie' to a 'poof' – but *then*, boy, *then* it was hard.) So, there's these youths just loitering around the exit. We could have risked it but it would only have taken one of them to ask a question and we would have been dead as none of us possessed anything that remotely resembled a decent Geordie accent.

We walked quickly on to the next exit, only to find the same thing. Not the same youths, obviously, but the same set-up. We groaned. We daren't walk any further because we'd be getting closer to the home fans which, in retrospect, might not have been a bad idea. So, instead, we doubled back and immediately caught the attention of the youths standing at the gate. One of them pointed and we scampered off and, suddenly, we knew that we could never get out of that gate now. We passed our first choice again and, although they may not have done, I couldn't help but feel that every one of the youths standing in the exit mentioned that we'd already passed by once. They probably didn't – they probably didn't notice at all – but I was starting to panic. The next exit was free and we ran out onto the street before things changed.

This was probably the first time I'd run away from a ground before the match was over. I wanted to put as much distance between me and Roker Park as was humanly possible. As we hit the top of the hill and were looking down towards the station, the game ended. A huge cheer went up. We smiled at one another and at what we considered to be a great escape. We could also hear the sporadic roars of fighting as fans left the ground. We started running again and didn't stop until we were on the platform.

Foolishly, I expected the shit-tip of a train to be there, ready and waiting to whisk us off home. Sometimes I'm so gullible it's frightening. I started to worry. There were no police and it wouldn't have taken a great deal to storm the platform. Chesterfield fans appeared on the platform in dribs and drabs and Sunderland fans appeared on the platform over the tracks in equal numbers – and a right aggressive bunch they were, as well. I just hoped no one from Chesterfield decided a round of *'Come and 'ave a go if ya think yer 'ard enough,'* was in order. Fortunately, they didn't; but I still searched the skyline for our train because until I was 20 miles out of this dump (which is exactly what it was) I wasn't going to feel safe.

Over the tracks, the Sunderland fans started to make gestures to the Town fans but without any real intent until, suddenly, this short, fat, round character steps forward and points to what I can only say was possibly the hardest Town fan there.

"Right, you! On the tracks! Now!" he said.

The lad from Town just looked aghast.

"Alright, then," he replied, and the pair of them started to climb down from the platform and onto the tracks.

Now, I'm no hero but I just couldn't see how it was any kind of a match. As I've said, the Sunderland fan was short (more so than me, believe it or not), he was fat and he looked like a little rubber ball in Doc Martens. He was probably as hard as rock but I still thought he was in for a pasting. *'You've picked the wrong one,'* I thought – but, then, had he? He'd probably picked the one he knew would take him up on the offer. Perhaps it really does 'take one to know one.'

Anyway, the buzz of possible violence rippled up and down the platform and I took a step forward to get a better look. (I hate football violence, me.) And I've no sooner taken this one small step for mankind than a bottle smashes at my feet. I looked across the tracks and there's just rows of grinning faces, like one of them has cobbed it and then they all put their hands behind their backs encouraging me to guess who did it. Next minute, another bottle smashes into the platform 5 yards to my right; then I can hear yelps as bottles smash down on people further down the platform. It was then that I realised they were coming from behind. I turned and looked through the rotting corrugated iron that formed the back of the station and there, on the field, were hundreds of Sunderland fans all throwing bottles over the station roof. If they'd taken the bottles back to the shop they could have bought a season ticket![3]

Every Town fan bar one was now pressed against the wall of the platform as bottles smashed down on the now deserted platform. I looked over to where the fight was taking place – and it wasn't! In fact, it never actually started as the police had spotted it early on and rushed

---

[3] Once again for the younger readers, when I was a lad, rather than place all our bottles in a blue bin on the yard, we used to take our empties back to the shop where the shopkeeper would give us 1p back per bottle. These empty bottles were then given back to the company to reuse. It was early recycling – only cheaper.

in to drag the short, fat guy off the tracks and do pretty much the same with the Town fan. I did think the police might just go round the back of the station and sort out the bottle throwers but they didn't – they left them to it.

Eventually, our transport arrived and, at that moment, I didn't care that the train was falling apart. All I cared about was the fact that it had an engine and would get us out of this God-forsaken hell hole. We did get a better look at the bottle throwers from the train and it appeared as if they were mostly girls and extremely young kids. The crazy thing was they obviously did this to everyone.

As the train pulled away they threw a few last bottles and then resorted to the two-fingered salutes that I could easily deal with from a five-year-old. We waved Sunderland goodbye from the discomfort of the train. A couple of bottles smashed overhead and, although I can't speak for everyone, I gave a huge sigh of relief. It had been a horrible day.

Sitting in my hard seat I dreamed of getting back into Chesterfield. What a day! But, then, that's the magic of the cup for you!

GRANNY STOPS THE AGGRO

January 25th, 1975 Chesterfield v No One – Postponed Game

One of my many boasts is that, in around 40 years of football supporting, I've never been beaten up at a football match. I've always maintained that football violence can be avoided by bringing a little commonsense and a great deal of fast running into play. So far, it has stood me in good stead and I can honestly say that no one has ever laid a violent finger on me at a football match. It's not something I should boast of – I'm sure there are individuals who can admit to a similar record, and probably over a longer period of time – but, considering that I can be a particularly stubborn and forthright distributor of views, then it's already a record that could be looked upon favourably. Add to that the fact that a great deal of my supporting was done amid the turbulent days of the 70's, and my choice of travelling companions was not what one might always class as desirable, I think you'll agree I have a boast that not only is impressive but sounds damn nigh impossible! Strange it may seem to you but true, nonetheless.

Perhaps, though, you've already spotted the flaw in my proud boast: "No one has ever laid a finger on me in violence at a football match." That particular quote is true but there is a hole in this seemingly perfect record. Unfortunately, a bunch of Forest fans happened to beat the shit out of me one cold winter's Saturday in Chesterfield when the game had been postponed. If it had not been for this digression into the land of the beaten up, my record would be all the more impressive. (Well, it would for me, I can tell you!)

I'll never forgive those particular Forest fans for their attack. I hope to this day that the bastards concerned are living thoroughly miserable lives and that their wives, if they have any, are having affairs with the household cavalry! It was a pointless, pathetic attack on an individual who had absolutely nothing to do with the events taking place (and I guess that probably sums football violence up in one sentence). At the time, it was particularly annoying. *Now*, it infuriates me so much I could swear – and very often do! 'Forgive and forget' was my mother's favourite cliché during my formative years but, then, *she* had never been beaten up by a bunch of Forest fans. So, I'm sorry, Mother; nothing doing on that one!

I was about 18 at the time and was as passionate about supporting Chesterfield as I am now, over 35 years later. Town were due to play Preston North End but the game was cancelled due to a frozen pitch; indeed, a great many games were off that day. I remember I had an atrocious bout of flu: my bones ached, my nose ran and my throat was sore. I'd been off work for about three days and, come the Saturday, was just about fit to stand. The three days in bed had driven me half mad and I was screaming for fresh air. I wasn't disappointed that the game was off; in fact, quite the opposite. We were having a crap season and I didn't need to be made even more miserable by watching us lose. However, I did need to get out of the house.

Around dinner-time, a friend, Steve Wright, better known as Pix, phoned to ask me if I fancied a jaunt into town with him and Rob Hill and, so, sickening for the great outdoors and fresh air, I joined them. I only ever intended my sojourn into town to be a brief one; long enough, in fact, to purchase an LP: *The History of Eric Clapton,* to be exact – a kind of 'greatest hits' thing. It was a bright day but extremely windy and I remember thinking that it was a good job the game had been called off as the wind would have spoilt it.

The town centre itself was in the pre-'knock-the-shit-out-of-it' days and, for those who can remember that long ago, you will recall the Police Station being a farty little thing where the Library now stands (roughly). *Boots the Chemist* didn't own half of Low Pavement either; they had a grubby little shop, which is now a shoe shop, on the corner opposite *Marks and Spencer* which was and always has been, to my knowledge, *M&S*. What Chesterfield did possess in those days were some excellent record shops; they hadn't been run out of town by the overpriced efforts that stand there now. Record shops with imaginative titles like *Some Kinda Mushroom*. Now, there's a shop title if ever you wanted one! In fact, you could always tell the music buffs in town because they never referred to this shop by its name but rather by the name of the guy who owned it; 'Dave McPhee's' they used to call it. I used to say it like I knew the bloke but all I knew for sure was that he had an ace record shop and was something of a Town fan himself! What a man! (Alas, *Some Kinda Mushroom* disappeared years ago, as did Dave McPhee, although he turned up later with a book shop in Hassop, rather unimaginatively entitled *The Country Book Store*.) But, I digress from the main topic on hand. Isn't nostalgia wonderful?

The chances are that it was to this particular record shop I was making my way that fateful day. A clue as to how cold it was, or rather how wretched I felt, lies in the fact that it hadn't needed my mother to moan, *'Why don't you put a scarf on?'* because it had already been done, which was most unlike me. I never wore a scarf. Well, not tied around my neck at any rate. I draped one around my shoulders for football games but that was about it.

As we strode past what was then *Wakefield's* (and is now *Santander*), a herd of youngish Chesterfield supporters came running down towards us. We had no idea what the commotion was. What's more, I didn't care what the commotion was, even when one of the youths stopped on seeing my blue and white scarf to issue scrambled warnings about someone 'coming along the top' and how everyone was meeting in *Polly's Parlour*: a bar which, if memory serves me correctly, was part of the *Portland Hotel* (now a big *Wetherspoon's* job!) None of this seemed to matter too much to me – after all, I wasn't a football hooligan and, on top of that, I had flu! How could it matter to me? If they couldn't tell the difference between a football hooligan and a quiet, peaceful youth only wearing a scarf because he was at death's door, then things were in a pretty sorry state! Things *were* in a pretty sorry state.

Following hard on the heels of the Town fans was a group of Notts Forest fans. Some ran straight past, as they should have done. Unfortunately, six or seven noticed my scarf and stopped as fast as their Doc Martens would allow.

It is, perhaps, at this point that you need to get a grasp of what the 18 year old me looked like. My height was pretty much the same as it is now: 5ft-4ins. I was much slimmer then, of course, as things like beer hadn't yet started to have too much of an effect, but the most important change over the years has been my hairline. At 18 my hair was long and thick; it was so long, in fact, that I could comfortably put my hand in the small of my back and grip my hair firmly. I suppose, today, hair that long would be put in a pony-tail but that was a girly thing to do back then (come to think of it, it is now), so it just roamed free.

Unfortunately, one of the Forest fans who had stopped in front of me was now making an attempt to take away my scarf. Was he stupid? Could he not see that I had a cold and needed this item of clothing? Obviously not; but then, he was a Forest fan, so need I say more?

"Gimme ya scarf, ya cunt," he said in a not too welcoming manner, and grabbed the scarf, trying to pull it away and throttle me in one single movement. Now 'brave' is the last word I would use to describe me. The words 'big', 'yellow' and 'shit-bag' are words that have been put together to form a sentence that describes me much more accurately. BUT – and it is a big but – I can be incredibly stubborn and at 18 years of age I was probably at my peak of stubbornness. Don't ask me why; I just was. Consequently, there was no way this youth was going to get his hands on my scarf. It was my best one, crocheted by my granny!

Aware that I might bolt from the scene, one of the other Forest fans, who was standing to one side and slightly to the rear (and who I shall now refer to as 'dick-head'), grabbed me by my much too long mane and yanked my head back. Having your hair pulled is really painful! Once again the idiot in front of me made a dart for my scarf. I might not have been able to run away, I might not have been a good fighter, but I could certainly floor him with my verbal dexterity!

"WHY DON'T YOU FUCK OFF?!" I screamed. As soon as the words left my lips, I regretted them – but it was too late. By now, he was wrestling with my throat and calling me all the names under the sun and I was just held there. The only things I could move effectively were my arms and they were busy trying to keep the moron off my neck.

I had flu, I had some wanker hanging on to my hair, while some other tosspot was trying desperately to get a blue and white scarf from around my neck that he would dump the moment he'd got it. This was turning out to be a pig of a day! When the idiot finally decided that he wasn't going to get the scarf, he decided that I might, after all, like to fight him. This was all I needed. He stood in front of me, thrust out his groin, dropped his arms down by his sides and beckoned me forwards with three fingers of each hand. (You know the pose!) God, he looked a twat! I'm sorry but there is just no other way to describe it.

"Come on, then," he said. "Come on, then, youth, 'ave a go."

I groaned. He obviously hadn't noticed that I had 12 stone of Forest fan hanging from my hair, so even if I had been of a mind to 'ave a go' it wasn't really an option.

"Come on, then, if ya dare. Come on, youth," he continued on in the same fashion. The pain from having my hair pulled was really starting to get to me and I wanted him to let go so much that I found it difficult, if not impossible, to concentrate on the idiot in front me. It seemed to go on for hours (although it was probably only a few minutes). I hoped he would stop; I hoped they would eventually get bored and move on to better sport. But I wasn't at all prepared for what happened next...

From somewhere at the side of me came a fist. It wasn't the lad who had been doing the threatening, or the one holding on tightly to my locks, but another; probably someone who had been watching and thought that this particular farce had gone on for long enough! I suppose I'd been watching, waiting almost, for the inevitable smack in the face. I'd been steeling myself against the impact, hoping I could numb the pain. However, when that smack did arrive it came as such a surprise that I didn't actually feel a thing! Having said that, I don't think I've ever been hit in the face as hard as that before – or, indeed, since. It sent me flying. I skidded down past *Wakefield's* on my back, my denim jacket protecting me from any injury that may have resulted in hitting the ground at too many miles an hour. Somewhere behind me there was a Forest fan with a handful of blond hair. The bastard! (Bitter? Too right I am!)

When I eventually came to rest, I thought, momentarily, that my ordeal was over but no sooner had the thought entered my head than it was kicked out by a large Doctor Marten in the ribs. Suddenly, they were on me, like flies around the proverbial shit heap, and yours truly was the shit! I was certainly having it kicked out of me, that's for sure. I'd never been in this position before and thought I wouldn't know what to do but I guess self-preservation is inbuilt. I curled into a foetus-like ball, wrapped my arms around my head and let five or six Forest fans kick the crap out of me.

I can't tell you what it was like because it was like nothing. Apart from knowing how it *happened*, I can't really remember how it *felt*. I can remember the feeling of injustice but that's about it. The body went into automatic pilot and I came out the other end devoid of serious injury. Perhaps the only reason for this outcome was down to the actions of a 70 year old woman who waded in with her brolly to get them off me. Again, I knew very little about that. I was helped to my feet and, then, Pix, who had done the right thing and ducked into the bustle of the market stalls, grabbed me and yanked me into the safety that the stalls held. He'd already rescued Rob who was now nursing a rather nasty-looking split lip.

The thing that really annoyed me, though, was that none of the market traders came to our rescue. I distinctly remember looking at a rather large butcher (this was during the days when you could sell meat on an open market), with meat cleaver in hand, looking up from his chopping and making some sarcastic (and not needed) remark; something along the lines of, *'What have you been up to?'*

I looked at him and replied, with as much restraint as possible, "And a lot of fuckin' help you were!"

His smile disappeared and my mate pulled me further into the market, probably before we got made into chops!

Later that week, I'm nursing my bruises at home when the phone rings and its Steve (aka Pix).

"Have you seen it?" he asked.

"Seen what?"

"In the *Derbyshire Times*..."

He was half laughing and I had the distinct impression it was at my expense.

"What?"

"You've made the papers, mate," he said, with a laugh that confirmed my fears.

I put the phone down and grabbed the *Derbyshire Times*. I hunted furiously through the headlines. *"Donkey Savages Woman in Street"* – no, that can't be it. Eventually, I found it; not exactly hidden away – **on the front page!**

"GRANNY STOPS THE AGGRO"

"Grandmother Mrs Ida Breckwell didn't think twice when she saw a young Chesterfield supporter being attacked by a mob of Preston North End followers last Saturday. She waded in...

"Mrs Breckwell, a widow, of 10 Baden Powell Road, St Augustine's, Chesterfield, was shopping in the Market Place just after lunch-time when she saw a young boy wearing a blue scarf 'come flying down the road.' 'He was only about 14,' she said, 'and there were about ten older boys chasing him. They flung him to the floor and started putting the boot in. So I turned away from the stall where I was buying tomatoes and walked between them and the boy. They stopped because they seemed flabbergasted, so I picked the boy up and told him to go. I don't know what made me do it but I couldn't just stand there like everybody else and let them kick the boy.'"

Now, the article says they were Preston fans; and, yet, I feel certain they were Forest fans who had come over, once their game had been called off, on the off chance of a rumble with fans from either Chesterfield or Preston. In some respects, it doesn't matter; the events are still the same.

To be described as a 14-year-old at the time was deeply embarrassing, although it would be a compliment now. I did write to the woman thanking her for her actions; I was eager to point out that she was braver than she thought as I was actually 18. She wrote back but I'm afraid the letter has got lost over time. But it doesn't matter because I won't forget her – just like I won't forget the bastard Forest fans!

On The Home Front

February 7th, 1975 Chesterfield 1 v 0 Port Vale

Port Vale arrived at Saltergate pushing for promotion. We were fighting to avoid the drop, so it was an important game. I arrived up at Saltergate expecting no trouble at all but, as I walked past the Social Club, a pint pot came flying through the closed window. With the gap in the window established, I could hear – if not see – all that was happening. Vale fans had taken up residence in one side of the Social Club and Town fans in the other. It wasn't long before someone threw something, and then it just deteriorated into a fist and glass fight. Eager not to get caught up in it, I pushed my way through the turnstiles and took up my usual place on the Kop. I was early. I was always in the ground early and I stood and listened to the fracas that was going on behind me.

Gradually, the ground began to fill up but things didn't quieten down. Fighting continued on the terraces throughout the game and it continued in the streets afterwards. I couldn't help but wonder what Mr Shentall made of it, especially after his stirring words of protest at the start of the season.

After the game, Chesterfield fans attacked the Port Vale players' coach, although some dimwit who threw a stone at it missed and hit a local bus. According to the press, Vale knew nothing about the incident and were unconcerned, although their manager at the time, Roy Sproson, came out afterwards with the comment of the season: *"It's a good job the stone didn't hit our bus – we've only had it 4 weeks!"*

A few weeks later, a Chesterfield fan appeared in court charged with smacking a Vale fan in the face. He claimed self-defence as it was a reflex action. He thought the other supporter was drunk because he was swaying a little and had a beer glass on his head. I'm not quite sure how that turns it into self-defence but you have to take your hat off to him for trying! The Vale fan was probably swaying because he'd been thumped and the glass had probably been broken over his head. Needless to say, the magistrates found him guilty.

The good news was that we won 1–0 and hauled ourselves off the bottom of the league.

March 1st, 1975 Chesterfield 2 v 4 Brighton

After a scoreline like this one, you always knew there was going to be trouble and, for some inexplicable reason, Brighton and Chesterfield have never really been bosom buddies. In fact, you could say that the rivalry existing between us is close to that of a local derby, yet it's hard to find two clubs geographically so far apart. I can't remember there being much trouble before the game but it certainly kicked off afterwards. Chesterfield fans chased a few Brighton fans through the centre of town and I remember very well them flying past me. However, most of the trouble seemed to be concentrated outside the ground.

Now, although I hated football violence, I wasn't half nosey when it started and I couldn't help but hang around to see who was doing what to whom. After this game, the Town fans, unable to get down St Margaret's Drive to attack the Brighton coaches, completely outwitted the police by going down the next street along, Tennyson Avenue. (As previously pointed out, the old Bill were still struggling desperately to cope with football violence and always seemed to be more than one step behind.) However, although the Town fans managed to surround the coaches, the Brighton fans were all safely loaded aboard and, so, a ruck seemed out of the question. As the Town fans became more and more agitated, a couple of coppers asked them to disperse but, 20 seconds after issuing the warning, the two officers must have really wished they'd kept their mouths shut because, rather than waste all that valuable time it had taken to get there, the Town fans decided to turn their attentions onto the two stranded bobbies! Eventually, after a massive skirmish requiring an awful lot of law enforcement to bring it under control, two youths were arrested: one for threatening behaviour and using threatening words (which, in case you're wondering, were, "Come on, let's get the bastards!"); and the other for possession of an offensive weapon. The biggest mystery after this was how the police only managed to make two arrests!

April 12th, 1975 Chesterfield 2 v 1 Crystal Palace

Palace were another side pushing for promotion in 74/75 and, like their manager at the time, were an arrogant bunch of nobodies. However, they did think their promotion was in the bag and, so, they brought a large contingent of supporters. Their manager, in case you're interested, was Malcolm Allison: more mouth and hat than talent but he managed to make a living. There was sporadic fighting on the terraces throughout the game but after the match it just went mental. We beat them 2–1, which just about ended their promotion hopes, and, afterwards, the two sets of fans battled it out in the town centre. There were so many brawls that day that it would be easier to tell you where they weren't fighting rather than where they were!

My walk back to the bus was extremely interesting and I made more than one detour. In fact, it was probably the longest walk back to Beetwell Street that I've ever made! In fairness, I don't think the Town fans were expecting such a turn-out and, again, if I'm being brutally honest, from what I saw we took a bit of a hiding that day. But the team were safe now; we weren't going down – so we could at least enjoy the last few games.

April 26th, 1975 Chesterfield 2 v 0 Charlton

Our last game of the season was at home to Charlton on April 26th. They'd missed out on promotion by just one place and I think the Chesterfield fans wanted to see the season out in style. The fans clashed before, during and after the game. There were nine arrests and thirteen ejected from the ground and the charges ranged from 'carrying an offensive weapon' to 'criminal damage.' We won 2–0, so I didn't care.

However, what was apparent – more so now, looking back – was the number of people starting to carry weapons. I'd seen it the previous season but, now, they were being *used*, not just *carried*. Earlier that season, a special train, making its way back to Leeds from Derby, had been stopped in Chesterfield after a Derby fan had been stabbed. A 16 year old youth was later charged with the offence. The people committing the crimes were getting more fearless and a lot younger!

But it was the end of the season. I could relax, go and play cricket and dream of the local derbies with Sheffield Wednesday, who had just been relegated. How we rubbed our hands with glee at that news!

It's All Gone Horribly Wrong
SEASON 75/76

Once again, Joe Shaw had assembled a squad of players which, he assured everyone, would be pushing for promotion and, once again, no one really believed him. Only two seasons ago we had looked to be genuine promotion contenders but 74/75 was poor and nothing had happened between that season and this to make anyone yelp with optimism. I suppose we wanted to believe we had a chance. (You have to think that otherwise you wouldn't bother getting out of bed and going to the ground.) Football fans don't need much to give them encouragement – a few well chosen words, a couple of good signings – and, suddenly, the bad days are a distant memory. The Chesterfield board of directors, however, were notoriously effective at delivering neither. Consequently, the crowds were down and no one expected very much at all from the season. The only bright spot on the horizon was the chance to play 'Fallen-from-grace Sheffield Big-club Wednesday' who had accompanied Rotherham into the murky depths of Division 3, so we figured there were 8 points in the bag to start with!

August 23rd, 1975 Chesterfield 1 v 2 Crystal Palace

For a warm up for 'The Wednesday,' we entertained Palace in our first home game of the season. If you wanted a fixture guaranteed to get the season off to a rucking good start, then the computer couldn't have done any better than pluck out this fixture. After the mayhem of the previous season, people were literally licking their lips in readiness and they were not disappointed. The previous season had seen us upset the form book and put a nail in their promotion push, and for this they had rewarded us with running battles throughout the town and basically given us a damn good hiding. However, this was a new season. There was no form book and, more importantly, the Chesterfield fans were more than ready and eagerly waiting.

You didn't have to wait for the end of the game to see that this was going to be vicious. Fans spilled onto the pitch during the game as fighting broke out on the terraces and there were definitely some old scores being settled. After the game, which they won, Town fans, being slightly peeved by this and still suffering the indignation of last season's beating, attempted to attack the Palace fans on their way back to the station but, with a large police presence protecting them, each attack, no matter which direction it came from, was beaten back by the police and I'm sure they thought they'd done a marvellous job at averting football violence. There is a saying, mind you, that there is 'more than one way to skin a cat' and, with that thought in mind, while the police were busy protecting and escorting the majority of the Palace fans, a minority of the poor blighters were getting the kicking of their lives down at the station from Chesterfield hooligans who had left the ground early. I can't be sure but I do seem to remember that one of the Palace fans was so badly beaten he needed hospital treatment. The others, not wishing to join their mate in A&E, ran back into the town centre looking for the police escort. A wise move? Well, it would have been if they had found the police. Unfortunately, all they managed to find was another rather hostile group of Town supporters. From the outside looking in – as I always tried to be – it wasn't a day to be a Palace fan. Okay, you go back down London with 2 points but, then, did you really need all that dental work? Some things never added up.

One Town fan, arrested after the scuffle with Palace, claimed he was a 'Junior Leader' in the army and had been trained to fight if someone got hold of him. "You have to fight back," he claimed, probably with a degree of confidence in his ability now that the government were actually paying him to learn how to fight. The JP was equally confident when he fined him £50.

Although the 2 points had gone south, it was a morale-boosting victory for the Town thugs who needed a good fight under their belts before the hordes of Dee-Dahs came down from Sheffield. With the Wednesday game just a month away, you might say Palace had been the perfect warm-up bout.

Wednesday On A Tuesday

September 24th, 1975 Chesterfield 1 v 0 Sheffield Wednesday

We played the Owls ten times between 1975 and 1980 and the five home games I witnessed between the two warring factions have to go down as some of the most vicious encounters I've ever seen; not on the field, you understand – they were just good games (sometimes) – but off the field it was, quite literally, a bloody nightmare!

It's also fair to say that most of the time we were on the receiving end as Wednesday had a reputation as bad as anyone in the Football League. The fact that they were just 12 miles up the road meant they turned out to be local derbies of unparalleled fear. Well, they certainly were for me! Now, I hate Wednesday (probably more than I hate Sheffield United, and that's saying something) and it still cuts very deep when I see spotty teenagers walking around Chesterfield in 'Wednesday' shirts. When I worra lad you'da gorra damn good kickin' for that; and that's precisely what used to happen – unless, of course, you'd arrived at Saltergate with about 5,000 of your mates!

As you will begin to realise, playing Sheffield Wednesday wasn't a barrel full of laughs. In fact, the only time it has seemed remotely funny is when you look back on it 25 years later because the fact is that for most of the time it was downright dangerous. Unlike their neighbours, the Urinals, Wednesday came with a government health warning strapped to each thug. I can't remember a game against them, at Saltergate at least, that wasn't marred by the most incredible football violence. It didn't happen at Hillsborough so much but, then, at Hillsborough, if you were foolish enough to go, you just stood there and kept your mouth shut.

My first encounter with the mob from north of the Derbyshire border was on September 24th, 1975 and was our, or at least *my*, first Football League encounter with them. Wednesday were newly relegated. How I had gloated; how I had taken the piss out of a Wednesday fan I used to play football with. He took all the punishment well. In fact, he took it too well: he just stood there and smiled. The Sunday before the game, a mid-week fixture, he fixed me with a steely smile and said, "We'll take your fuckin' kop, Radford, so just make sure you're near a bleedin' exit!"

How I laughed. "No chance," I replied. "There'll be far too many police."

I'm not quite sure why I trusted the police so much. After all, I'd seen them fuck up more than one supposed 'operation' to combat hooliganism. I don't want you to think I have anything against the police because I don't; I just think that in the early days of football violence they were bloody useless and the hooligans weren't half as stupid as most media people portrayed them to be. But I still couldn't see Wednesday taking the Kop. The fact is, I hadn't seen anyone take the Kop since Villa, and they were a proper big club – not like this pretend outfit. Huh, as if they could take our Kop! But my friend said nothing and just reiterated his earlier warning that I give the Kop a miss.

"We'll be straight across the pitch," he smiled.

He wasn't issuing a threat; he wasn't even being particularly nasty; he was just giving a piece of advice to a friend. But, as I said, I just couldn't see it happening. Villa did it but they were a case apart. I *just* couldn't see Wednesday doing it. The main reason for my optimism lay in the fact that to get out of the Cross Street end in those days you didn't just jump over a low wall and sprint off towards the Kop. You first had to jump up and onto the wall and heave yourself over. The wall was quite a size and I always thought the police would see this occurring and then act accordingly, hopefully by kicking the bastards back onto the terrace below. It would seem an appropriate piece of action to take against a Wednesday fan, I thought. In fact, if I had dreamt for one minute that Wednesday would take the Kop, then I would, indeed, have heeded his advice and gone in the stand or in the Compton Street end but I decided there was no chance and, consequently, no real threat.

So, on that Tuesday night I thought nothing of taking my usual place on the Saltergate terrace. In retrospect, I should have realised what might happen because the guy I played football with in the Chesterfield Sunday League was very often late for the kick-off, or he'd miss the game completely, because he'd been detained in a police cell somewhere as a result of his exploits following the Owls the day before. In fact, now I think about it, his tales of Wednesday's shenanigans had warmed us up on many a cold Sunday morning, but as I made my way to the ground it never crossed my mind that they might transfer those same exploits to Chesterfield. Who said hindsight was a wonderful thing? I was excited and in good humour. We were all keen to see the game and, hopefully, beat them into the bargain.

On entering the ground, I was amazed to see how many supporters had made the short journey from Sheffield. This was our fourth home game of the season and the three previous games had seen us average around 4,000 per game. The attendance for the Wednesday game was a whopping 12,899 which set the scene for a barnstormer: local derby, big crowd, electric atmosphere. It was brilliant – and this was before the players had run out!

Now, on seeing such a large away contingent, I was slightly concerned but, equally, I was exceptionally pleased to see that they were all tucked up nicely in the Cross Street end of the ground. I figured that if we made it to kick-off without incident then it would be a trouble-free night, or as trouble-free as you're going to get in the 70's. The thought had no sooner entered my head than a cry of *"The Wensday!"* went up from the back of the Kop. Not a massive chant – about 20 or so youths – and it did, indeed, lead to the inevitable skirmish. I turned round to check the progress of the fighting and make sure it wasn't coming anywhere near me. It didn't look good. A load of Chesterfield fans, mostly young lads as the real thugs were still fighting in the pubs at this stage, came tumbling past me, trying to avoid the marauding mob. There were more Wednesday fans than I had expected. I turned around to see how those on the Cross Street end had welcomed this attempt on the Kop, only to find them half-way across the pitch. I was literally frozen to the spot.

It was an odd sight. It was as if someone had pulled a plug out in the Cross Street end. It was like sand spilling from the top half of an egg-timer and, as it emptied, a bare terrace was left behind as the pitch slowly filled. And all the time this huge, black, menacing wave of destruction flowed towards us. Mind you, I say 'us' but when you see that happening it is most definitely every man, woman and child for themselves, so I suppose I should really say 'flowed towards me.'

It seemed ages before my mind registered the seriousness of the matter, although it probably only took two seconds of thought before I legged it. The big problem was where to run? They were everywhere. The gang of lads I was standing with all ran in different directions. I remember running along the front of the Kop and then realising that this was the bit the Wednesday fans would eventually jump down onto. So I made a detour and ended up round the back of the Kop, only to find Chesterfield and Wednesday fans slugging it out toe-to-toe – and we didn't appear to be doing too well! Beyond the fighting youths, I could see Town fans actually climbing over the gates to get out. This caused a degree of confusion for the supporters still trying to get in and I dare say some looked at the scene, pushed their money back into their jeans and headed back to the safety of the pub – and who could blame them?!

I looked over to the wall at the side of the turnstiles and saw my mate Rob scaling it, his Oxford bags billowing out, snagging on the pieces of glass embedded in the top of the wall, and tearing. I wanted to shout things at him, tell him not to be such a bloody coward, but he'd just lost most of his trousers so I figured he'd suffered enough. And it is fair to say that I only wanted him back in the ground so I wouldn't feel so alone – but I was also mean enough to realise that I'd be able to use this against him the following day, if I ever made it that far. And it is, perhaps, fair to mention that, even if I'd wanted to get out of the ground, with me 'weighing in' at just 5ft-4ins in height I would have needed crampons and a 10ft rope! So staying was always going to be much easier than leaving, which is just as well because, despite everything, I actually wanted to stay and see this game; I just didn't want my face rearranging in the process. With this in mind I took a deep breath, walked calmly back onto the terrace and found a 'dad-like' figure to stand with. I just leaned on the crash barrier near him and made it look as if we were together. He did have a young lad with him and I hoped that even the louts from Sheffield wouldn't stoop so low as to pick on a father and son combo.

I'd been split up from the lads I was standing with but one of them eventually found me. He'd taken one in the chops but was basically all right. Like me, he also adopted the surrogate father and together we got ready to watch the game in as close to a trouble-free environment as we were likely to get.

The pitch was still covered with fans from both clubs. Wednesday fans were still running across the pitch and Town fans were still trying to evade them. Although the gate for this game was an official 12,899, there were probably nearer to 15,000 there as Owls fans broke down a gate and forced their way into the ground. The kick-off was delayed and there was a continued plea by club officials and the police for fans to calm down and clear the pitch. It goes without saying that none of this made the slightest bit of difference.

How long it took before relative peace was restored, I can't remember. It seemed forever but that's probably because I wanted the game to kick off and finish so that I could get home and be safe. But when you're waiting for something like that to happen, it's incredible how slowly the fingers on your watch turn. Eventually, the pitch did clear and the game did get underway and, joy of joys, we won! As

Malcolm Darling's free kick swung into the bottom corner of the net, I punched silent celebratory holes in my pockets! I even managed to suppress the frenzied leap in the air until I was walking through Chesterfield 20 minutes after the game and was sure there was no one near me! With about ten minutes to go, Wednesday fans were leaving the ground and with good reason: they were shit! Honestly! I know I'm biased but they were absolute cack! To be fair, I'm sure many were leaving so they could go and phone 'Praise and Grumble' on Radio Sheffield and complain about how poor their side were. But some were leaving with other thoughts on their mind...

Outside the ground, Wednesday fans had left a trail of damage right through the town centre. Corporation Street had borne the brunt of it with around £2,000 worth of damage caused to premises and shops, according to the press. The railway station was also given the once-over. There was some trouble at the bus station but not a great deal and, more to the point, I managed to avoid it.

The bus home was full of bloodied noses and closed eyes and all the talk was about what a bunch of wankers they were and how we'd get them next time. Somehow I didn't think so. It was bravado talking and it's easy to be brave when you're on the bus home. While others talked of getting them back, I decided that if our footballing paths were to cross in the future, you could put me down for a stand ticket.

The local press had a field-day with it and, rather surprisingly, made a great deal of a combined operation between Chesterfield and Sheffield police to combat the violence. And, yet, when one looks at the trouble that was caused, the havoc, the destruction to premises, then one can only assume this so-called police operation was dreamed up on a Monday afternoon by a couple of bobbies who were after an hour's overtime but decided to jack it all in after five minutes. This wasn't a police operation: it was a complete and utter shambles. You can, perhaps, forgive the Chesterfield police for being caught on the back foot somewhat but one would have thought their Sheffield colleagues might have just had a word in their shell-like. I mean, the guy I played football with knew what was going to happen, so why didn't the police?

Over 22 people were treated by *St John Ambulance* staff, including two policemen injured in the fighting. One of them needed stitches to his face and neck after being struck by a bottle. Ten people were taken to hospital to receive treatment, most of them Town fans, and their injuries ranged from facial lacerations to head injuries. One Town fan was kept in hospital for the night after being stabbed in the head. Doesn't get much more serious than that, really, does it? So, as you can see, the police operation to combat violence was an unprecedented success!!

Questions were even raised at local council level. One councillor wanted the club to take steps to make sure that such scenes were not repeated, and he also wanted them to get more turnstiles open as a friend of his had queued until half-time, couldn't get in and, so, had gone home. Incredible how he could turn something as important as the safety of his voters into making sure his mate got in the ground on time!

That Sunday when I turned up to play football, my 'Wednesday' footballing friend looked at me and said with his usual steely smile, "What did I tell you, Radford? What did I tell you?"

I didn't have the bottle to get on at him about the scoreline but, then, the scoreline for him was almost of secondary importance.

October 25th, 1975 Chesterfield 2 v 2 Millwall

The town was still talking about, and still taking stock of, what happened after the Wednesday game when Millwall came to visit – and they are just what you need when you've had the hiding of your lifetime. It may well have had something to do with the beating that Town fans had taken at the hands of their dearly loathed neighbours that they were out in force for this one, the one game when you really want to be hiding in your bedroom. Now, if Wednesday are bad, then I'm not quite sure how you would even start to describe Millwall. One thing *is* for sure: you know that if you go head-to-head with their firm, then the chances are you're going to end up in hospital! And that is pretty much what happened.

There was fighting before, during and after the game and two Chesterfield fans were both rushed to the intensive care unit at Chesterfield Hospital with head injuries. A Post Office was attacked on Foljambe Road, with the owner and a scared woman trapped inside. A Millwall fan was attacked with a knife and two Town fans were arrested for that. The game was great: we were 2–0 down and came back to draw 2–2 with goals from McEwan and Shanahan, the latter hitting a post in the last few minutes. It was, perhaps, as well he did because I dread to think what they would have done if we'd come back and won it.

Once again, it was one of those home games where you just wanted to get the bus and go home. I must admit, I did breathe a sigh of relief as the bus pulled out of town and Wynnie, recognising an easy target when he saw one, asked if I wanted to go on one of his two coaches to Bradford for the first round of the FA Cup. How could I refuse? After these two home games, that was going to be a breeze, wasn't it? Wasn't it?

Radford In Bradford

FA Cup First Round

November 28th, 1975 Bradford City 1 v 0 Chesterfield

My trip to Bradford City with Wynnie's Tours was my first visit to their ground but, then, a lot of my sorties with Mr Wynne had been firsts. For a young, reckless (well, sort of) Chesterfield fan, despite the threat of violence, it has to be said that it was a good and somewhat interesting way to travel. As I've also pointed out numerous times, I'm sure, it was also safe – in a ridiculously violent and hooliganistic kind of way.

It was a grey November day as we rolled out of town on a bus packed to the luggage racks with thugs. I'm not quite sure who Dave Wynne had as contacts but they were hardly reputable – something I and the softer element of travelling fans had come to be extremely glad about. There was a general consensus that this was going to be a tough one but several of the back seat mob were adamant they wouldn't leave without making a serious attempt at taking the kop. I wondered if it was, perhaps, a little early for making those kinds of promises; it might be better to see how many Bradford fans were on it to start with. But, then, I was thinking like a coward, not like a nutter!

Hooligans are, indeed, a strange breed. A few weeks earlier (I think) Wynnie had problems getting enough people together for a trip to Rochdale. The reason, it seems, was simple: no one from the hooligan fraternity expected much trouble in Lancashire and, so, as far as they were concerned, the trip was basically a waste of time. I suppose this highlights the difference between a fan and a fighter: one goes to see a football match and the other goes to inflict pain and suffering. On this journey, trouble *was* expected and so Wynnie filled the bus easily – so easily, in fact, that he was forced to take two! I will never understand why the thought of being beaten up appealed so much. Football violence was (still is) a very strange phenomenon.

Footballing-wise, I think we were slight favourites as Bradford were going through a rough patch with financial difficulties, poor league form and they were in a division below us. A draw we fancied, win at best. **BUT**, this was FA Cup territory. Even back in the 70's our cup exploits were legendary – or, rather, the lack of them was.

Nothing much happened on the way up there; the usual hurling of abuse and obscene gestures at complete strangers but, apart from that, nothing out of the ordinary. Even on entering Bradford itself, although the scarves were still hanging from the windows, no one thought to pull them open and announce our arrival, which was most unlike Wynnie's Tours. As the buses pulled up quietly outside the ground, the supporters dismounted and walked straight into the away end. I was flabbergasted. No one mentioned looking for a pub or a chip shop, no one mentioned looking for a few stray Bradford fans to give a seeing-to; they just paid their money and walked in. I couldn't have been more pleased.

What Bradford's ground looks like now is completely different to how it looked then. It had a kop (a little shallower than the one at Saltergate, I think), a run-down stand on the right-hand side and an uncovered terrace for the away support. The left-hand side was, I think, the wooden stand which burned down many years later, although I can't be absolutely sure about that. My memory seems to be governed by the things my eyes directly witnessed and the possible consequences those things might have on me. To be fair, only the kop and the away end were likely to affect me and, so, I paid very little attention to the rest.

Once everyone had gained entrance – well, everyone from our two buses, anyway – someone decided that we really ought to take the kop, and I now realised that the earlier talk had not been idle boasting or threats. This was probably also the reason why they decided to enter the ground as soon as we arrived. Now, for those of you not in the know, 'taking the kop' was the ultimate in hooligan activity at a football ground. It was a scalp. If you went somewhere and took the kop, then you were (perhaps in your own eyes only) the proverbial *dog's bollocks*. However, having your kop taken was terrible: it was a sin, something you never talked about and something you tried to make sure would never happen again. Getting the Bradford scalp would, no doubt, increase our standing in the hooligan world. It's a bit like being seeded at tennis, I assume. Being your average shit-bag, I didn't very much care and I thought the whole idea was a really terrible one but, then, I always thought that. I just wanted a quiet life; to stand safely in the away end and sing the Blues to victory. But when your sole purpose is simply to make up the numbers then you have little say in these decisions.

So, with the Bradford end looking more or less empty, 40 or so Chesterfield hard nuts climbed over the wall onto the pitch. Suddenly, it looked much bigger than I had at first thought. It's incredible the tricks that fear will play. They waited a moment till all had grouped and then started to run towards the kop, shouting that old Chesterfield battle hymn: **"AAAAAAAAAAARRRRRRRRGGGGGGGGHHHHHH!!!!"**

I didn't want to follow but I had to make a decision quickly. I looked around the away end and there were several groups of youths I didn't know and had never seen before. They could have been Bradford fans and could, if I stayed, have kicked my head in. The one or two youths I did recognise were easily outnumbered, so I took what I considered to be the safest option: I jumped onto the field and jogged slowly after the hooligans who were now breaking out of their own penalty box and making good ground in midfield.

You may question my decision but remember that, although clubs allocated a certain amount of terrace to away fans, it didn't mean that this section couldn't be used by home supporters. They weren't prevented from standing on it and many fights started because of this. For some reason very few clubs had complete segregation and the police were almost powerless to stop home supporters infiltrating the terrace intended for away fans. The fact that clubs didn't ban supporters back then probably didn't help the police much either. They would throw them out one week but the following week the same lunatics would be back and the club would accept their money again. I've walked into many grounds and found that the first thing to greet me on my entry was the sight of ten 6ft skinheads all wearing scarves differing in colour to the one I would have been wearing if I'd been foolish enough to put one on.

But I digress. As I say, the Bradford end was empty, or at least it was when I jumped onto the pitch. Unfortunately, by the time I hit the 18-yard line (still 20 yards behind the advance party) I could see Bradford fans running in from the side. I couldn't believe where they were coming from. They were obviously eager for the fight. Now, if I'd been in charge of the Chesterfield fans, I'd have made a simple and painless decision: I'd have stopped, stuck two fingers up at the Bradford contingent, who were obviously relishing the contest, and walked back to the away end. I'd have called it a 'tactical withdrawal.' My pride may well have been dented slightly but it would have made a full and painless recovery – which is more than one can say about a dented head! Alas, I was not in charge and whoever was, well, he wasn't paying much attention to the physical pain aspect. I thought that, on seeing the Bradford fans, they might at least slow down but, no, like everything else, that would have been too simple. There is a theory commonly known as 'Twats Complex' which explains how one group of football supporters, when faced by a larger and more aggressive looking bunch of football supporters, instead of running away (as is the norm), will actually take to running *at* the enemy with increased speed and a marked increase in the volume of the battle hymn being sung. It's as if the increase in speed and noise will frighten the larger group into running away. I can't say I've ever seen it work – and today wasn't going to be a first time, either.

And so it was that the Chesterfield fans were sorely affected, all except one rather lame hanger-on at the back: ME! By now I was trying to catch up with the party in front by running backwards. I was like Michael Jackson in denim and for every backward step I took it seemed as if I was gaining on them. I'm sure I wasn't but, when consumed by blind panic and fear, that's how it appeared. Mercifully, the police got off their idle arses and intervened and the Chesterfield supporters were headed off at the pass, so to speak, and, boy, was I glad!

It was a victory, of course, and had it not been for the police we most certainly would have hammered the City fans who, by now, were climbing over their wall to meet us. (As you have probably noticed, 'they' had suddenly become 'we.') Knowing it was all over, I could join them and tell my tale of bravery to the other Chesterfield supporters who might have come late. (Yeah, right!)

Fighting is one of those things that has never come easily to me. I've never had the ability to walk up to someone and hit them just for the sheer hell of it. I remember my school fights so well because there were so few of them, and in them all I had to be bleeding, crying and terribly upset before I would even dream of hitting my protagonist back. (I was the school walkover.) So, quite what I was doing half-way across a football pitch in Bradford, attempting to take the kop with Wynnie's ne'er-do-wells, is anyone's guess.

We sung our way back over 70 yards of Bradford turf. Some, like me, I'm sure, were delighted that we'd been stopped; others really were pissed off. If this happened at a football match today, then we would all have been ejected, banned, electronically tagged and given a curfew on a Saturday afternoon but, back then, we were simply cobbed back in our end and told to behave. I didn't really need telling to behave myself because I had an awful feeling that today might not be our day – in more ways than one.

Being an FA Cup tie meant a larger than average crowd and, perhaps more significantly, a greater number of travelling supporters. Despite our dismal record in the cup up to this point, we always managed to maintain our excellent support away from home. I cannot imagine why because, although the chances for victory should remain the same, in our case, when the cup came around, our chances somehow diminished. Perhaps people went along in the hope of being there at the start of the great cup run? Whatever the reason, the vocal support was more than adequate and had been whipped up into an aggressive frenzy by the hooligans that had attempted to run across the pitch.

The game got under way on time and the usual skirmish was not far behind. A few Bradford fans, standing among the Chesterfield fans, started singing; they were chased and then got the kicking they'd more or less been asking for, before being hauled back to their own end by the police. Both sets of fans viewed it as some sort of victory: the Chesterfield contingent because they had vanquished their foe; and the Bradford fans because they had simply been standing among the Chesterfield fans singing – although how getting a good kicking can ever be seen as a 'victory' is a mystery to me. The supporters on the Bradford kop welcomed their heroes with the same passion and aggression with which we had said goodbye to them. Skirmish followed skirmish throughout the first half and what really annoyed me was how the next load of Bradford fans to reveal their identity always seemed to know exactly where I was standing. They would sing, I would move, they would get chased-punched-kicked and I would look for another space that offered a decent view and complete safety. Ten minutes later, some skinhead would whip out a Bradford scarf, shout **"C-I-T-Y!"** in my ear and the whole process would begin all over again. By half-time I was knackered. The only place I hadn't stood was the Bradford kop, the one place I'd been heading for at the start of the game. I was beginning to wonder if I might not have been safer had I made it there!

The first half of football was poor. In fact, it was so dismal that people were wondering if we could, perhaps, go out to the cinema rather than stay and watch the match. Something had to be done to relieve the boredom and that made half-time very interesting indeed...

Usually, it was ten minutes of boring records but not at Bradford. Some exceedingly bored Spireite had discovered that if you kicked at the terracing for long enough, then it broke up into bite-sized lumps. Coinciding with this discovery, it was announced that the 'Save Bradford' appeal would be getting under way as usual and the 'blanket' would be coming round.

The 'blanket' turned out to be just that. A large piece of material, supported at each corner by a thick-necked, crash-helmeted Bradford fan, was paraded slowly around the pitch for fans to throw in whatever spare cash they could afford. This would, hopefully, be collected in the aforementioned blanket, taken back to the office and probably buy a bottle of scotch for the next directors' board meeting! The crash helmets were obviously in place to make sure these youths were not injured by any stray coins. I'm certain that the whole concept would fall foul of Health & Safety nowadays but, back then, you could do just what you liked! If a coin missed the intended target, then the lad nearest the misplaced monetary unit would drop his corner and scamper after the misdirected donation.

I was surprised they even bothered to bring the sheet to the away end – but they did. The immediate thought was to throw money – not at the sheet, of course, but at each of the corners. However, with the crash helmet protecting the only part that anyone wanted to hit, then throwing *money* did seem to be a bit of a waste. [Enter, the crumbling terraces.] I seem to remember the four lads moving a whole lot quicker as half a ton of assorted terrace rained down from the fast-disappearing away end. If we'd continued at this rate the terrace would have been no more than a ramp, come full-time.

With this new pastime taking up most people's attention, very few of us even noticed that the second half had actually commenced. Eric Winstanly did manage to put the ball in the net but his effort was disallowed for offside. I can't say that many people really cared and I must admit that my attention span had been severely dented because the cheers that were starting to permeate down from the very back of the terrace were far more intriguing than anything happening on the pitch.

As I got to the back of the terrace I found I could actually see out over the wall. The streets of terraced housing ran away in all directions, the rooves clearly visible from the back of the away end. Not content with breaking up the terrace for small arms fire, someone had discovered that the wall itself was not exactly made of solid stuff, and with the right amount of pulling and tugging they had managed to build up a small amount of heavy artillery. I suppose it still puzzles me as to why the police didn't get involved. Let's face it, if you're at home and your child is in the corner being very, very quiet then there's a good chance they've done something wrong. The same thing applies to 50 or so hooligans staring out over a wall and sniggering. Still, that was not my problem.

The problem, at the moment, was working out how far from the ground the nearest house was. It wasn't a case of, *"How many yards?"* It was quite simply a case of, *"Can I hit that house from here?"* Of course, there's only one way to answer such a question and it isn't by waiting for a reply, either. There was a hush as the stone wobbled through the air and clattered down the slated roof of the terraced house. There was a cheer and, suddenly, an awful lot of interest. Well, the football was rubbish so they had to have something to do! There were youths here with much stronger arms; youths who, without putting too much of their mind to it, could easily hit the houses across the road and, indeed, houses quite a way into the terrace. For now, though, the first house was the target – after all, it did have a skylight.

The news of what was happening spread quickly (although, to be fair, it didn't need a rocket scientist to work it out) and it wasn't long before every Chesterfield fan present that day was looking out over the back wall. It must have been disconcerting for the players, who were used to being the centre of attention, looking up and finding out that the supporters who had travelled all this way to see them were now far more interested in what was happening on the street. It was the first time I'd ever paid to go into a football ground and then spent half the time looking out of it! The police appeared to remain ignorant before, during and after the fact but, then, it could simply have been a case of 'anything for a quiet life.'

The skylight on the first house was the main target, although every piece of terracing and back wall thumping into the roof drew polite applause from those of us too scared to throw anything. The cheer that greeted the skylight breaking was the loudest thing I heard that day. In fact, someone quipped that when we cheered the Chesterfield players lined up to kick off again! It wouldn't have surprised me to see the two teams clambering over the wall and up the terrace because curiosity had gotten the better of them!

Shortly after the skylight went through, three or four people ran out of the front door to see what was happening. They ran back inside, covering their heads, as a hail of concrete rained down upon them. I half expected people to start aiming for the house windows themselves but no one actually did. Instead, someone pointed to a large Ford Zodiac of various colours parked at the end of the road. Although I'm not a car person, I remember this model for being about as ugly as you could possibly get a car to be (although I now think they're brilliant – in a retro sort of way). It was also noted that a few of the wayward stones hurled at the disgruntled family had, in fact, hit the car. A fresh smile was born, along with an urgency to smash the windscreen but, try as they might, no one could make a single stone do the job. Plenty of stuff whacked into the bodywork, chipping off several different paint jobs and getting down to the real rust. With their means of transport under attack, five or six people set off from the front door of the once besieged house, only to be beaten back by the intense bombardment of 9mm Bradford terrace.

And then it happened... Someone lifted what seemed like a huge piece of wall above his head and hurled it into the distance. We stood open-mouthed as it soared through the air, almost in slow motion. There was silence as we watched it glide towards its target and then there was a massive cheer as the chunk of stone crunched down onto the car's bonnet. It nestled there like some fat, overweight cuckoo sitting in a badly-formed bed of rusty steel. The car was fucked! Two minutes later a missile of similar size and weight caved the windscreen in. You'd have thought we were 4–0 up by the noise we were making. When the windscreen went, three men made another attempt to rescue the battered car – although for the life of me I can't think why. One jumped inside it, while the other two dodged and skipped around the incoming flak before realising it was far too dangerous and heading back to the house. The chap in the car stayed put, perhaps under the misguided belief that we couldn't hit him while he was inside his car. It was difficult, admittedly, but it didn't stop people from trying! With the state of his car getting worse by the minute, he eventually leapt out and fled across the road, claiming the sanctuary of the house opposite – which, in turn, drew the fire away from his own house. Boy, I bet his neighbours loved him! We never saw him again but a side window was smashed in the house and a tile was sent crashing from the adjoining house which was now coming under increasing fire, probably because it was closer. Once again, four people were quick to run from the house wearing a 'what-the-bloody-hell-is-going-on' look and four people were very quick to run back indoors wearing an expression that looked more like 'bloody-hell-it's-raining-concrete!'

As I said earlier, from a footballing perspective very little happened. Bradford scored four minutes from time but no one really cared and once they were in front the chances of us getting anything out of the game were about the same as my chances of getting into Nicole Kidman's knickers! But, as the game drew to a close, most supporters turned their backs on the war-torn Bradford and watched Chesterfield disappear from yet another cup competition.

There had always been an atmosphere surrounding this game and trouble was never far from the surface. It was one of those things you just knew – a sort of sixth sense. This part of the game was always an important time; this was the time to take stock of potential trouble areas and groups of fans I'd not seen before. I noted that the police, although present, were keeping a very low profile, which worried me a little. I also noted that our exit gates were open and the police were doing very little to dissuade anyone from walking into the Chesterfield end from the outside. I watched several youths walk in, followed by several more, and then several more. This wasn't looking good.

Then I saw a Bradford fan I knew. He wasn't difficult to spot as he'd been carrying the sheet round at half-time and I think I would have recognised that burly frame anywhere. It's also not very often that you get supporters standing there in crash helmets. He wandered around for a while before settling for a place next to the much-too-small exit gate and leant against the wall. He stood there, completely ignoring the football match but concentrating very hard on seeing who was leaving the ground. As he saw the first Chesterfield fan attempting to leave he watched him closely and, as the fan drew level with him, he leaned forward and head-butted him. Now, being nutted is one thing but being nutted by someone in a crash helmet takes it to whole new dimension. I imagine it's a damn sight more painful for a start. I watched the Town fan lie on the floor and receive the obligatory kicks in the stomach before getting up and staggering away. No, this really wasn't looking very good at all!

My first instinct had been to leave the ground early but this particular incident put a new light on the matter and gave rise to second thoughts. I had absolutely no intention of fighting for the cause: helping your fellow Chesterfield fan is one thing but the prospect of getting head-butted by a twat in a crash helmet is taking the whole concept of help a little too far. So, rather than leave, I walked down the terrace to where a bloke stood with his young son. They were both Bradford fans and I sidled up to them and leant against the crash barrier pretending to watch the match. (You will have noticed, I'm sure, that this wasn't the first time I'd used this particular 'get-out-of-jail card.') However, I was actually watching the build-up of Bradford fans by the exit gate and it would be a fair description to say I was absolutely shitting myself.

Behind me, on the terracing, little skirmishes had already broken out but most of the Bradford fans were chomping at the bit by the exit gate, waiting for the final whistle. When the bloke at the side of me decided to leave, he didn't realise he had his surrogate son with him. I was dreading walking out through that gate. Seeing one Town fan make it, I breathed a brief sigh of relief. I say 'brief' because the next Town fan wasn't so lucky. The evil bastard with the crash helmet was actually enjoying this. I'll never forget the fat swine's chubby chops quivering as he sent people flying to the floor.

And then it was me. Obviously, my foster father and stepbrother made it through easily; but then it was my turn and... I made it! I walked out of the ground, my heart beating so fast I was sure someone would hear it and recognise it as the heartbeat of a frightened Spireite. I turned left, only to find that the buses weren't there! I carried on walking down the hill and just hoped. It was all I could do since I had absolutely no idea where the buses were. I was passed by several Town fans who had also made it out of the ground and were now running down the hill hoping, like me, to find the buses. But running can be a big mistake: it's a dead giveaway. It doesn't matter if you're wearing your club's colours or not; if you're running, you're the enemy and you get hit – it's that simple. Today proved to be no exception. The Chesterfield supporters sprinting down the hill just ran into a whole heap of trouble: a big bunch of Bradford fans. The fear that courses through the veins at times like this is enough to make anyone run but somehow I managed to retain my composure and keep walking. Not so much 'composure,' perhaps, but more frightened rabbit syndrome. The battle at the bottom of the hill was now well underway. The Chesterfield fans who were not into fighting had turned tail and were now running past me back up the hill, although others had decided that a good kicking was in the offing anyway so stayed and swapped blows. Me? I just carried on walking. Punch-ups were now taking place all down the road but I just carried on walking, hoping that I would soon find where the buses were stationed and, more importantly, that no one would decide to pick on *me*. Although some Town fans were giving a very good account of themselves, this was rapidly turning into a pretty poor day all round.

A friend of mine, Steve Wright, eventually joined me in my amble down the road. He told me he knew that the buses were at the bottom of the hill because he'd asked a policeman. I can't imagine why I hadn't thought of that – it *was* the sensible thing to do – but when I left the ground I think I'd lost the ability to speak. Together, we talked as if we were just leaving the game and, fortunately, weren't troubled by anyone. Together, we witnessed a friend of ours, Rob Hill, literally being carried down the hill after having the capacity to walk kicked out of him. He was screaming to be released so that he could go back and 'have another go!' It was surreal. The youth could hardly walk, and he had taken more than one smack in the face, but would he give up? It really surprised me as I'd never thought of Rob as a hooligan – far from it, in fact – and to see him behave like this was a bit of a shock to say the least. Personally, I would have let him go; in fact, I would have pushed him back in there because, at that time, he deserved to get hit for sporting a really crappy Rod Stewart-style haircut. Now, if anything deserves a beating that does! But it was a shock. I thought he was a coward like me. But, then again, perhaps I'm doing him a disservice; perhaps he was simply retaliating, protecting himself – although at the time I did think, "What a berk!" Today, that very same berk is a centre stand season ticket holder and his mother is very proud of him. I know she is; she told me. I also know that she would *not* have been very proud of him on this occasion.

There was still quite a bit of brawling going on behind me, although I didn't want to turn around and have a look. Occasionally, a bloodied and battered Town fan would stagger past me and, more often than not, he'd be followed by two Bradford fans attempting to make his injuries even worse.

Even when the buses were sighted, they were still much too far away for comfort, and why they had been parked this far away from the ground I couldn't imagine – unless, of course, the police were actively encouraging violence on match days. All in all, it was a horrible, scary afternoon and the Chesterfield fans took what can only be described as a right shoeing!

Once we actually made it to the bus, the full extent of the damage could be seen. Fortunately, our transport was unscathed but, inside, it looked more like a World War I field hospital! Youths were bleeding freely over the upholstery while others checked the swellings on their eyes and cheeks in the driver's mirror. They knew that minor problems, such as black eyes, would be the centre of bar room conversation back in Chesterfield. Of course, the story accompanying the black eye wouldn't be quite as one-sided as the actual acquiring of it had been. A good story around a battered face must be worth a pint in any pub!

On the front seat of the bus I noticed Wynnie looking decidedly dejected. Somewhere along the way he'd collected a smack in the mush and it had shaken him up somewhat. He sat with his head in his hands – not literally, of course, although anything would have been possible on this trip – and watched as his empire crumbled around him. For the first time ever I realised that Wynnie was just the same as me: a big shit-bag. He arranged these bus trips to gain street cred (and this was long before street credibility had even been invented) and, sitting there sporting a swollen cheek, well, he probably realised he never really wanted any street cred anyway.

The only difference between Wynnie and me was that I was soft and I knew it but Wynnie was soft and he didn't want to be. He wanted to be a hard-nut like everyone else but, on the wrong end of a good hiding, he was beginning to find out what being an 'ooligan was all about. It was more than just organising a bus: oh yes, you had to be a bit of a bastard on the side as well!

In a last desperate attempt at false bravado, some Town fans made out as if they were trying to get off the bus to re-attack the Bradford fans, but most had had enough and were just eager to get out of that shit-hole. Eventually, we pointed the bus home and sung our way back to Chesterfield as if we'd won. We may have lost, we may have taken a right hammering into the bargain, but it hadn't been all bad: we'd made an attempt on the kop, half demolished a couple of houses and all but destroyed a Ford Zodiac. Wasn't that enough? And, anyway, everyone was determined to make the next set of fans pay for it.

Wynnie sat down on the front seat, nursing his bruised cheek and probably wondering if there would be a next time.

Going Out With A Whimper And A Bang

In January, Chesterfield sold goal-scoring legend Ernie Moss to Peterborough for £25,000. I don't think many supporters were surprised by this but they were somewhat annoyed; not because we all thought Ernie was the greatest thing on two legs, nor because we saw it as an end to our promotion ambitions (because very few people thought we had them anyway), but more because Peterborough had offered £40,000 for him at the start of the season. At that time our board of directors had turned it down, saying that the offer simply wasn't big enough and that Ernie was worth more. Six months later and that very same board had devalued Mossy to the tune of £15,000. This great piece of business acumen proved still further – if, indeed, any more proof was needed – that the board of directors at Chesterfield just weren't up to the job.

Joe Shaw was adamant that promotion was still on the cards and, as if to prove that we were going for it with all guns blazing, we paid a club record fee of £15,000 for the talents of one Steve Cammack. Of course, it would take more than a club record signing to get this team promoted: it needed three or four – and we all knew that wasn't going to happen. We'd gone into something of a downward spiral and the football on the pitch certainly wasn't anything to write home about. The season was petering out, the cricketing season beckoned and I expected very little from the remaining few games; but, as the pundits are always quick to tell us, "Nothing is certain in football!"

March 6th, 1976 Chesterfield 1 v 1 Cardiff

So there I am, expecting a gentle run-in to the end of the season, when hoards of slavering Welshmen descended on Chesterfield. Cardiff were in something of a promotion race and when I set foot in the ground they were already fighting on the terraces. The police had adopted a 'no nonsense' policy as regards matters pertaining to football violence and everyone involved in it was taken down to the police station and charged. Or, at least, that was the general idea. On this occasion, they had two warring factions and elements from both sides had been ejected from the ground and transported down to the station for processing. Unfortunately, so many of the police were at the ground enforcing the 'no nonsense' policy that there just weren't enough police left at the station to prevent the two sets of fans from continuing the fight inside the nick! Being arrested for football violence is one thing, being arrested for committing that same crime whilst in a police station is something else, and I can only assume that there were more than a few red faces amongst the Derbyshire Constabulary come Monday morning!

After the game, the Cardiff fans who hadn't been arrested went on the rampage and, this time, Marsden Street (a small side-street just off Saltergate) took the full force of the attack. Bricks, stones, lumps of concrete and even a dustbin were used to smash windows. The vandals attacked several cars, the Chest Clinic and the Conservative Club. (I doubt very much that the latter was a football-related incident. In fact, it was probably a good excuse for Chesterfield fans to get in on the act!) There were several arrests for 'grievous bodily harm,' not to mention 'being in possession of a Welsh accent!'

A Beautiful Whimper

March 24th, 1976 Sheffield Wednesday 1 v 3 Chesterfield

With just the Wednesday game to go, I felt I could relax. Not quite sure why when one considers the happenings earlier in the season but there was no way I was going to miss the game, even if it did mean going alone – which is exactly what happened. The scoreline that night was quite incredible, one I certainly didn't think we were capable of achieving, but I walked out at the end of the game having watched Town pull off a memorable 3–1 victory.

I stood on the Leppings Lane end, alone and away from anyone else, and said nothing for the whole 90 minutes. Watching your side win and not being able to cheer the fact is one of the most annoying things imaginable. It looked like it was going to be a bad night when the Owls took the lead after 20 minutes. However, Darling soon equalised from the penalty spot after Fern had been brought down. When the penalty went in I did start to cheer but I stopped myself quickly and turned my rapid arm movement into me trying to smother a cough. There were some Town fans singing that night and they attempted to cheer – but only briefly. It wasn't a particularly hostile night but Wednesday were being hammered and, let's face it, it doesn't matter how hostile you are as fans, if your team is being taught a lesson on the football field it can be difficult to conjure up hatred for the opposition as you're more inclined to want to give your own players a good slap. The truth is: Wednesday were being played to death. Fern had one disallowed and then he gave us the lead before half-time. The interval was really quite relaxed – nothing happened – and Chesterfield, for a glorious moment, were in the ascendancy; we were playing like a team that was 10 points clear at the top. The second half kicked off and within four minutes Malcolm Darling got his second of the night to put us 3–1 up and virtually kill the game.

I walked out into the Sheffield evening having stayed mute for the whole game. I didn't want to do that again but it had kept me safe, so perhaps the ends had justified the means. Having said that, I think I was fairly easy to spot as a Chesterfield fan that night since, while the Wednesday fans trooped off home with faces longer than a tramp's dewdrop on a frosty evening, I walked away looking not so much like the cat that got the cream but more like the one that had relieved the family fridge of all its meat and dairy contents *and* helped itself to next door's as well! I was bouncing along to get my bus home with a smile on my face that stretched all the way back to Saltergate.

That season Wednesday missed relegation to the Fourth Division by just 1 point. How I wanted them to go down! How fitting it would have been had our 3–1 victory been the nail in their coffin; but they were still there to fight again and, more importantly, to fight next season. We lost just two of our remaining nine games and clambered up to fourteenth in the table. Of course, that little run-in at the end gave us all hope for the following season.

Wednesday And Everything After
SEASONS 76-80

On September 11th, 1976 we lost 6–0 at home to Wrexham. It was just about enough for most fans and turned out to be more than enough for Joe Shaw who, shortly after the game, tendered his resignation which was eagerly accepted by the Board. Joe's last match was away at Sheffield Wednesday in the 76/77 season where we sunk without a trace, appearing on the wrong end of a 4–1 scoreline. From what I can remember, there wasn't any trouble. Chesterfield put in a largely inept performance and there was nothing for anyone from south of the Yorkshire border to get excited about at all. To find out it was Mr Shaw's last game was probably more exciting than the game itself. The Chesterfield Board then astounded everyone as they broke with tradition and actually appointed a manager, Arthur Cox, who many thought might actually do something! If he didn't, at least we could keep ourselves amused by shouting, "Cox, out!"

Over the next four years, Sheffield Wednesday were to figure in a large way in the violence that took place at Saltergate. I'd already witnessed the horror of the first encounter with them and I witnessed many more over the following four seasons.

As, hopefully, many of you will have noticed, this book is a chronological tour of those dark days of being a football fan. However, for the games against Wednesday I'm breaking with the current format and lumping them together into one horrendous mass. In some ways it's more therapeutic for me to do it like this: like anyone who has suffered any degree of trauma, I need to get these games out of my system so that I can 'move on.' The games against the Owls were never ones to look forward to and my therapist has said that if I deal with them in one complete chapter, then perhaps I can rid myself of the bile that congregates in my chest every time I think about them!

February 26th, 1977 Chesterfield 2 – 0 Sheffield Wednesday (76/77)

I'd tried to get my hands on some stand tickets for this one thinking that, in doing so, I would remove myself from the dangers of the Kop but it appears that everyone was thinking the same thing and the stand was sold out in a matter of days. They were Chesterfield's equivalent of gold bullion; Ronnie Biggs would have had a field day! Actually, it always amazes me that the Wednesday games were never made all-ticket. The police were desperate to cut down on violence, and yet neither the police nor the club ever thought to make them all-ticket affairs. I suppose, in some respects, it didn't really matter where you positioned yourself for a game with Wednesday, one never felt completely safe. How could you with all that violence happening around you? It would take a special kind of idiot to feel safe in that environment, I can tell you.

But this was a new era for Chesterfield: we had a new manager; we had hope; and making his home debut for us that day was the new £50,000 signing from Scunthorpe, Rick Green. Heady days, indeed! Very few Chesterfield fans could ever remember the club paying more for a player. Mr Cox had obviously loosened something in the Board Room. In fact, some Scunthorpe fans were so disappointed they had let their best player come to us that they continued to support him, and a bus-load of them arrived for his first game with Chesterfield against Wednesday. In retrospect, they probably wished they'd stayed at home.

Wednesday were chasing promotion and we were struggling to fend off relegation yet again. Although Cox had taken over as manager early that season, he hadn't really shown us that he was the man to change the expectations of a success-starved bunch of supporters. Okay, we hadn't yet shouted "Cox, out!" – but there was still time for that. To be honest, I thought this game against our loathed neighbours was hilarious. We hammered them 2–0 in front of a crowd of 15,113; and 'hammered' is a fairly good description of this one-sided affair.

Before the game there had been the usual round of fighting on the terraces but what was noticeable was how many Town fans had turned out for this one. Considering the thumping we'd taken the previous season I'd almost expected everyone to stay at home, but nothing could have been further from the truth. The season before was a shock; no one was prepared for the invasion that happened. This season it seemed as though everyone was ready. Wednesday fans were still on the Kop in rather large numbers but this season we were giving as good as we got. Okay, that's perhaps a little over the top. Let's just say we were giving, and leave it at that. Fighting in the ground started as early as 2pm and, although it was sporadic, the police never managed to bring it under control and it continued throughout the 90 minutes. The major plus for me was that the Old Bill at last managed to get something right and stopped the Wednesday fans from invading the pitch.

When Rick Green's goal went in on six minutes, there was a brief yet noticeable moment of silence as everyone breathed in at the same time to celebrate the goal. The noise that could be heard when we all exhaled was deafening and the Kop appeared to implode as if everybody had suddenly lost their legs. The mixture of fighting and celebration greeting that goal caused the crowd to collapse. It's difficult to describe but it was like being in a washing machine, being thrown first one way and then the other. It was as if someone had thrown a giant rock into the centre of the huge crowd of people causing the crowd to ripple outwards, crashing into barriers, falling in waves down to the front of the Kop before bouncing back off the wall at the bottom. It must have looked very exciting but it was horrible to be a part of. There were 23 people injured in that incident and I'm only surprised it was so few. When Green got his second goal the game was as good as over; but we just had time for the immaculate Rodney Fern to hit the post and it became a thoroughly miserable day for the Owls fans.

A huge cheer greeted the final whistle and I expected fighting to break out again but was pleasantly surprised to find that most of the Wednesday fans had long since disappeared. *"Yeah, well, I wouldn't have hung around long myself after being creamed like that,"* I thought to myself. However, there was an alternative reason for them sodding off early and I should have realised: they were waiting outside! The police did their best to keep the two sets of fans apart after the game but fights broke out in the car park above the Town Hall and there was also fighting at the rail and bus stations.

I walked slowly down to Beetwell Street for my bus and prayed that the Wednesday fans would either still be fighting in town or have long since gone. Of course, my prayers weren't answered and the walk to my bus-stop was like walking down the main street in Beirut. Bricks and bottles smashed and clattered all around and I managed to hold the surging panic that was rising in my chest at bay and walk nonchalantly onto my bus. I watched the fighting continue and I watched the police chase after and scatter groups of fans without getting hold of anyone. The third cheer from me that day was a silent one as my bus pulled away, leaving the fighting mob behind.

An article from the *Sheffield Star* just after the game bore the rather strange headline: ***"Sheffield Fan Tried To Bite First-aiders!"*** It went on to say:

"Ambulance men trying to help a Sheffield Wednesday fan injured at the Chesterfield v Sheffield Wednesday match had to call for police assistance when the fan became violent and tried to kick them. Eventually they lashed his feet together and handcuffed his arms behind his back before carrying him away on a stretcher, Chesterfield magistrates heard. The Wednesday fan was fined £75 and ordered to pay £20 costs after admitting to using threatening behaviour likely to cause a breach of the peace. Tony Reid, prosecuting, said police who broke up the fight on the terraces found the Wednesday fan lying on the ground shouting obscene language. They helped him to his feet and carried him to the side of the pitch where St John's Ambulance began to attend to him but as he lay on the stretcher he began to lash out with his feet and tried to bite the ambulance man. The Wednesday fan told the court he had turned violent because he had been kicked in the back."

To be honest if someone had attempted to bite me while I was trying to help them I might just have been tempted to give them another kick – especially if they had their hands tied behind their back and their legs lashed together. I don't know what the ambulance man was thinking of.

Mind you, it wasn't just the Wednesday fans that were slightly naughty... Oh, no! An article from the same paper had this headline: ***"Man Waved Axe In Air After Owls Derby"*** and was reported thus:

"A man from New Bolsover was fined £20 with £20 costs after admitting to possessing an offensive weapon in a public place. Prosecution said police had been informed that a youth in the Town Hall car-park was waving an axe about. The police officer found the man carrying a spanner, and found a hatchet on top of a nearby car. The man told police his car was parked next to a minibus full of Sheffield Wednesday fans who threatened to attack him, he took the items from his car in self-defence and gave the hatchet to a friend." He obviously wasn't believed but, then, that's hardly surprising.

In the days following the game, the police were patting themselves on the back and saying what a tremendous success their operation to cut football violence had been, how the trouble had been cut to a minimum and how everyone was really happy with the way it had gone.

If this had been a tremendous success in their eyes, it makes you wonder how they viewed an unmitigated disaster?

October 8th, 1977 Sheffield Wednesday 1 – 0 Chesterfield (77/78)

After having spent a silent away day on the Leppings Lane end the previous season, I decided that my next trip to Wednesday would be one where I could at least shout and enjoy myself – if that was at all possible at Sheffield.

A friend suggested that we try the cantilever stand as he thought we should be fairly safe in there and, just to make sure, he took his girlfriend and I took my dad, both our idea of a deflective shield – although I'm sure that if any trouble had arisen it wouldn't have mattered if I'd had my granny with me because we would still have got our heads kicked in!

I still have my ticket to this game and I can't believe the price on it. Catch a load of this: *'Reserved seat, including VAT, £1.60. Juveniles and O.A.P's £1.20.'* It takes some believing, doesn't it?

Anyway, back to the story. We took our seats in the all but empty stand (there were 13,093 at the game but the stand looked empty) and awaited the game. I must admit I was concerned as we entered the ground and, although I did my best to look casually nonchalant (or was it nonchalantly casual, I forget which), I couldn't help but notice a large gang of youths sitting in the back few rows of the stand. In fairness, they were hard to miss. But I was in the stand, my dad was with us, my mate's girlfriend was there: what could go wrong? I thought I could handle them being so far away but after about six minutes we had our first chance on goal and Stuart Parker really should have scored. My friend remained seated but threw his hands in the air, I leapt to my feet and threw my hands in the air, my dad applauded sportingly and my mate's girlfriend yawned. Stands make me feel safe, as I've said, and once we'd had a shot on goal I was really starting to encourage from my 'safe' seat. After about 15 minutes the seats behind me started to fill up. *"People coming in late,"* I thought. Oh, if only I'd been right! Unfortunately, the great gang of lads seated at the back as we arrived, were now sitting virtually on my shoulder. Needless to say, my encouragement subsided, my mate's encouragement did the same, my dad continued to applaud sportingly and my mate's girlfriend shit herself; well, almost – but, then, so did I!

For the sake of those who didn't go to this game, we really played well that day and could have been four up by half-time. It's perhaps as well we weren't, though; I hate to think what would have happened. My dad would have applauded sportingly, no doubt, but I'm not sure I could have.

Jack Charlton became manager of Wednesday after that game. He'd obviously seen enough to think they were worth taking on. I just thought he was an arrogant dick looking for a club to take on that had an ego as big as his. In retrospect, they were perfect for each other.

I remember worrying briefly about how we would get out of the ground, especially now that we'd been 'found out' but I can't remember any specific incident so I suppose we must have done it easily, if not a little cautiously. I also remember my friend telling me off for encouraging the team so vocally and nearly getting us into trouble. I hadn't thought I'd been that vocal, certainly not up to my usual standards. I remember shouting once and then I thought I got rather subdued (but that can happen when you have a bunch of hooligans sitting on your shoulder). The way I saw it, once we'd been found out it was hardly worth the effort to keep the noise down; the planks behind us would have battered us if they'd wanted to whatever we'd said or done or whatever the score. We must have crossed them on a good night. My 'mate,' if you can call him that, came to very few football games with me but if he was going to be like this every time, I remember thinking I might be better coming on my own. There was enough aggro from opposing supporters; I didn't need any from one of my own.

March 4th, 1978 Chesterfield 2 – 2 Sheffield Wednesday (77/78)

Chesterfield were now showing genuine signs of improvement. Wednesday, on the other hand, hadn't had a great season and, although this game carried very little significance, other than the fact that it was Wednesday – which is perhaps about as significant as it can get, I suppose – I imagine both sides were eager to win and finish the season in some kind of style.

Having said there was very little significance to the game, it still attracted a crowd of 12,495 and those who attended went on to witness one of the most brutal football matches ever seen. This was your original blood and thunder local derby. Mostly blood. I remember it because I don't think I've ever seen so many supporters carted out on stretchers either before or during a game. The *Derbyshire Times* very rarely did pieces about crowd trouble but it would have been impossible *not* to write about it on this particular day. I'd been fortunate enough this year to gain a ticket for the Saltergate wing stand – Row E, Seat 9 (yes, I still have the ticket stub) – and it remains one of the most sensible purchases I've ever made!

You knew it was going to be rough just walking up to the ground. The violence had started early in the morning in the pubs in the town centre. (You could usually tell how close it was to kick-off time by the pub the violence was in. For instance, if they were fighting in the *Market* or the *Fleece* then you were all right for an hour's shopping before nipping up to the ground. However, if they were brawling in the *Barley Mow* or the *County* then you only had about 15 minutes to take your place.) But there was a really nasty atmosphere to this one and the visual signs of violence were everywhere: broken windows, smashed bottles and groups of women in *M&S* tutting about how disgraceful it was. Some bright Herbert of a 'Bowels' fan even nicked a charity box out of the *Barley Mow*. Yes, it had come to that. Apparently, the less brain dead of the Wednesday contingent in the pub had a whip round for the stolen box and the landlord at the time rather hoped they'd come and pinch it every week! And what went off on the pitch matched what was happening on the terraces. It was violent and ugly: lunging tackles, players booked. In fact, I can't believe that both sides managed to keep a full complement of 11 players on the field.

As I've already mentioned, the Chesterfield supporters had been taken by surprise on that opening encounter but each year after that they were ready; not in the same numbers perhaps but there were always some Town fans on the Kop singing. I've tried to show the odd, sometimes funny, side of football violence but there was nothing funny about this encounter. It was, quite frankly, sickening. It said in the paper that 16 people were treated by the St John Ambulance with a further three requiring hospital attention and that didn't take into account the five policemen injured.

The Wednesday fans were mostly congregated on the Compton side of the ground and we held most of the Kop. From the stand I could see great chunks of rock flying onto the pitch. Most of it was stuff being thrown between the warring factions. At one stage a toilet chain came swirling onto the pitch; I was somewhat surprised that the toilet never followed it!

Chesterfield took a 2–0 lead through Hunter and Green, and then Wednesday had two goals disallowed (one for pushing and one for off-side); decisions I greeted with the same joy as I'd greeted Chesterfield's goals. But it was these moments that led to a further upsurge in trouble. One of the linesmen was hit by a missile and the police had to protect him from the slavering beasts standing down his side of the Compton. In the end, the ref had to shift him over to the other side of the pitch for his own safety. A pitch invasion looked like an odds-on certainty and I doubt being in the stand would have made that much difference had it happened. Some dork of a Wednesday fan marched onto the pitch to remonstrate with the referee (or perhaps that should read 'chin the referee') but, fortunately, the police managed to stop him.

Thankfully, the pitch invasion was halted by two things: the police and some incredibly dodgy refereeing, to say the least. To say Wednesday's come-back was controversial is something of an understatement. The first goal was fine, nothing wrong in that, but I'm still not sure they actually scored a second. The ball looked to be going in but Les Hunter did this phenomenal overhead kick to keep it out. Well, that's how it looked. In the stand I was on my feet praising 'Good old Les.' On the pitch the ref, or the linesman, or both, were signalling a goal. It's doubtful if either of them could have made any kind of decision. When one considers how referees struggle with goal-line debates nowadays, then there's no way on God's green earth that either official could have given the goal; but, then, it's easy for me to say that as a Chesterfield fan. Allowing the goal was the only way these two officials were going to get out of the ground alive, so they probably figured it was worth it – and I for one can't blame them for that either. They knew which set of fans were causing the bother. I'm not saying the Town fans were without blame, far from it, but the Wednesday fans were crazed. Their actions throughout this game made what happened during that first encounter look like a girl guide's picnic. Even Jack Charlton was worried about any action the Football League might impose upon the club as they weren't just causing trouble at Saltergate; they were doing it everywhere!

Soccer violence erupts at Saltergate during the 2-2 draw with Sheffield Wednesday. Poor quality picture plucked from the back issue of The Derbyshire Times, but it gives a taste of what those games were really like.

The *Daily Express* reported that: *"Those fans whose magnificent support persuaded Jack Charlton to take over at Sheffield Wednesday are now giving him cause for concern."*

"They behave at home. Why can't they behave away?" Jack told reporters but, then, perhaps he didn't realise they only behaved at home because everyone else was too shit scared to go there.

Chesterfield's secretary, Arthur Sutherland, put it quite simply: *"If there was any trouble from the Chesterfield side, it must have been very minimal indeed."* Good old Arthur!

I thought the ref, Bert Newsome, was useless but I must admit I wouldn't have liked to have been refereeing that one. It was frightening enough watching it. And all this happened after the lead headline in the *Derbyshire Times* before the game of ***"Major Police Operation for Derby Match."*** The article went on to say:

"A major police operation is planned for Saturday's Chesterfield v Sheffield Wednesday derby clash at Saltergate. Last year 15,000 people attended the match and the police prevented any serious trouble by having extra men on duty. In the previous season's clash soccer hooligans ran riot causing large-scale damage to town centre properties.

Chief Superintendent Ken Unwin said, 'We shall mount an operation on similar lines to last year's. There will be many more additional officers in the town including uniform, plain clothes, mounted police and dog handlers.'"

Well, if that was a major police operation aimed at curbing violence all I can say is it failed miserably. The problem was that after the game the police thought it had gone swimmingly, mainly because the majority of the trouble had seemed to be contained within the ground. Whichever way you looked at this one, though, it wasn't pretty.

One Wednesday fan, arrested for threatening behaviour, told how he lost his temper on finding that his friend who'd gone for a hot drink had been set upon by Chesterfield fans and had his legs broken with an iron bar. I can understand why he might lose his temper but, unfortunately for him, his defence, rather like his friend, didn't stand up in court.

On the same court billing, a Town fan was sent down for three months for assaulting a police officer. I always find this rather strange: if you're going to get sent down, then get done for hammering an Owl. We had enough on in these games without turning on the police.

One of the papers said: *"The antics of the minority were in danger of seeing Wednesday fined by the Football League."* I was there! If that was Wednesday's minority, I would hate to be in a game where their majority started to cause a rumpus!

December 26th, 1978 Chesterfield 3 – 3 Sheffield Wednesday (78/79)

The early encounters with Sheffield Wednesday had been the worst by far and, thankfully, last season's encounter was never topped. I had a kind of love/hate relationship when we played Dee-Dahs.[4] Loved the atmosphere – it was always electric; and I loved the fact that they never seemed to win at Saltergate. Hated the fact that I had to go and hide in the stand; there was always loads of trouble and it was always quite frightening. Having said that, it was always the first game you looked for when the fixtures were announced.

---

[4] Less than affectionate nickname for anyone who comes from Sheffield.

Another reason for loving the Wednesday game was the big crowd and this one was no exception as 13,332 snuggled very nicely into Saltergate. Perhaps 'snuggled' is the wrong word against Wednesday. Whatever, it was a helluva game: a 3–3 draw with Walker, Fern and Prophett getting on the score-sheet. There had been the usual bout of fighting, both outside and in, but nothing like the previous year. With Chesterfield fans gearing themselves up for this clash, the Kop was never going to be handed over as easily as it had been in the first fixture. This game stands out in my mind as I got a right mauling in the stand from two geriatric Town fans. Hey, that sounds about right: I buy a ticket for the stand so I can keep out of trouble and then get turned over by a couple of pensioners.

As it was Christmas, I'd taken my sister to the game. She'd been missing from the Saltergate scene for far too long and we sat down to enjoy the ritual humiliation of Sheffield Wednesday. Unfortunately, it didn't quite materialise. We had the makings of a half-decent side but we were very poor at the back. Nevertheless, we had enough to beat this bunch of muppets and it wasn't long before I was punching holes in the air in celebration as we took a deserved lead. Now, Chesterfield scoring usually fills me with joy and excitement but on this occasion all I could feel was a searing pain down the back of my neck; most unusual, I have to say. I looked at my sister and, after a brief chat, discovered that she had suffered similar discomfort. We were totally mystified as to what strange phenomenon had overcome us. Sometime later, we scored a second goal and, once again, up we go in delight and, once again, we both succumb to this incredible pain around the neck region. We looked around to see if people were throwing things at us or if we were the victims of some cruel practical joke, but there was nothing. When Prophett netted the equaliser in the dying minutes of the game I was slightly worried, not because I was concerned about football violence but because I was concerned that my sister and I had contracted a crippling disease that was causing us to waste away from the neck down. There was only one way to find out and, again, we hit the air in celebration only to be greeted with incredible pain and discomfort. On this occasion, however, I'd had the forethought to turn around quickly and, to my horror, found an old git had got me by the hair and another one was trying desperately to get hold of my sister's in a similar fashion. As he pulled on my hair, he was muttering something and trying desperately to yank me back down into my seat. Boy, it hurt!

The man must have been out of his tree; it wasn't as if he was missing anything. He saw the whole game; just missed the players hugging each other. And it wasn't as if I was the only person in the stand who had raised their bum off the seat; everyone had.

Now, normally, I think of pensioners as being kind, winsome, old characters who love to chuckle and reminisce about what it was like in their day; people who smell of wee and *Werther's Originals...* I'm sure you know what I mean. However, these two old geezers were the most annoying, obnoxious, old bastards I've ever come across. I must admit, it hadn't struck me until I started writing this bit that they might well have been Wednesday fans. As I said, at the time I assumed they were Chesterfield followers because they were sitting in the Saltergate wing stand; but perhaps this was the pensioner branch of the Wednesday firm? Anyway, I faced my two aggressors firmly, all square-jawed and indignant. One of them had a face like a corpse's shoe and the other one looked more like a constipated hamster's arse. They did have two things in common, though: both had flat caps and both had fists full of hair torn from the scalps of my sister's head and mine!

Eventually, I managed to say something along the lines of, "What the bloody hell are you on with?" to which the corpse's shoe replied, "Sit daaaan." (He was nothing if not eloquent.)

"You bloody idiot! Touch me again and I'll..." 'Tell my mum' might have been the most truthful ending but, instead, I just left the words hanging there as if it might frighten him, although all it really did was make me look an even bigger pillock for not having a decent put-down for the barmy old bleeder.

"Sit daaaan," he said again, as if I might not have heard him the first time.

"Is that all you can say?"

"I can't see. Sit daaan!"

Obviously, it was pretty much all he could say! I was furious. I was so mad I would quite willingly have stopped his pension, refused him a hip replacement and quadrupled the tax on flat cap sales! That would have shown him. But I couldn't do any of that. In fact, the pair of them had so little to say for themselves I couldn't even argue with them, so I just turned around and 'sat daaaaaaaaan.'

But it wasn't just the OAP's that were causing trouble that festive day. According to the *Derbyshire Times* over £1,200 in fines were handed out to five hooligans. Apparently, by imposing such hefty fines the magistrates were indicating that they were determined to stamp out such behaviour which *"spoiled the pleasure of the general public."* Two of the youths appearing before them were fined £300 each, while the other three were each fined £200. All were ordered to pay court costs and bound over *"to be of good behaviour"* for a year. The odd thing is that their behaviour didn't appear to be that alarming; it amounted to little more than sticking two fingers up and shouting abuse. Okay, one lad did actually punch someone, but the rest... As I say, it was for very little indeed; certainly less than what the old gits were guilty of on me in the stand that day and an awful lot less than I actually do from my position in the main stand these days!

April 14th, 1979 Sheffield Wednesday 4 v 0 Chesterfield (78/79)

This was, perhaps, one of the most embarrassing moments of the Spires v Owls clashes. Originally, I wasn't going. We were playing shite at the time and I decided that I didn't need to see us lose and run the risk of getting my head kicked in. After all, a man can only take so much. So, Saturday morning I'm in town doing my shopping: those important few items that a man-around-town needs, like shaving foam and records and stuff like that. (I think I used to spend all my wages on a Saturday morning. Trust me, it wasn't difficult.) With what passed as a spending spree over, I walk down to the *East Midlands* bus station to catch the bus home and who should I see but a friend of mine, John Day.

"Are you going, Dave?" he said in his usual cheery manner.

"You have to be joking," was my honest response.

The conversation went on like this for some time until said supporter, who always should have been a salesman, eventually convinced me that going to Hillsborough on a bright April day was just what I needed. How I agreed to it I'll never know. Well, actually, that's not strictly true. I do remember exactly how the lying git managed to talk me into going. He told me – nay, assured me – that the massed ranks of Chesterfield's finest were descending on Hillsborough for some pay-back. Now, can someone please tell me why I believed that so easily at the time and, yet, reading it back now, it seems about as likely as Mrs

Thatcher (spit) shagging Arthur Scargill? It's just so ridiculous; in fact, more than that, it's bloody incredulous!

I should have realised something was amiss because as soon as I'd succumbed to John's sales patter, a young lad, who had obviously been listening in to our conversation, pushes himself forward and offers me his bus ticket. Not only that, but the lad in question was so eager to rid himself of the bloody thing that he knocked 50p off the price! So I had my bus ticket but I also had my shopping, so I rushed back home and then caught the bus back into town, just in time to get the *East Midlands* 'crammed-to-the-rafters-with-thugs' battle-wagon to Sheffield.

Now, as I said earlier, I should have known. Yes, I really should have known. But there we are, waiting for this special bus and I'm looking around me all the time expecting to see hordes of Chesterfield hoodlums, all the better for a few pints of Dutch courage, making their way from the good hostelries of Chesterfield in time to do battle with Wednesday. I should have known. It worried me that no queue was starting to form. It worried me that everybody looking anything like 'hard' was walking straight past. It worried me, and I should have known.

Eventually, this dirty great double-decker pulls up down the side of the *East Midlands* office. Very few people moved. I looked around but saw nothing: no gangs of hooligans; no thugs; in fact, hardly anyone. In all, there were ten people on the bus. Eleven if you count the driver. TEN! I kid you not. I was destroyed. We sat upstairs with a young lad and his girlfriend while the other six sat downstairs. At first I gave John a hard time: "So, a lot going is there?" etc, etc, etc. But he said nothing; just sat there smiling. In the end, we both cracked out laughing and continued to do so all the way into Sheffield. It was the laugh of the condemned man. Once at Hillsborough, the driver dropped us off with a cheery smile and said he'd see us after the game. Somehow I wasn't so sure.

Where to stand was the next problem. Neither of us fancied the Leppings Lane end so, as the day had been nothing but a farce so far, we decided that the best options were the East Bank and tight lips. This was in the days when the East Bank was uncovered and it was a really good view. In fact, the view was too good because Wednesday turned us over 4–0 and we had to stand there and politely applaud. It was made worse by this bloke who would insist on turning round after every good move/goal and ask our opinion: "Great goal that, eh? Just great, eh?" (Yeah, mate, we're so thrilled we could just shit.) It's really hard trying to be happy when you're as miserable as sin!

To make matters even worse, I nearly cocked the whole thing up, as well. On the terrace, near to where we were standing, was a small piece of the East Bank with railings round it and a policeman – just the one. Inside these railings was some bloke giving it some, "Come on, Chesterfield!" For a split second I thought, *"Oh, a section for away fans."* (I was told later that its purpose was just that, although it never attracted any. Wonder why?) I even considered going in to join him but a split second later it hit me that he was a Wednesday fan and would have kicked the fuck out of me had I gone in there. After ten minutes of singing 'Come on, Chesterfield,' he gave up and walked back into the middle of the East Bank with the rest of the thugs. This was one of those days when you were glad we hadn't scored. Cheering a goal is often an automatic reaction but we were so bad on this day that scoring was never really an option, although a shot on goal might have been nice. It's also fair to say that I was more than a little worried about how we would get back to the bus after the game. It turned out that I had every right to be.

Once outside the ground, we walked to where we'd been dropped off but I was still worried. A double-decker bus is fairly visible and I was concerned that a few Wednesday fans might just bump into it on their way out. But perhaps I shouldn't have been concerned at all because when we got to where the bus should have been, it wasn't there! The only good thing about this was that if we couldn't see the transport, then the Wednesday fans couldn't see it either. Now a double-decker bus takes some hiding and, as things stood, all I wanted to do was climb aboard it and go home with the minimal amount of fuss. As we continued our walk, we saw a couple who had been on the bus with us and, quietly, we expressed our concern. They were as mystified as we were. We walked a little further round, seeing other people who had been on the bus and gradually feeling more and more out of place with every step. We were trying desperately not to attract attention, which is difficult when you appear to be standing out like a sore thumb! It felt as if we did two circuits of the ground without finding either the bus or a policeman upon whose mercy we could throw ourselves. People started to talk about getting the train home, which was a bit of a worry for me as I just didn't have the money – and I wasn't the only one in that particular boat. So we just stood there, like lemons, waiting for a smack in the gob or the bus driver, whichever came first. We looked like tourists who couldn't speak the language and didn't know where to go.

After about 20 minutes, which seemed more like two hours, we heard someone calling to us from the road: "Hey, you lot! Oi!!! Hey!" It was the driver. "Come on. The police made me park the bus down here!"

I cringed and couldn't imagine why he didn't just shout, 'Hey, this lot are from Chesterfield and they're a right bunch of cowards!' We half ran, half walked to our saviour, got there and found him standing there caressing a fucking wheel! In my memory he was holding a bus wheel but I don't think that would really have been practical. I mean, they're pretty big things, aren't they? So it was probably one he wanted for his car. I honestly don't know. What I do know is that, on seeing him, my first thought was, *"FUCK, is that all that's left of the bus!?"* Whatever, there he is lumping this wheel back to the bus while we follow in a nice little line. What was that I said about drawing attention to yourself?

"I had to park down here," he said. "The police made me. All special buses go in here so they aren't damaged."

And he kept going on about Chesterfield and I just wanted him to shut his bloody mouth. It was all very Pied Piperish. He was dead jolly and nice and thought life was wonderful, especially now that he'd got his bloody wheel! But we were just following, trying not to notice the stares from the other side of the road.

We got in and out of Sheffield safely but, to this day, I will never know how. The driver wasn't really the plonker I've made him out to be; in fact, he was quite a nice bloke. But the whole thing was surreal. If anyone out there was on that bus, give me a nudge; we ought to have a reunion. Let's face it, we wouldn't need a big room!

September 29th, 1979 Chesterfield 2 v 1 Sheffield Wednesday (79/80)

By 1979, Chesterfield were playing some of the finest football I've ever witnessed from a Chesterfield side and we had very real promotion ambitions, rather like our dearly beloathed neighbours. Consequently, the first encounter of the 79/80 season turned out to be a real stormer!

Once again I was in the stand, the Cross Street wing stand; not the bit for away fans but further on, against the centre stand partition. Despite our ambitions, our season hadn't started so well. (We actually lost to Rotherham, so you can see how bad it had been!) The attendance was 14,950 and I was unfortunate enough to have a real mouthy Owl (some might say it's the only sort there is) two rows behind me, on the other side of the partition.

The game was great and Town won 2–1, Walker and Crawford the scorers, but the bloke behind, for some reason, decided that I was to be the brunt of Sheffield's frustration and kept giving me grief throughout the game. It wasn't that he had a personal problem with *me*; he just seemed to hate everything about the club. He went on at length about what a shit club we were, how we didn't deserve to do anything and never would, what a crap ground we'd got, and how we had no right to be playing the likes of Wednesday who were a great club (some might even say massive). Anyone who has listened to Radio Sheffield at any time will realise that this rant epitomises everything about Wednesday and its fans. For some reason they just can't get their heads around the fact that, occasionally, the footballing gods decree that they will have to play little sides, like us, who will then turn them over and remind them just how big they really are (not).

But I digress. As I say, behind me was the S6 Gob. I hated him. I know he was winding me up – or, at least, I know it started out that way – but, in the end, he was starting to believe his own propaganda. Although I prided myself on managing to keep out of trouble regardless of the situation, I couldn't resist letting him have a verbal volley back. Well, be honest, Chesterfield are the club I love, right? I mean, would you stand for someone saying your wife was rubbish? Okay, for some that might be a bad analogy but you know what I mean. Without thinking about the possible consequences, I decided to unleash my own unwieldy gob and start trading insults with this idiot. I can't remember everything that was said verbatim but it ran along these lines:

"Why don't you shut your mouth and bog off back to Sheffield?"

"Don't talk to me like that, son."

"Piss off! Don't call me son! You just don't like losing, do you?"

"I shan't lose in a minute because I'll come and sort you out."

"Yeah? I'm shaking. Frightened to bloody death."

By this time he was getting really angry and he didn't like the fact that I was now the one doing the 'winding up.' Of course, I loved the idea and rather than leave it, as anyone with a modicum of sense would have done, I continued to bait him, making up, no doubt, for all those years of Owl oppression. I should add that it wasn't as if I was getting on to a hooligan here: this was a man in his mid-forties, sitting with his young son (who, it has to be said, had been forgotten by his father a long way down the argument). But, despite him having a look like thunder, I felt reasonably safe. Well, how many responsible fathers do you know who would abandon their young son just to give a lippy Chesterfield fan a walloping? Exactly! And it was that kind of reasoning that inspired me to continue this verbal battle.

Every time Wednesday went close, he was up, bawling at the ref: "With decent officials we'd be 5–2 up!"

"With decent officials you'd get relegated!" (Large guffaw from my side of the stand.)

"Poxy club. You haven't even got a decent stand."

"You didn't have to come. In fact, you could have given that seat to a supporter."

"Just you watch your mouth. I'm sick of you."

"Yeah? Yeah? Well, I'm bloody sick of you. Just sod off!"

"I'll bloody have you in a minute," he said, and stood up, leaning forward as if he was going to reach down and get hold of me.

At this point I got slightly worried because he did actually mean it. His fists were clenched and his argument, which had never been reasoned (but, then, neither had mine), became very, very personal indeed. I never expected him to get quite so worked up but, call me a fool if you must – and heaven knows enough people do – I felt I just had to have the last word. He was hating every minute of the game and I was loving it. Wednesday never actually looked like getting on level terms, and we both knew it. So, when he moved as if to get me, rather than sit down and smile, knowing that I'd wound him up good and proper, I stood up, leaned back towards him and said, "When you're fuckin' ready, mate. Any time you like."

This time there was a sharp intake of breath from my side of the stand. It wasn't the most sensible move I've ever made; in fact, it has to go down as one of the most stupid. I abhor violence. I'm a quiet, reasoned soul at heart but I love my club and sometimes I say things that come straight from the heart and never pass through brain central at all! I had absolutely no idea who I was trying to kid. I certainly didn't fool myself because it was one of those statements you make while at the same time thinking, *"NO, NO, DON'T SAY IT. PLEASE, DON'T SAY IT......... Ooops, too late."*

The lad sitting with me, Brock (what an obvious nickname for a lad named Badger!), grabbed hold of my arm, pulled me down into my seat and told me to stop being a bloody idiot. And although I knew he was right, the one thing I didn't need was a supposed mate telling me to stop being an idiot; he should have been on my side! So that just made me worse. I wanted support, a bit of backing here. So, as soon as the man opened his mouth again, and I didn't have to wait long, I stood up and faced him. This time, however, I didn't say anything to him. I never got the chance. He just looked at me, wagged his finger, said a few choice words and then the line I least wanted to hear.

"I'm fuckin' having you outside after, ya bastard!"

I was momentarily gobsmacked – but just couldn't sit down. I knew that I really would lose face if I did. (And, what the hell, it looked like I was going to lose it after the match anyway.) I needed to have that last word. That's the kind of idiot I can be.

"Right! Outside! I'll be there!" The words just echoed in my head. I wanted them to sound positive and cocky. But they didn't; they sounded hollow and empty.

The collective mouth of my section of the stand hit the floor. My mate put his head in his hands and sighed. Behind me, I could hear the bloke trying to explain to his son, in the nicest possible way, what 'having him after' actually meant; but, in the end, he gave up and told him to sit and watch the match. My ex-mate, who, curiously enough, I've never been to another match with (but, then, he was a half Spurs fan anyway, so it was no big loss), just gave me loads and loads of grief. Why had I got *him* into this situation? Excuse me, did I miss something here? For some strange reason he thought I'd expected him to get involved – and I didn't. I really didn't! *I* had dug this hole and I knew *I* had to get myself out of it. I certainly didn't expect him to climb in and lend me a hand (although, as a mate, you'd have thought he would have offered). But he just went on and on and on. I didn't say anything; I think I was too frightened to speak!

When the ref finally ended the game, I walked tentatively outside. I honestly expected a huge mitt to grab me from behind and ask me where I was trying to sneak off to but I think he was as big a shit bag as me because there was, thankfully, no sign of him at all. (Good job, cos I'd have given him a right good hiding... in my dreams!) Patience was never my strong point but days such as these soon turned me into the tolerant individual you know today.

I'm not quite sure why I got so worked up with this guy. Perhaps it was a number of things: perhaps I was sick of watching Wednesday fans come to Saltergate and cause so much trouble; perhaps I just wanted a little retribution of my own. Whatever it was, it was most unlike me.

Wednesday, on the other hand, went about their usual business, which led the local paper to run with the report of: *"Traditional enmity flared into hooliganism over last Saturday's game. Trouble at the Kop and in the town centre led to several arrests involving Chesterfield and Sheffield supporters on various charges – mainly threatening behaviour."*

It was strange how supporters were charged with threatening to behave badly but the ones who actually did behave badly seemed to get away with it. Thankfully, that day I wasn't among one of those arrested for threatening behaviour and I suppose it's fair to say that both of us had crossed that line. But, then again, I'm sure the police had more serious things to deal with: like the man who used karate-type kicks against Wednesday fans; and the one man who dived into around 50 supporters and started kicking and punching out at them. Yes, that makes my actions seem rather timid indeed.

February 16th, 1980 Sheffield Wednesday 3 v 3 Chesterfield (79/80)

The last Wednesday battle was away at Hillsborough and I shall remember it, not for the small amount of trouble but for the game of football itself. Quite simply, this was the finest game of football I've ever seen Chesterfield involved in. In fact, it's not far short of the best game of football I've ever seen! There were 23,637 at Hillsborough that day and, for the first time ever, we actually took a load of fans; so many that the police had tried to make the Leppings Lane end for visiting supporters only. They failed.

There were a few skirmishes early on and I lost the lads I'd gone with. So there I was, standing on the Leppings Lane end, feeling a little bit frightened and very alone. My first thought was to applaud sportingly everything that happened; but I couldn't. When Kendall saved a penalty, I went wild. A gang of youths in front looked at me. One of them whispered to his mate, in a voice loud enough for the whole of Sheffield to hear, "There's one behind us." That kind of statement really puts you off your game but I couldn't move, so I decided to stick it out and see what happened and, as it turned out, nothing did. Perhaps they realised there were bigger fish to fry in this particular net and, eventually, they moved away in search of them.

In the end, it looked like I was going to go home safe but miserable, 3–2 down with about two minutes to go. Then we got a free kick on the edge of their box. The ball broke to Salmons and he curled it into the top corner. I went mental. It was actually worth getting beaten up for. No, really it was. We deserved a draw, if not the win. But the quality of football on show that day was probably better than anything either of the two sides has conjured up since. So why should I care what the hell happened to me? We had a vital point and I'd seen a great game. That really is what football is all about. So, thankfully, I was able to jump around and sing inside the ground and I didn't even care if they were waiting for me outside.

Once I'd applauded the team from the pitch, I made my way to the bus with relative ease. Not everyone did. You could hear the odd shouts as fights broke out in the distance. But it had been such a good game and we'd played so well. You couldn't help but think we were even winning the fights at last. We probably weren't but, then, who cares?

Unfortunately, Wednesday made promotion with Blackburn and we missed out by one sole, solitary point. It was the most heartbreaking season of my footballing life. It hurt more than any hooligan's punch. At least, that's how it seemed. And just to rub salt into the wounds, at the end of the season the Football League decided to move the goalposts for the following season and give 3 points for a win. If they'd made that decision one year earlier, we would have been promoted instead of Wednesday. I've never liked the Football League!

David Radford

It Wasn't All Beer And Wednesday
SEASON 77/78

Although it might be fair to say that the majority of the trouble during the late 80's came from Sheffield Wednesday and, indeed, disappeared when they rode out of town, it would be wrong to assume that nothing else happened apart from the weekends we played them. In fact, nothing could be further from the truth. Having said that, it would also be wrong to assume that football violence happened every single Saturday because, to put it simply, it didn't. The violence, certainly in those days, had two major contributing factors in my opinion: (1) how well your team was doing in the league; and (2) who you were playing. For instance, we could have been bottom of the league and, yet, a scrap was guaranteed with that lot from north of Dronfield and those yellow and blue scum from near Nottingham. Equally, if we were near the bottom and were playing some non-descript bunch of no-hopers, such as Barnet, then you had more chance of getting into a fight in the local chip shop than at the match. Clubs that were doing well but no one cared about would invariably come to town and cause a ruck, mainly because no one expected it. But, in the main, football violence in our division was fairly sporadic.

During the late 70's Chesterfield were in a state of flux: we had at last appointed a manager who looked liked he knew what he was doing; but whether the Board were prepared to back him with the funds he required remained to be seen. We were 'rebuilding,' I suppose. It's just that, as a Chesterfield supporter, there is only so much rebuilding you can take. There does come a point when you wish that all the building was finished and you could actually get down to some serious decorating!

Season 77/78 was nothing to write home about really. The team flattered to deceive throughout, but inconsistency saw us flirt briefly with the top of the table before succumbing to a comfortable ninth position. One of the few highlights was our League Cup encounters. We had managed to draw 4–4 with Barnsley over two legs before whooping them 2–0 on their own cabbage patch. The reward for this win was a plum second round tie against the rather magnificent Manchester City, which boasted people like Dennis Tuert and Brian Kidd. The police had set a ground limit of 19,000 for the game, with City getting 5,000 tickets, and, although they continually asked the club for more, they ended up returning 3,000 unsold which meant that a lot of Chesterfield fans didn't get to see the game. As usual with games of this nature, the local press had a headline field day and the *Derbyshire Times* came up with the fantastically unimpressive, ***"Aggro-phobia grips town as big match looms."*** The article that followed was equally hysterical:

"Aggro-phobia will bring the shutters down in Chesterfield next Wednesday when thousands of Manchester City fans pour into the town."

I think you'll agree that this is somewhat over the top. In fact, it makes it sound as if we were about to be overrun by the combined forces of the Roman Empire, the Vikings and the four horsemen of the Apocalypse. The newspaper article went on to say that pub landlords had threatened to vet anyone resembling a football fan (which probably translates to: 'Pub landlords will only serve people if they have enough money for at least six pints of ale').

Anyway, the aforementioned apocalypse never happened. City won the game 1–0 and there were only four arrests – although, to be fair, it should have been five because Sean O'Neil's tackle on Tuert was enough to get him sent down for a couple of months, never mind arrested. A couple of the arrests were on City fans who decided it might be a good idea to smash the windows of *The Chesterfield Arms*. When they appeared in court, one of them said, "I did it because I felt like it." I assume that by that stage he'd figured it was pointless trying to make up some lame excuse about how he'd been trying to throw his favourite brick to his best mate.

For Chesterfield, well, we had seen the emergence of yet another new goalkeeping talent that night. I suppose the regulars all knew he was good but that night he was exceptional and it wasn't long before Steve Ogrozovic was sold to Liverpool for £65,000. He had played just 18 first team games for Chesterfield. His replacement was Glan Letheran from Swansea and the poor lad just couldn't win, really. He tried, bless him, but he just wasn't good enough. Perhaps it was no surprise that our slip down the league coincided with the signing of Mr Letheran.

As I pointed out earlier, football violence didn't always occur and, apart from our 'big game' with Man City, it had all been fairly quiet. The only thing I could find in the papers was that one Chesterfield fan went berserk after a home game in October. The man pleaded guilty to the charges and his defence was that this was his first taste of freedom since he'd been released from borstal. I don't know about you but, had I been defending the lad, I would have been embarrassed to have come up with that as a defence. Surely the solicitor could have come up with something a little more plausible. I mean, *I'm* glad to get out of work each day but it doesn't mean I want to go into town and run amok! I'm much happier going home for 'me tea.'

The FA Cup was, of course, our big chance to shine and, after seeing off Halifax in the first round, we were drawn away to Blyth Spartans. With a name like that I wasn't even sure they were a proper football team. I had certainly never heard of them and assumed that after the second round I would never hear of them again as we would undoubtedly cast them back into the bin from which they had appeared. Now, for a game like this I would normally have been on a coach and heading north but, for some reason, whether it was financial or just plain apathy, I decided to give this one a miss and, boy, am I glad I did. That evening, as I watched the results come in on the teleprinter, I was gutted. We'd lost to a bunch of non-league muppets! I mean, how inglorious can it get? Being a Chesterfield fan, there are some things you expect – things that don't exactly take your breath away but leave you shrugging in that, *'Well, I expect nothing more from my club'* sort of way – but losing to a non-league side was beyond my thought processes. I wasn't sure that I could ever remember it happening before. To be fair, we seldom got beyond the first round anyway, but to be knocked out by a non-league side… well, I was speechless.

The following day, as I set off to play football, I saw my mate Higgy.

"Did you go yesterday, Stan?" he asked.

"No," I replied, "and I'm bloody glad I didn't either."

"I did," he said. "It was fuckin' murder. Absolute mayhem!"

At first I thought he was talking about Chesterfield losing but it soon became apparent that he was actually talking about the events surrounding the game. Apparently, we got a hiding that ranked up there with the best of them. The rumours I heard over the next few days all seemed to say the same thing: it seemed that a large number of Geordies had turned up and given us a spanking we didn't want and certainly didn't expect.

It was interesting that the local papers never mentioned these events. In some ways it's understandable but the stories I heard were that most people were glad to get away from the place that night and the match really was of secondary importance. Perhaps the papers in Blyth gave the violence better coverage, although my bet is that they just revelled in the fact that they had turned over a league club – and who can blame them?

More To Pompey Than The Chimes

January 28th, 1978 Chesterfield 3 v 0 Portsmouth

Portsmouth were in freefall. They'd dropped down to Division 3 the previous season and had avoided the drop to Division 4 by just one point. This season, they were just as poor and looked to be the side most likely to go down when they came to Saltergate in January. No one really expected this to turn into anything. This was a club near the bottom of the league. They were also coming all the way from the south coast, so you have to ask yourself if *you* would really have made that journey. Well, while I might not have bothered, the Pompey firm decided that there was more fun to be had in Chesterfield than hitting the January sales!

I suppose I should have figured something was wrong when a gang of youths in strange scarves singing, *"Hi-ho, Pompey. Pompey, hi-ho,"* walked along Saltergate and up to the Kop turnstiles. The police, however, were wise to them – or at least they should have been. I mean, it wasn't as if they were trying to disguise where they were from, and those Pompey scarves were a dead give-away. Now that I had seen and heard them (and I figured the police had recourse to pretty much the same information that I had), the fact that a couple of them started singing *'Chesterfield'* as they approached the turnstile didn't throw me in the slightest, especially as they were asking the turnstile operator if this was the home end.

I expected these interlopers to be laughed at and sent packing round to the Cross Street end – but perhaps I expect too much. Instead, the Chesterfield police gave these youths the once-over, yawned, farted and let them onto the Kop. Incredible! Okay, so I might be exaggerating slightly when I say they yawned and farted but for all they seemingly cared they may as well have done. Sometimes one couldn't help but feel sorry for the police. I mean, controlling mindless thugs must have been a thankless task at the best of times but, then, you look at the actions of the police on this occasion and wonder if they were really helping themselves at all. They might argue that they thought these were Chesterfield fans messing around but I think this defence can only be used if you are clinically insane and have never attended a football match before in your life.

Naturally, I was a little shocked and somewhat perturbed to see these youths gain entrance to the Kop but it didn't stop me from following them through the turnstile. (What was that I was saying about being clinically insane?) I suppose I hoped that, once inside, they would make their way round to the Cross Street end or that the police would do their duty and get rid of them for me. I honestly can't say. All I know is that I walked onto the Kop, shaking my head that these hooligans had been let onto it. I was probably constructing a letter to the *Derbyshire Times* as I did so; one from *'Shocked of Wingerworth!'*

To be fair, I'm not quite sure what happened next. I didn't see the Pompey fans and so I went and stood in my usual place. It was relatively early: around 2.15pm. I was always in the ground early in those days. I wanted to take in the atmosphere long before it appeared. I met up with a few friends, we talked about football, the day's game and tomorrow's Sunday football match and we had a quick look through the programme. In those days, reading the programme was akin to inwardly digesting the back of a matchbox but, more than anything, it was, or at least I thought it was, just another Saturday. I told my friends about the debacle I'd witnessed when entering the ground and we laughed about it. In fact, we were still laughing when the Pompey chimes rang out again from the back of the Kop. At first I took no notice but my friends did and I could tell by their expressions that things didn't look too great. I turned to see about 20 youths battering everything that moved – and most things that didn't. At the head of this gang was a tall, slim youth in a fawn or light-grey suit, with a large, green umbrella rolled up at his side. He marched confidently down the centre of the Kop and walloped anybody close enough with his umbrella. I'm not quite sure what it was made of and I didn't think of it at the time but, in hindsight, most umbrellas crumple simply at the sound of a good gust of wind, so to use one as a weapon makes me think that he may have had a conveniently stashed piece of metal down the middle of it!

My friends immediately ran away – and one can't blame them really – and I'm not quite sure why I didn't do something similar but I didn't. Oh no, that would have been too easy. Instead, I buried my head in the programme and made out like I was reading some epic novel rather than what the players liked as a pre-match meal. Quite why I didn't get the hiding that everyone else got I can't imagine but it was more by luck than judgement, that's for sure.

As more Chesterfield fans started to filter onto the Kop, the fighting did increase a little as one or two of the Town fans, who were more than happy to trade punches, got involved. Unfortunately, it was very one-sided. Town fans occupied the sides but Pompey certainly had centre stage, particularly their leader who seemed to be orchestrating everything. Before the police had chance to move anyone to the Cross Street end, a few more Portsmouth fans started running across the pitch. The few Chesterfield fans left on the Kop soon disappeared with this new attack. It was quite frightening.

Eventually, as the hordes from the south coast were removed from the Kop, my mates returned in dribs and drabs. One of them, Frisk, had twisted his ankle as he made his escape and that left us short of a centre-half for Sunday's game. (Typical! Why couldn't they have picked on someone who wasn't in the side?) We won the game comfortably 3–0, with Rodney Fern getting two and an own goal adding insult to their injury.

There was only one arrest that day: a 17-year-old who had run across the pitch. He argued that he'd actually been trying to get away from the trouble rather than cause any, although surely that would have meant him running away from the Kop and not towards it. (I could have made a fortune as a solicitor!) I think it's safe to say that no one believed him.

March 1978

A trip to struggling Hereford really shouldn't have been anything to worry about, not for a side that still thought it could make a challenge on the top places. Hereford were so concerned about losing their league status that they hired international hypnotist *'Romark'* in a bid to improve their confidence – and their chances. Indeed, *Romark* predicted that Hereford would win the game, with their centre-forward scoring the winning goal. He was actually right as they won 2–1 with the centre-forward getting the second goal. Mind you *Romark* had also used his powers to make the Spireites' back line act like headless chickens every time they attacked – but you won't read that in the papers, will you?

Overall, though, it had been an interesting season and, with the summer a stone's throw away, I decided that a trip to Tranmere might be a good idea. It was the last away game of the season. Neither side had anything to play for – except pride.

Lose Or The Minibus Gets It!

April 28th, 1978 Tranmere 1 v 1 Chesterfield

In all fairness, I remember very little about the actual game. Cammack scored to get us a point and the crowd was really poor at somewhere around the 2,000 mark. I don't remember receiving a particularly hostile reception and I don't remember feeling as if my life was in danger at any point during the game. That changed as soon as I was on the bus to go home. A gang of Tranmere fans appeared from nowhere (it was actually doubtful that they'd even been to the game) and they looked rather menacing. They didn't actually do anything; there was just a lot of reciprocal gesticulating. But I was thankful when the police, somewhat taken aback themselves by events, finally came to our rescue and moved the mob away. We greeted their departure with the customary two-fingered salutes and a smile that meant, *'I'm on my way home – you can't get me now.'* It was a brief and totally unexpected blot on what had been a particularly ordinary match day and was slightly more frightening, perhaps, because of that.

But what happened to *us* paled into insignificance when I got back home and found out what had happened to a minibus full of Town fans leaving the same game. I assume they'd been attacked by the same supporters who attacked us, and maybe we were second on their list, I really don't know. What I do know is that the minibus was close to being written-off: the windscreen and a couple of side windows had gone through and the bodywork had been kicked into a new, less aerodynamic shape. They were less fortunate than we had been in that there were no police to assist them out of the car park. The minibus contained members of the supporters' club football team who, earlier that day, had played Tranmere's supporters' club and won. The *Derbyshire Times* reported it thus:

"A group of Chesterfield football supporters came under siege in Birkenhead on Friday when their minibus was attacked with bricks and stones. The fans were leaving the main car park at Tranmere's Prenton Park after Chesterfield's 1–1 draw. The windscreen and two windows were smashed and the bodywork was badly dented. Chesterfield supporters had beaten Tranmere supporters 6–1 earlier. 'It's a miracle no one was injured,' said Mr Howard Borrell." (Wonder what *he's* doing now?)

I have to say that seeing what happened to Mr Borrell's mob made me appreciate the larger vehicle I had travelled in and the thickness of its glass, and how being sworn at doesn't really amount to much in the end!

And that was more or less that for another season. We beat Swindon 3–1 in our final home league game and finished a respectable ninth – but everyone knew we were capable of more. The last decision the board of directors made was to finally agree that our kick-offs would be at 3pm, like everyone else", from the start of the following season. We were, perhaps, the last football club to move to 3pm kick-offs. Now, why isn't that a surprise?

Chesterfield fans going mental behind the goal at Shewsbury in 77/78

One To Forget
SEASON 78/79

Like most new seasons 78/79 was eagerly anticipated. The supporters, along with the Board, expected Cox to improve on his ninth position of the previous season. However, arming Cox with the necessary tools would mean taking the chains off the Chesterfield wallet and I'm not sure anyone knew where the key was! Consequently, the side didn't really change much and so it was unlikely that anything else would; but if you don't have hope then it's hardly worth going to the match in the first place, is it?

October 1978

We started the season fairly well by knocking Barnsley out of the League Cup and then going down 'the Smoke' and dumping Leyton Orient out by 2–1. Suddenly, we were in the third round. This was scary. Our reward was a home tie with Charlton which produced an absolute classic but, then, how else can one describe a nine-goal thriller? I suppose it would have been a little more of a thriller had we been on the right end of the 5–4 scoreline, but we weren't, and we bowed out in style in front of 6,500 screaming fans.

Back on the league front, we managed to beat Swansea at home. There was a miniscule amount of violence, with one Welsh fan being arrested for spitting at Chesterfield fans although, in fairness, he probably just covered the poor lads in spittle while he was trying to explain whereabouts in Wales he lived.

The fun really kicked off when promotion favourites Watford strode into town. Elton John was now running the show at Watford and maybe it was for this reason alone that Chesterfield fans turned out in their thousands to give Watford a good hiding. There were eight and a half thousand at the game, which we lost 2–0, although I doubt that any of the hooligans who turned up that day left the ground either knowing or caring what the scoreline was. The *Derbyshire Times* also decided that the game was a mere triviality and went for the more eye-catching headline of: **"Policeman Hurt In Clashes With Fans."** The article went as follows:

"Three policemen were hurt during struggles with Chesterfield football fans on the terraces at Saltergate on Saturday. They suffered cuts and bruises and one officer was off sick for two days as a result. The game with Watford attracted Chesterfield's biggest crowd of the season and the trouble lasted for about 20 minutes. Police made six arrests inside the ground and two in the town centre after the match. Superintendent Norman Rushden said, 'The trouble was caused by a small unruly element of Chesterfield supporters. The Watford supporters were excellently behaved. All those arrested were charged with public order offences and one fan was also charged with assaulting the police.'"

I have to say, it wasn't a game that has stood out in my memory but it is worthy of a mention, if only to show how all the hooligans appeared for the big games. Whilst I can remember the match and the events, it wasn't a game where I felt particularly scared or worried but, then, that might have had something to do with the fact that I was at home on safe(ish) ground. My hapless memory seems to remind me that most of the commotion took place on the Compton Street end and I do recall a few missiles being thrown. But, most of all, I remember that we were beaten by a bunch of soft, southern, shandy-swilling bastards!

Now, as you will be aware, all of my experiences up to this point had occurred while following Chesterfield FC and so far I had survived without serious injury. However, March 3rd, 1979 in particular has left me wondering how I can still sit here today and write that.

Stanley, I Presume!

March 3rd, 1979 Leeds Utd 2 v 2 Norwich City

I'm not quite sure when we decided to go to this game; all I know is Town were having a crap season and my best mate Richard Norman (aka Spiney Norman, aka Rinner) asked me if I'd go to Elland Road with him. Rinner was a bit of a Leeds fan although he'd never actually been to Elland Road to see them. With Chesterfield playing away at Watford and with it being highly likely that they would lose, I said yes.

At the time I had this idea that I'd like to do all 92 league grounds but with a difference: I wanted to do them all having seen Chesterfield play on them. But I guessed I could make one exception for this match.

After all, I was counting Charlton as a ground I'd been to and I'd gone there to see 'The Who' and 'Lou Reed' – so sometimes you just had to take the opportunities as they came along.

The journey up to Leeds was fairly unadventurous. We got a straight-through train going and we knew there was a train straight back to Chesterfield about 20 minutes after the game. And that was all we thought we needed to know. I hadn't given any thought to the possibility of football violence, but why would I? I was going to watch a game that involved two clubs I really couldn't give a monkey's about. I was a neutral and surely everyone would be able see and recognise that fact.

Leeds were a good side at the time and were close to the top of the First Division. Their supporters, though, had a terrible reputation and were hated by most clubs and other supporters throughout the country. Even I could remember them coming into Chesterfield one Saturday afternoon on their way to a football match somewhere and smashing up the odd pub or two.

There had also been quite a bit on TV about their supporters throwing missiles onto the pitch. The club had been warned by both the police and the FA regarding the behaviour of its supporters and, despite several announcements/pleas, nothing had really changed. Thinking about this now, and knowing about their reputation at the time, I can't imagine why I agreed to go to this game. The chances of there being trouble at Elland Road were quite high and this would be a big crowd and in a place that wasn't familiar to me. In retrospect, I would have been safer if I'd stayed at home and stuck red hot knitting needles into my eyes and dashed my head against a wall until my nose bled! But none of that crossed my mind on the day; it's only now, as I write this, that I wonder what on earth I was playing at! As I've said before, isn't hindsight wonderful?

We arrived in Leeds really early, about 12.45, and we took a leisurely walk up to the ground. We wanted to keep out of the pubs and suchlike because we didn't want to be mistaken for Norwich fans, and so we found ourselves entering the Elland Road end at 1.30. This was early by anyone's standards but, having said that, there were several people going in at that time. It wasn't as if we were the only ones.

As I handed over my money at the turnstile, the operator handed me back my change and a piece of paper, which was a surprise as I hadn't been expecting him to slip me a note. I mean, I hardly knew him; we'd only just met! On closer inspection, the note was an instruction to all Leeds fans not to throw objects onto the pitch. I was half reading it as I pushed my way through the turnstile, only to be blinded by a really bright light. I was pretty sure that God wasn't a Leeds fan (we all knew he was a Spireite), so I figured it was something else. I looked up and was confronted by a BBC television camera filming Leeds fans or, more precisely, filming me – someone who didn't care one hoot about Leeds – reading the notice that had just been handed to me. Realising that this was my big opportunity, I gave a performance second to none. My interpretation of 'man reading slip of paper at football match' was, although I say so myself, simply breathtaking. To this day, I am just amazed that some big film director has not spotted me and thrust me into the limelight that I so obviously deserved!

In truth, I had to give a *performance* of 'man reading slip of paper' because the light was so bright you simply couldn't read under it. In fact, I came back from Leeds with a sun tan, the light was so hot! The note didn't say much and, just in case you managed to squeeze through the turnstiles and not get one, they reprinted the instruction in the programme.

The game itself was an interesting one. Despite my fading memory, I can recollect Leeds going into a two-goal lead and squandering many more chances to increase that lead. Their inability to kill Norwich off came back to haunt them as John Bond, the manager of Norwich at the time, brought his son on as substitute (I think) and within minutes, Norwich had pulled one back. Then, with about 15 minutes to go, Kevin Bond himself put an absolute screamer past the Leeds keeper for the equaliser. The Norwich fans in the far corner went berserk – and who could blame them?

The mood on the Elland Road end changed significantly. What had been a fairly happy day suddenly didn't look too bright and the Leeds fans wanted some sort of retribution. The kop immediately began to sing: *"South Stand, South Stand, do your job. South Stand – do your job!"* And, so as not to let anyone down, the South Stand went to work. From my very safe vantage point in the Leeds kop you could see the mêlée that suddenly broke out among the travelling fans. I could only assume that Leeds fans were among them from the start. Then, while the police were busy trying to drag people out, more Leeds fans started to scale the fences, penning the Norwich fans in. The poor buggers had nowhere to run and looked to get a hell of a beating.

But the Leeds fans, to their credit, didn't throw anything onto the pitch. The only things they did throw were a few well-directed punches and kicks and so there was no way the Leeds Board could consider closing the kop. Perhaps they should have addressed the whole issue of violence rather than just the issue of objects being thrown. From what I could see, closing the kop would be of no benefit to anyone – certainly not the travelling supporters. It would have made much more sense to close the South Stand where it appeared that the majority of the Leeds hard core were situated. I don't think for one minute your average Leeds hooligan cared one hoot whether they closed the kop or not. Threats like that only ever really hurt the genuine fans that turned up and hurled abuse but, then again, when was the last time someone got a black eye from being hit by abuse? The hooligans would always be hooligans; it didn't matter where they did it. But, to be honest, as long as we remained safe I didn't care. Rinner looked at me and smiled. As strange as it may seem, violence was fine when it was 100 yards away and not likely to interrupt what you were doing.

When the final whistle went we left the ground quickly, not because we were concerned about the violence but because we had a train to catch. Being young, fit and healthy we ran all the way back to the station and made it with about five minutes to spare. Five minutes isn't a lot but it was enough, and we would have caught the train easily if we had been standing on the right platform. Despite collapsing in a heap of giggles on realising this fact, we managed to establish from a British Rail worker that there was a train to Sheffield in about ten minutes. We could get that one instead. You would think that was straightforward enough but we waited, and waited, and waited, and waited, and then we realised that the Sheffield train had also gone from another platform! Being on the wrong platform once was excusable (it *was* our fault), but twice? Come on, do me a favour! This time it wasn't our fault: the British Rail guy had told us the wrong platform. So we went back to the information desk and established the time of the next through train to Chesterfield but, more importantly, which platform it would be leaving from.

Since we now had an hour to kill, we walked back out into Leeds, round the corner and past the *Queen's Hotel*, and found a little café down some stairs in a basement. It wasn't exactly salubrious but the food was good and we had a good laugh about how the day had gone so far.

After filling ourselves and passing the hour away in the café, we went back to the station and managed to climb aboard the train to Chesterfield – at last! By this time I had managed to find out that Town had lost 2–0 at Watford and, so, considered it a poor day. What I didn't realise was that it was going to get a whole lot worse.

Once we'd finished laughing about the day's escapades, we travelled back in relative silence. By the time we reached Sheffield I had taken to reading the Leeds match day programme yet again. I didn't pay much attention to who got on or off the train but, then, who would, in all honesty? I was too engrossed in Eddie Gray's team notes to notice the youth walk past me but Rinner saw him and tried to attract my attention by looking out of the window and pretending I wasn't with him! Suddenly, the programme was snatched from my hands and I looked up to find this huge Man United fan glaring at the front page. He threw the programme back at me.

"I fuckin' hate Leeds, I do!" he snarled.

A little bit of my brain was saying, *"Yes, I'm not fond of them either because I'm a Chesterfield fan,"* but the stubborn part of my brain – which, unfortunately, tends to override almost everything I do – just picked the programme up from the seat where it had landed and glared back.

The reason I glared back wasn't because I was hard or anything stupid like that; it was because I was sure I knew this youth. I was sure he was a Town fan. It has been said that it could well have been Gessler. To be fair, it could have been anyone. I wasn't well enough in with the hooligans at Chesterfield to have recognised Gessler if I'd fallen over him, so this is all supposition. But the supposed self-styled leader of the Chesterfield Kop *was* quite a bit of a Man United fan on the side. All I can say for sure is that, whoever he was, he was a big bugger and he was a twat. I may not have known who this big idiot was but I can say with some degree of certainty that he didn't like being glared at by a little runt like me, and so he leaned towards me, his forehead nearly touching mine, and said, "Listen, ya Leeds cunt, I hate Leeds. I hate Leeds being on my train. There isn't the room."

Well, I was sure pleased we'd cleared that one up. For one minute I thought he was going to take me out and buy me a pint! I swallowed hard. The foul smell of fags and alcohol on his breath made me cringe but I figured this wasn't the time to recommend *Listerine*. As he leaned back he flicked his fag ash at me. It landed softly on the table in front of me and, without thought, I very deliberately wiped it away with the back of my hand and watched as it cascaded down his Levis and crashed onto his Doc Marts. In terms of 'smart moves I have made' this has to be rock bottom; it really has. It has to be the most stupid, idiotic, ridiculous thing I've ever done. Talk about 'red rag to a bull.' This unwitting matador (me) appeared to be minutes away from being trampled on by a bull that was already pawing the aisle of the train in anger. But, apart from being annoyed at being picked on like this, I was quite speechless. I wanted, I suppose, to protect myself without it being seen as if I was begging for mercy but, at that moment, I couldn't think how to do it. Every instinct told me to stop being so bloody pigheaded and apologise – but I just couldn't.

'Bollock-face' was mad now. He looked up the train and shouted, "Ere, Mickey! We've got Leeds!" almost as if they had contracted a disease – and, I suppose, in some respects, you could say that was how it was viewed. Moments later, Mickey appeared and I had to smile. I was expecting another big, strapping Manc – all bald head, braces and boots – but, no. Mickey was a small, willowy figure and he looked about as threatening as a tub of *Flora*. He smiled at me and now I was really concerned because this wasn't a smile that said, *"Hello, I'm Mickey. Are you having a nice day? It's a pleasure to meet you."* Rather, it was one that said, *"Hello, I'm Mickey and I'm a psychopath and when I'm not at Man United games they put me in a straightjacket for the nation's protection."*

Mickey and 'Shit-for-breath' were joined by a couple of other youths who stood behind them, filling up the aisle. I looked across at the passengers in the other seats, probably for some help, but their noses were buried further into their broadsheets than they'd ever been! This didn't look good. Mickey pushed his way onto the seat beside me. He smiled again; he was pure evil. My guess is that if this youth is still alive today he's in a maximum security prison, strapped to a bench, doing a passable impression of Hannibal Lecter. And if he isn't, well, then he ought to be. I'd never seen him before. Like I say, I only vaguely recognised 'Nobhead' because I thought I'd seen him either at Town games or in town itself, but I didn't know any of the others.

Mickey looked at me and whispered, louder than I would have liked: "Would you like to meet Stanley?"

Now, this really confused me because my nickname, at the time, was Stan. So this youth is asking if I'd like to meet Stanley and all I can think is, *"But I am him."* Then I wondered if there was someone else on the train, even more evil than they were, whose name was Stanley and, if I wanted, they could fetch him and he could deal with me.

"Well, do you want to meet Stanley?" he repeated. This time it wasn't so much a question but more a case of *'You're going to meet him'* and, with that, he put his hand in his pocket and pulled out a Stanley knife.

"Oh, for fuck's sake!" was about all I could come up with as a reply.

It went very quiet and I thought that this was it. I genuinely thought I was going to be butchered on the train. It wasn't a time for heroics or stubbornness anymore; it was obvious that no one on the train was going to stop these mindless morons, and so it was time to do a bit of backtracking.

"Look," I said, "I'm no Leeds fan. We've just been up there to watch the game. We're from Chesterfield. I'm a Chesterfield fan."

'Manure-face,' who was quite obviously the leader of this happy bunch of travellers, took a step back in horror and then leaned forwards and pulled Mickey up from the seat beside me.

"Oh, mate ..." he said, wrapping a big arm around my shoulders. "Oh, mate, why didn't you say so? Oh, fuckin' 'ell, I'm so sorry. If I could get down on my bended knees and apologise, I would."

Actually, he could have done. There was plenty of room. Mickey and the other two disappeared back up the train but 'Twat-head' stood there apologising for several minutes more.

"Why don't you just fuck off?" I said, as one final act of defiance – and he did!

To this day I have no idea who he was and I really don't care if he was Gessler. And, for once, I really don't care who knows it. But that thick, pig-necked tosser wanted a right royal kicking – and in my dreams he gets it! The most annoying thing about that trip was having what had been a really good day ruined; although if I hadn't been so belligerent, stubborn and, above all, stupid then it might not have been as bad as it was.

Once the dust had settled, I sat there for a minute or two, completely numb. I couldn't believe – and still don't know – how close I actually came to getting razored into slices. Was it all bluff or was it for real? Looking at the youth, I would say it was for real. And how I managed to hang on to the contents of my bowels during those seemingly endless few minutes, I will never know.

After a short spell Richard burst out laughing although I'm afraid I just couldn't join him.

"It wasn't funny!" I said rather indignantly. I was, perhaps, somewhat aggrieved that the focus of attention had been on me when it was Rinner who was the bloody Leeds fan! He wants to think himself lucky I didn't tell on him.

Just to rub salt into the wounds, on the BBC's *'Look North'* programme on Monday night they covered the riveting saga of Leeds United giving out notices to their supporters before the game with Norwich and there, for all to see, giving a command performance, was me! I cannot begin to tell you how many times people came up to me and said, "I didn't know you were a Leeds fan, Stan."

"I'M NOT!!!" was my usual bellowed response.

If this was what happened when you went to a football game as a neutral, then give me travelling with a bunch of hooligans from Chesterfield any day!

1979 – On The Home Front

A miserable season had seen us slip down the league and attendances had fallen away. However, that didn't stop trouble from occurring in the town centre as supporters from other towns had decided that Chesterfield was a good place to stop for a little ruck and rumble. Leeds, Sunderland and Forest had all stopped off and done a fair amount of

David Radford

damage, so much so that Chesterfield's landlords had decided they'd had enough.

The *Derbyshire Times* ran the following article:

"'JAIL SOCCER THUGS' PLEA AFTER VIOLENT WEEKEND

"Soccer fans passing through Chesterfield could find all pub doors shut in their faces in future and local landlords are demanding jail sentences for hooligans after a weekend of soccer violence. Trouble flared again in the town on Saturday night when a gang of Sunderland supporters stopped off on their way home from the match at Leicester. Police were called after one landlord locked himself, and his customers, inside the pub as the visiting fans, threatening to wreck the bar, tried to kick their way in.

"All this came just a few weeks after a 'Wild West' brawl at a town centre pub involving Forest fans. Tommy Morris of the Corner House pub said, 'Leeds fans give us trouble regularly, then there was the Forest lot – and now this – they're all crackers! The Sunderland fans filled the street; there must have been about 50 of them. Two of them had knives; they were shouting, "Let's wreck it," and kept kicking at the door.'"

But, as I said, Sunderland weren't the only fans who took a shine to the town centre: Forest fans came one night and decided to smash up the *Painted Wagon*. Now, many of you will have no idea about the *Painted Wagon* but salubrious it wasn't. According to the press, they did £750 worth of damage although, to be honest, I think you could have demolished and rebuilt the place for half that amount!

Violence aside, the team was struggling. We were in very real danger of getting relegated. In April, three straight losses to Hull, Swindon and Wednesday did nothing to ease our fears – or our goal difference.

April 16th, 1979 Chesterfield 1 v 0 Mansfield Town

Stories about victories against Mansfield just have to be told, whether anything happened in them or not, and this is no exception. Fortunately, we avoided our fourth successive defeat by snatching a victory with a Phil Walker goal that sent the majority of the 5,000 crowd into ecstasy.

From what I can remember, there wasn't a great deal of trouble before the game and there didn't appear to be a great deal during it. Still, nine people were ejected from the ground so something must have kicked off somewhere; but, then, this was Mansfield so there was no real surprise in that. However, the fact that one 'soccer special' needed a police escort when Chesterfield fans boarded a Mansfield supporters' coach gives you some indication of what it was like after the game. I dare say this also had something to do with the busmen saying they were joining the landlords' 'Ban the Thug' campaign. Indeed, after the Mansfield derby game, a spokesman for *East Midlands Transport* said, *"Our drivers are reluctant to take on the work. We ran four specials on Monday and there was trouble on all four."*

Violence was something I could do without quite easily and, yet, for some strange reason I was drawn to watch it. I became something of an expert in negotiating my way around fights. Just like a good footballer might read a game of football, I could read a ruck really well, and it always left me well placed to see a lot and do absolutely nothing. Not the greatest pastime in the world, I agree, but it beat the hell out of stamp collecting. Of course, you ran the risk of some fed up copper hauling you in for doing nothing – but I guess that just added to the excitement. If you were to do it now they'd call it extreme sports watching! I wasn't a hooligan, so I wasn't quite the lowest form of life... yet.

April 28th, 1979 Chesterfield 1 v 0 Rotherham

When Rotherham rolled up we'd seen a setback against Lincoln but had managed two draws on our travels. Slowly but surely we were easing ourselves out of this mess. A win against Rotherham wouldn't assure us of Third Division football next season but it wouldn't half help.

It was at this game that I saw one of the funniest sights I've ever seen from my vantage points on the Kop. It was a bright, sunny day and the Rotherham hordes were well assembled on the Cross Street. There had been a few little spats on the way up to the ground and I'd heard talk of some skirmishes down at the station but nothing that would worry you.

Suddenly, a fight broke out on the Cross Street. One solitary Chesterfield fan, arms flailing and boots flying, was lashing out at anything that came near. He was massively outnumbered, about 1,000 to 1, and so he couldn't keep this up for very long. Recognising his days were obviously numbered, the youth ran and a long snake of Rotherham fans set off in pursuit around the Cross Street terrace. Realising he had nowhere to go but along the back and down the side, some Rotherham fans doubled back to cut him off and it seemed as if our hero, who was now being applauded all around the ground for his efforts, was going to get the inevitable kicking. There was the usual stand-off: the Town fan, with his back to the wall, surrounded by at least 100 Rotherham fans, all keen to make him pay for being where he shouldn't.

We watched and waited. His only way out was to jump over the wall but you knew that the moment he turned his back they would have him – and I guess he'd figured this out for himself. Without warning, he did what no one expected: he ran at them. Just charged them, all on his own. Now, this is an interesting move because, in fairness, no one wants to get a smack in the mouth, and if this lad was going to stand and fight, then one of the Rotherham fans was going to get smacked. As no one wanted to be the first to feel this youth's fist, they all backed off, some of them stumbling back and falling over. With his opponents on the back foot, he then turned, jumped over the wall and walked casually round the ground to the Kop. I don't recall him getting arrested – but I could be wrong. He was applauded all the way back to the Kop where he received something of a hero's welcome and, I dare say, he was bought more than one pint that night! In some ways that one moment encapsulated football violence: all the hooligans were keen to do a bit of smacking but no one really wanted to get smacked!

Perhaps suffering from the ignominy of being outsmarted by one single Chesterfield fan, after the game a gang of Rotherham fans chased a couple of Town fans down St Helen's Street. The lads dodged up an alleyway and, quite sensibly, in my opinion, asked an old woman to let them in. Again quite sensibly, perhaps, she declined the offer of having her house targeted by football hooligans and left the two lads on her doorstep. When the Rotherham fans finally caught them, one unfortunate victim lost consciousness when a Rotherham fan swiped out – but that was probably because he'd been stabbed in the throat! Eventually, the old woman decided that she really ought to let them in. When the ambulance came, the Rotherham fans became ambulance chasers in the sickest sense of the word.

In total, five people were arrested for incidents in and around the town centre before the game, four were ejected during the game and three were arrested after the game.

The police managed to persuade the Town fan who had been stabbed to take part in some kind of sick, twisted experiment and three days after the assault the lad was escorted around Rotherham's terraces in the hope that he might spot his attacker. Whilst I can appreciate that he might want justice, it does seem a rather awful way of achieving it. As it was, the lad saw nothing and the person who had done the stabbing was probably at home watching TV. So nothing at all was accomplished from all this – apart from scarring this lad both physically and mentally.

Back in the league, a 0–0 draw away at Peterborough was enough to see us stay in Division 3, which is just as well as we lost the last three games quite easily.

And If The Kids Wanna Fight You'd Better Let 'Em
SEASON 79/80

After just missing out on relegation the previous season Arthur Cox was on the look-out for players to boost his squad and we saw more transfer activity that summer than we had over several decades. Bill Green was signed for £40,000 and Alan Birch came from Walsall for a similar fee. Alan Crawford and John Ridley were each signed for £35,000. Leaving the club was my favourite, Rodney Fern, who went to Rotherham, but we also unloaded Bobby Flavell (to Barnsley), Cottom (Chester), Cammack (Scunthorpe) and, shortly after the season had started, Letheran went to Swansea for around £60,000. It was good business but Cox hadn't finished spending, not by any means. Early in 1980 he paid £40,000 for John Stirk, a club record fee of £50,000 for goalkeeper John Turner and then smashed that record by signing Phil Bonneyman for £150,000! It wasn't so much the amount we paid for these players, it was the wages they were on. Some of the players, Turner included, were on more money than some First Division players, so we needed success. Having put all our eggs in one basket, we desperately needed to get promotion – and we didn't have the best start.

Three Go Mad In Mansfield

August 18th, 1979 Mansfield 3 v 2 Chesterfield

Now, as we all know, Mansfield are scabs! We all know this and we all accept it; but what we called them pre-miners' strike, well, I just have no idea. I don't even really recall viewing them then with the disgust and mistrust that we do now. In fact, if anything, they were just 'this club down the road.' (To be fair, most of my spleen-venting went towards the two Sheffield clubs.) Given the close proximity of the yellow peril and given the fact that we had both spent our footballing lives in and around the bottom two divisions, you would have thought there might have been numerous tales of massive punch-ups between the two clubs. Unfortunately – or fortunately, depending upon how you look at it – this hasn't always been the case. I'm sure there have been plenty of altercations in back alleys but, for me, Mansfield were always just a team we hated because of local rivalry; a rivalry that escalated and became more significant since the miners' strike, and I have seen a tremendous amount of pure hatred towards these hapless supporters, particularly at Chesterfield, purely because of this. But this tale happened before all that, so this was just hooliganism. There was nothing political behind it at all.

Getting to Mansfield shouldn't have caused too much of a problem really since it's only 15 miles down the road, so if you didn't want to go on the supporters' club bus you could walk it. But, with Wynnie's Tours taking a well-earned rest, the onus on getting us to Mansfield lay with the *East Midlands* battle wagons.

A fortnight before the game I did a round-up of who wanted to be a part of this thrill-a-minute, roller-coaster ride to Mansfield and, as was usual with local games, there was a fair amount of take-up. So two weeks before the game I rushed into town, strode purposefully into the *East Midlands* booking office and demanded eight tickets for the coach to Mansfield. God, I was excited. Two weeks to go and I was excited. I put it down to not having family holidays as a child but I was making up for it now. I started to empty my pockets of all the cash I'd collected.

"We aren't taking any coaches," the woman replied.

I smiled, cleared out my ears and continued to hand over the money, albeit a little more slowly. She smiled back, shaking her head slowly. I was worried.

"I said, we aren't taking any coaches," she repeated calmly.

I looked at her quizzically. I thought I'd heard her but, then again, I could have been wrong and all of a sudden I didn't want to speak. I pushed the money towards her as if this would emphasise what I wanted and perhaps change what she had said. It didn't.

She repeated it slowly, emphasising each word as if I was a deaf child from another country who couldn't speak English and needed the chance to lip read: "WE – ARE – NOT – TAKING – ANY – COACHES."

"But, why?" I asked, eventually, still really unable to take it all in.

Before she had chance to answer, two more youths came into the office, both wanting to book seats for the coach to Mansfield that was no longer running. The woman went through the process with them, as she had with me, only this time sighing and giving us that 'if-I-have-to-say-this-one-more-time' look.

"Why not?" the three of us demanded as one voice.

"Because you keep wrecking the bloody buses!" she said, starting to lose her patience. I don't think her friendly customer service routine stretched as far as football supporters.

"*We* don't," we said rather indignantly, emphasising the 'we.'

"We don't care who it is that does it," she quite rightly pointed out, "but every time we put a coach on for a football match it comes back vandalised. It costs us more to put them right…" Her voice trailed away at this point and I think we all got the picture.

In fairness, the previous season *East Midlands* had stressed that they might not run football specials for this very reason. They had difficulty getting drivers to take the job on and even greater difficulty replacing the seats. Looking back on it all, if I had been running a bus service I wouldn't have dreamed of putting a football special on – and we were, perhaps, lucky to have had them for as long as we did. But, that kind of thinking didn't help me one iota. This was Mansfield. The bloody hole didn't even have a railway station! So, although it was only 15 miles up the road, suddenly it wasn't as easy to access as I'd thought. Trust me to have friends that couldn't drive. This was something I needed to review – and quickly.

"How are we going to get there, then?" I said out loud, although I'm pretty sure I'd meant to just think it.

I don't suppose the woman actually gave a shit but she did provide us with the answer to the problem.

"You could always get the service bus," she said.

I cheered up immediately at this and went home to deliver the news. I thought it was an excellent opportunity, and it would probably work out cheaper, but out of the eight that had originally expressed an interest, only Rich Norman (Rinner), my best mate at the time, Richard Good (Goody), a twat who everybody hated because he was doing some wanky geology course at Aston University and loved everybody to know it, and I were left. The rest saw it as more of a hindrance and took their money back.

I should point out that I have nothing against people who go to university to further their education. Good luck to them. I just had a lot against Richard Good. Here was a youth who said to me, during an argument: "At least I'm doing something with my life – unlike you." (Last I heard he was working in a bank. Mmmm, did you a lot of good that geology degree, you tosser.) Richard Good didn't just piss me off, he pissed everyone off – even his own brother! He scraped into university and did the only degree his grades would allow and then spent the next three years talking about how brilliant he was and what a swell life it was being a student. Twat! Hopefully, he'll never read this but, if he does, at least he'll know which rocks are the best ones to use to stone me to death! I know I've mentioned this particular individual before, and I know that he seldom comes out of it in a good light, but, then, perhaps that should tell you something about the boy. By now, he may well be a fine, upstanding citizen but, back then, he was just a jerk who supported Liverpool. I'd better stop: I can feel my spleen starting to rupture at the thought of him.

Anyway, come the Saturday, the three of us set off for Mansfield. Finding the right bus bay in Chesterfield was the first obstacle to overcome but it proved to be quite easy as we just joined the end of a blue and white snake that wriggled slovenly and unevenly down the pavement edge. It was about 20 youths long when we joined it but it continued to grow long after we had taken our places. Eventually, we were settled on the top deck of the bus to Mansfield and, as it pulled out, the chant of *"Ches-ter-field"* rang out. It felt like any other away trip really, except that the passengers on this bus weren't entirely made up of football supporters: you'd got shoppers on there as well. We were still singing heartily as the bus pulled into Doe Lea, and we carried on for a little while after that, but it came to an abrupt halt when the bus pulled up a few miles further on for three lads wearing yellow and blue scarves! Now, this hadn't crossed my mind at all. I mean, why would anyone who lived an equal distance from both towns choose to support Mansfield? I just couldn't understand it. Surely that has to go down as bad parenting and maybe Social Services should have been involved to put a stop to such ludicrous behaviour! Either way, the thought of

Mansfield fans actually getting on a bus to Mansfield had never once crossed my mind. (Mmmm, so who's the dope now?)

I did wonder at the time if the sight of the three Mansfield fans had caused a little fear to run through the bus, and that this might have had something to do with the cessation of singing, but the fact is it had more to do with the Chesterfield fans not wanting to let the three lads boarding the bus know just what was waiting for them on the top deck. They came up the stairs, all smiles and excitement. Obviously, none of them had considered that Chesterfield fans might be on their regular bus to the match either (the dopes!) but if I say they were surprised by what faced them once they got to the top of the bus, then it would be the most massive understatement of all time. Their smiles disappeared, along with their excitement, and they sat down and said nothing. If it had been me, I would have turned round and walked back downstairs.

The songs soon started up again and everyone was making the most of it but it never crossed my mind that this might get out of control. It didn't even click when we pulled up two stops further on and picked up two more Scabs fans. It never even entered my head that, as we got closer and closer to Mansfield, we would undoubtedly pick up more and more Mansfield fans; but we did, and eventually the bus was evenly split between Scabs and Spireites.

The singing was now being traded. We sang *"We hate Mansfield"* and they called us *"Sheep-shaggers."* They've never quite understood that was a name for Derby, not us. It would, perhaps, have been churlish to remind them of how inaccurate they were in their choice of insults, so, instead, we just carried on. Gradually, the insults became a little more personalised and a porky Scab at the front was picked out for a rousing rendition of *"You fat bastard."* They came back with the beautifully reworked *"Sheep-shaggers"* and, then, we replied by smacking one of them in the face. I really hadn't seen *that* coming.

The singing was getting more and more aggressive and the atmosphere on the top deck more and more uncomfortable, so I suppose I should have known that things would deteriorate. Like any disagreement, it only takes one person to make a move before full-scale war is declared and the Scabs fan with the bloody nose was all that was needed. Suddenly, people were trading punches and kicks up and down the aisle of the bus – which is never easy. I looked at Rinner and he was smiling. Behind me, Goody was white and it was he who suggested we get off. Rinner told him not to be such a twat as we were nearly there and so, ever the diplomat, I suggested we at least go downstairs. We weren't the only supporters making this decision but, now, I felt the same way those first three Scabs fans who had come upstairs must have felt because, now, it was our turn to be completely outnumbered. On the plus side, there were a good few old women who I was sure would step in and stop a fight if anything happened. I just had to hope the grannies weren't part of the Scabs firm! Sitting down, it felt as if every Mansfield fan on the lower deck was imagining kicking my head in and enjoying it – but I wasn't too bothered, as long as it remained part of their imagination!

Upstairs the battle raged on and the bus actually swayed alarmingly from side to side. Rinner was still smiling but, then, he was 6ft tall and the last person you'd go and belt. I, on the other hand, was 5ft-4ins and was the first person you'd smack, so I think I had every reason to be a little more concerned. One person more frightened than I was – and, trust me, that takes some doing – was Goody. He had now turned a deathly shade of white and couldn't even raise one of those fake smiles.

I can't say we found this journey as safe as usual but we did arrive in Mansfield in one piece. However, I was somewhat concerned about what might happen once the bus had disgorged its contents onto the Mansfield streets as we were ripe for the slaughter. Thankfully, nothing much actually happened. Once on the streets, the Scabs fans disappeared and we were soon caught up with a drunken contingent of Chesterfield thugs. Sometimes running into hooligans – as long as they're your own – did have a plus side!

If I was to describe the pre-match entertainment as 'fraught,' then I can only describe the post-match as 'fuckin' mayhem!' Considering I paid so much attention to not getting my head kicked in, I can't believe I was so lapse in preparing for this game: I hadn't considered the possibility of Scabs fans getting on the service bus on the journey there; I'd paid absolutely no attention to what time the bus left for home; and, even if I had known the time, I had absolutely no idea where to catch it from. I hadn't exactly cocked it up but, then, you couldn't really say it was going to plan either. I had assumed that it would all be very straightforward and that there would be thousands of Town fans to follow but, once out of the ground, everyone seemed to disappear in different directions.

As we walked up a busy Mansfield street, I was well aware that we were lost. I'd been to the place many times before but only ever to watch football. I'd never walked its streets but, then, who'd want to? We walked quietly up the road, mainly just following a couple of Town fans, but everything seemed to be fine; we just needed to come across a bus stop. Then, just as I was beginning to think nothing would happen, all hell broke loose. A shit-load of Scabs (one of the many collective nouns for Scabs fans) came storming up the road and it was at this point that we saw where all the Town fans were. We stood and looked at the pitch battle taking place in the middle of the street before legging it further up the road. The need for a bus stop was now very urgent indeed. I even asked a policeman but he seemed more concerned about making sure he avoided the brawling fans as they moved slowly up the road. However, he grunted and pointed in a general direction. I wasn't convinced but, equally, had very little in the way of an alternative. So we did what anyone would do: we ran. Eventually, we came to the bus stop where a good few Town fans were already waiting impatiently in line. As we looked back down the hill the fighting was getting ever closer. Across the road, a lad about the same age as ourselves watched as his dad got kicked to the ground. The Scabs were all over him. The chap had, in fact, broken his leg and, realising this, his son ran around, frantically shouting for help but getting none. The policeman had disappeared. And the lad's cry for help didn't last long as someone whacked him on the nose. Whether his father's leg had been broken by some Neanderthal or because he fell awkwardly, I couldn't say, and it hardly matters really, but it just looked awful. I felt for the lad. The really funny thing, though, was that a couple of years later this youth turned up to play football in the same Sunday side as Rinner and myself and he recounted the story one day in the pub. I didn't have the heart to tell him we'd witnessed the incident.

But there we were, standing at the bus stop, watching the thuggery getting closer and closer. Everyone not wearing a Mansfield scarf was smacked. Youths out with their girlfriends to do a bit of shopping were getting punched; in fact, some of the girlfriends were on the receiving end, too! All we could do was watch as the fight got closer and closer, knowing it would eventually consume us. Even Rinner was worried; his cheeky grin no longer in evidence. Goody, white and worrying, was beginning to fray the nerves: "What are we going to do? Shall we run?" Christ, I really needed questions at a time like this! It did cross my mind that if I started to beat the shit out of Goody, then not only would everyone be eternally grateful but the hooligans might just think I was one of them and leave me alone. I mean, it seemed really senseless us all getting hurt. I'm sure Goody would have understood.

Then, suddenly, steaming up the road like the Magnificent Seven, with Clint Eastwood at the wheel, came an *East Midlands* double-decker. Would it get to us before the fighting did? It was going to be mighty close. Rinner smiled. Goody jumped up and down like an expectant puppy. And me? Well, I just stood there, hoping that nobody thought this idiot was with me.

We didn't care where the bus was heading, we were just going to get on it but, as luck would have it, "CHESTERFIELD" was the name on the destination board. The bus pulled up, the brawling mass just yards behind, but our jubilation quickly melted away when the doors opened and the driver screamed, "Room for three upstairs!" A dozen people pushed their way on board, the twelfth being Rinner. It was like a scene from a play: the doors closed behind him and Rinner turned to see my frightened face staring at him from the pavement. I just stood there, my heart pounding, and I couldn't think what my next move ought to be. I just couldn't think.

Clint Eastwood put the bus in gear and revved to pull away. I just stood there, blank. I couldn't believe it. I'd even lost the will to run. Suddenly, the bus shuddered as it tried to pull away and then the doors opened again! A massive fist attached to a long, strong arm shot out of the doorway, grabbed me by the denim lapel and dragged me on board. The doors closed behind me. I turned and, together with Rinner, we watched the shocked face of Goody disappearing into the distance as the bus moved off down the road.

We laughed till it hurt. We stood there on that bus, packed to the rafters with Scabs *and* Spireites, and tried to talk to each other about the look on our 'friend's' face but words just couldn't do it justice – they never will. Our sides ached and tears literally rolled down our cheeks. Perhaps it was an adrenalin release mixed with pure unbridled relief? It's hard to say, but we both knew it couldn't have turned out better – for us. It still remains, for me anyway, one of the funniest moments at a football match ever! Why the doors opened, I don't know. Perhaps the driver opened them by mistake. Or maybe someone leaned on the emergency lever. Whatever the reason, I was safe and, I have to admit, didn't give a fuck!

When we got into Chesterfield we did wait at the bus station for Goody; we weren't that rotten. Well, no, that's not true: we only waited because we wanted to hear what he had to say. We wanted to see if he'd been smacked or had managed to avoid the trouble but, most of all, we wanted to take the piss. He arrived on the next bus. Big smile, the one that says, *"I was crapping myself back there but I'm not going to let you know that."* Apparently, after the bus had left the police had arrived and everything settled down. Being the extra special friends that we were, we continued to rib Goody mercilessly and laughed about it for many a long season.

John Motson Knows Jack Shit!

League Cup Third Round

September 25th, 1979 Liverpool 3 v 1 Chesterfield

I've been to Anfield twice to watch Chesterfield. The last time we went there we stuck four past them and the only fists thrown were the jubilant ones puncturing the still Anfield air.

How different it was, though, the first time I went, on our encounter with Liverpool on September 25th, 1979. It was the third round of the League Cup. We'd dispatched Hartlepool over two legs (5–1 and 1–2) and murdered Shrewsbury in a similar fashion in the second round (3–0 and 0–0), so we went to Anfield with a fair amount of confidence. I had this feeling in my gut that this was going to be the major upset of the year, so I dragged my travelling companion, Spiney Norman, into Ladbrokes for that all important bet.

"A pound on Chesterfield to win the League Cup," I said.

The woman looked at me and laughed.

"I'm serious," I said, over her rebuff, and I was.

"Can't do it," she informed me. "You have to pick three clubs."

Now, I had no idea if this was true or not. I think she was probably trying to save a poor unfortunate from throwing his pound down the toilet. But I *was* serious. With just one hour to go before the coaches departed, I thought we were a good bet for the League Cup.

"Look!" I reasoned. "What is the point of me picking three clubs when only one can win it? And I happen to think that will be Chesterfield."

She looked to both sides and, when no assistance came her way, she called the manager. She explained to him, in great detail, that the runt out front had no idea about betting shop protocol and the manager turned, fixed me with his best 'fuck-off-and-stop-wasting-our-time' stare and said, "We just don't have a price. It won't happen."

I went through a similar argument with him as I had with the woman, that I wanted to make the bet a simple Chesterfield to beat Liverpool one. Once again, no joy. Similar obstacles applied and I was getting really pissed off. They told me I could put a bet on the first player to score but, hell, how could you do that? In our first 11 games of that season we had scored 24 goals, shared out among Moss, Birch, Walker, Hunter, Crawford, Salmons and an own goal. Be honest, who on earth do you pick? So I left the bookie's with the pound still in my pocket and still sure that the League Cup was as good as ours.

If memory serves me correct, we travelled with the AGD. (For those too young to know what the AGD was, well, it changed its name to the PFD just to confuse you but, to all intents and purposes, it was the admin department of the Post Office. After being given flash offices and a new road name, 'Future Walk,' it was then sold to whoever would have it!) My sister Jennifer worked there at the time (along with most of Chesterfield) and, so, getting a seat on one of the coaches was easy. It was a light-hearted and uplifting journey and the road to Liverpool was one long HONK as cars pipped at buses, and buses at cars, vans at minibuses, and so on. Apart from the myriad of coaches descending on Scouse Central that day, British Rail had organised not one but two special trains. Yes, it was migration time. The town must have been damn near empty.

We arrived in plenty of time and the coach parked alongside the road at the bottom of some park. Stanley Park, perhaps. Who knows? Who gives a toss? We were there. I walked along the road and counted 72 coaches. This isn't a jest, this is honest. I admit that my maths abilities always have been a bit of a grey area but I can count quite proficiently. I was amazed. Even now, as I write this, I'm thinking I must have got it wrong and, yet, I know I didn't. I'd go as far as betting the pound that Ladbrokes wouldn't take on it. We walked up through the park in the dying September sunlight, butterflies ploughing around my insides. I was tense. This was the big one.

"Don't fancy walking through here tonight," Rinner said, thinking more of himself than the match. *(Typical!)*

"I shouldn't worry. Liverpool are the best behaved supporters in the land," I said, believing every word John Motson uttered on *Match of the Day*. That just shows what a twat I was but, more importantly, it shows that John Motson knew bugger-all about football supporters! Just because Liverpool supporters sing *'Walk On'* doesn't make them well behaved; well, not in my book anyway. And I certainly don't recall any Scouse fans inviting me into their house for a friendly, cosy cuppa before the game started.

There are certain things attached to a particular area and Liverpool has some of the most annoying, in my opinion. For a start, as I've said, its supporters are reckoned to be the best behaved in the land when they are clearly just as big a bunch of hooligans as any other club's supporters in the football world. Let's face it, they do have a certain record. On top of that, if you come from Liverpool you are immediately a comedian; you have a God-given right to perform 'stand-up' comedy on stage, apparently. Well, here's a news flash: you aren't funny, you aren't well behaved and no one owes you anything! Tossers!

But what did I know? I was a mere third division football supporter stepping out into the big time for what seemed like the first time. As far as I was concerned, the only thing separating the two clubs was Division 2. I'd seen our supporters at work and I knew we could be as good, or, more appropriately, as bad, as the rest.

As we came out of the park I expected to see a line of turnstiles neatly clicking round as we filled their away end. What I actually saw was a line of supporters stretching down the road, turning round and coming back again. Liverpool, for all their majesty, had one gate open. ONE BLOODY GATE! I mean, this was the kind of service I expected at Rochdale or Matlock. In fact, that's doing both those clubs a disservice as I'm fairly sure they both would have managed more than one chuffing gate. When we joined the queue we were only about 20 yards from the actual turnstile – but that was only if I looked to my right. If I looked forward and followed the queue, I was about 200 yards away! It was a very depressing sight. We moaned and cursed at the scouse mounted policeman and were fortunate enough to hear that much-sought-after scouse wit!

"We didn't think you'd bring this many," he said with a chuckle.

"Oh, the long winter evenings must just fly by in his house," I thought.

Well, I can tell you here and now that no one laughed because it just wasn't funny, he wasn't funny, and there was nothing funny about this situation at all. The chances of getting in before the kick-off were non-existent. In fact, looking at the queue, I'd be doing well to get in before the end of the game! Someone suggested that, instead of trying to entertain the troops, he should go away and get someone to open up a few turnstiles; although I think the actual words used were more like, 'Why don't you fuck off and get someone to open some more bleedin' gates?!' But, surrounded by so many people, he had absolutely no idea that *someone* was me, thank goodness.

The 'mountie' was put under even more pressure when a couple of bus-loads attached themselves to the end of the queue and wanted to know what was going on. The comedian on the horse tried again but his line wasn't funny the first time round and it positively died on the second.

"I thought thawa supposed to be in fost fuckin' division," someone yelled (which I thought was a damn sight funnier than, 'We didn't think you'd bring this many') and then followed, rather aptly, with, "Tha gunnarav problems when Man U come."

"Oh, we'll have more gates open for them," Mr Wit replied, which really pissed everyone off because that was it, really; that was how much thought Liverpool had put into our arrival. We weren't Man United, so we didn't count. It's one of the reasons the scouse bastards have gone on to be one of my most hated clubs. They didn't give a toss.

But, suddenly, after much shouting and annoyance and, who knows, maybe even some radioing by the policeman with the famous scouse wit (the mounds of crap his horse was leaving in the street were funnier), another gate creaked open and a doddering old fart prepared to let us in. On seeing the gate opening, the lads at the back of the queue made a dash for it and, before I knew what was happening, everyone was making a dash for it. Being an honest, upright, 'you-were-here-before-me' sort of chap, I stayed where I was. When the queue reformed, I was alone, standing in the middle of the street like a pillock. I was further back now than when I started! However, Rinner was from the 'see-a-chance-and-take-it' school and he'd made a run for the gate, ending up about 30 yards away. It was some time before my eyes married with the scream of, "Stan!" (for 'twas my nickname). "Come over here!" (I may be slow but, on this occasion, the words 'gift-horse' and 'mouth' were something not to be ignored.)

It must have been the longest 30 yards in history and we ended up missing a comfortable 20 minutes of the game. I'm not sure if we were 1 or 2–0 down when we got into the ground but, already, there was fighting at the back. The Chesterfield supporters had been apportioned a corner of the ground opposite the kop and, for some really strange reason, Liverpool fans were standing at the back. As the first supporters got in, they were able to keep out of the way. The Liverpool fans licked their lips, obviously thinking this was going to be the night they beat up a bunch of third division minnows. But when 'the lads' got in – the Chesterfield supporters who enjoyed confrontation – things changed somewhat. We needed more room anyway and, so, the lads spread their wings, boots and fists and cleared the offending scouse debris. Had I been in the ground, I'm sure it would have been fun to watch. I know I shouldn't say it but, come on, be honest, own up, it would have warmed anyone's heart, especially if you'd been standing outside like a muppet for the best part of 30 minutes.

The support from Chesterfield was excellent. We sang the night away as if we were playing our way to victory when, in actual fact, at 3–0 down it's fair to say we all knew we were on our way out of the Cup to one of the top sides in Europe. It was no disgrace: Liverpool *had* put out a top side. There was no such thing as squad rotation then, you just picked your best side; and, apart from Souness (who, I believe, was injured), their side was pretty much at full strength. While I started the evening thinking this was going to be the upset to end all upsets, I was now thinking that I'd just settle for a goal. We had played quite well – in fact, so well that we'd given Liverpool more than a scare – and, had Mossy not missed his obligatory sitter, then the scoreline would have been a whole lot closer and, perhaps, a fair reflection of the game. And, with the game drawing to a close, Birch gave me everything I'd been asking for as he hammered a free kick past Clemence from 20 yards. It was all we wanted. That and to applaud our team off the field.

After the match, that genial Irishman-to-be, Jack Charlton (yeah, right), commented on how we must have been relieved to have come away on the wrong side of a 3–1 scoreline, which only goes to show: (a) that he wasn't at the game; and, (b) what an arrogant idiot he was! (But, then, as he was manager of Sheffield Wednesday, I guess we already knew that.)

So, despite losing, we were more than proud of the Spireites. We had looked a good side and had absolutely nothing to be ashamed of. All we wanted to do now was applaud our team off the pitch, get on our buses and trains and go home. But it didn't quite go as I'd expected. It was the sound of breaking glass that first alerted me to a disturbance at the back of the terracing and I instantly resorted to panic mode. All too quickly I'm wishing the players would run off the pitch and thinking, *"Go on. Get off. You were great. I've seen enough now!"* Then there was a surge of fans from the back as fighting broke out behind us. This was getting very scary very quickly and I pushed and scrambled my way to the front, away from the flying boots and fists, and outside onto the road. In retrospect, I don't know why I got so worried *inside* the ground because we'd left it to face the biggest, most disorganised shambles it has ever been my misfortune to encounter.

The police just stood and watched, both inside and outside the ground, as if nothing was happening. I had expected to be walking back through the park but, once we were out of the ground, I discovered that the park was locked; instead, we had to walk round it. By now, there was a mass brawl in the road. It appeared as if everyone was engaged in fisticuffs of some sort or another. Most were probably like us: trying to get out of the way. We ran to the end of the street, the noise of the fighting a little too close for comfort, and I didn't rate our chances of getting to the bus without some sort of problem. In the mayhem I picked out three Liverpool fans: a young lad and two girls. I was looking for a safe harbour and these were the best I could find.

"Hello," was my rather blurted introduction. "Good game, wasn't it?"

They were young and were wearing Liverpool scarves, and my biggest worry now was getting smacked by a Town fan. But they were friendly (or, perhaps, just as scared as we were) and they managed to escort us down the road in one piece. We did well because all around us people were getting decked and nobody was doing anything about it. For the police it was a night off as they were just standing there, in twos, watching it all happen!

Ever the pessimist, I was sure we would get a thumping at some stage; it was just a matter of time. I looked around and saw a friend of mine being pinned to the railings of the park by some Liverpool hooligan and, much to my delight, also saw him escape by first whacking the hooligan in the mouth and then running off down the road. This may have been a normal Tuesday night in Liverpool but it bloody terrified me. This wasn't even one of those situations where you were glad you'd lost because it would have been so much worse had you won. This was just normal. These were the 'best behaved supporters in the land' doing what they did every week. Wankers!

As we reached the road where the coaches were parked, we said goodnight to our escorts, thanked them and thought we'd cracked it.

"Oh, you aren't going down there, are you?" one of the girls said and, before I had chance to confirm her suspicions, she added, "You want to be careful, then."

I hardly dared to ask why but thought it only right.

"Well, they ambush you down there," she said.

"Oh, great. Right. Thanks."

That was all we needed to know. Was this the famous Liverpool goodbye: escort you down Bedlam Road to Ambush Corner? Having said all that, it did sound rather far-fetched. I mean, ambush? As if! No sooner had I allowed the thought to creep into my mind than the night air was filled with high-pitched screeching. I had no idea what it was; well, not until a dozen scousers came tumbling over the fence and jumped onto a Town fan two yards in front of us. They knocked him to the floor and had the lot: money, watch, trainers, jacket... They left him with a kick in the nuts, a couple in the ribs and a smack in the mouth. And we walked past! Sorry, whoever you are, but I was in self-preservation mode. I think everyone was.

It wasn't as if those doing the ambushing were thugs; they weren't. They were just young lads. On their own you would have slapped 'em round the ear 'ole and told 'em to bog off! But as a group, you couldn't do anything. It was absolutely ludicrous. I mean, this wasn't even football violence; this was robbery. If mugging had been invented back then, well, this was it. I dare say the goods they stole would have been sold the following day in the school playground, that's if the little runts ever went to school in the first place. Jeezus, what a place! And to think they made it the European city of culture! They would have thought twice about it if they'd been with me that Tuesday evening.

We made it to the bus unscathed, which in itself was something of a minor miracle, but it wasn't over yet as our next obstacle was that two lads were sitting in our seats. I looked at them, not really knowing what to say. It was obvious they were from Chesterfield but I didn't recognise them from our bus. It seemed rather petty to make a point of asking for our own seats back but, before I got chance, one of them looked at me and said, "Are these your seats?"

I nodded and they politely stood up and went to sit in the seats behind. I knew they were from Town so I wasn't worried but I had to know where they'd appeared from. It transpired that they'd made the outward journey by train and when they'd arrived at Liverpool, buses had been supplied to take them from the railway station to the ground. Unfortunately, or ridiculously, no buses had been supplied to take them back to the train station or, if they had, no one knew where they were. The police had told them what number service bus to catch and where to catch it from. Then, as they had stood in orderly queues waiting for a number 64 or 27, or whatever it was, the police had just stood about and watched the best behaved supporters in the land pour out of the ground or pub and kick the shit out of them!

It was a riveting story which had most of the bus listening in with varying degrees of wonderment but, eventually, the lad in charge of our bus (and I do believe it was none other than the infamous Howard Borrell) broke the news to these two lads that 'we couldn't possibly take them' and they 'would have to go back home by train.' They shook their heads.

"Look!" he said. "If I get someone to take you to the station, will you go with them?"

The lads agreed and our hero jumped off the bus (rather him than me) and returned five minutes later.

"I've got someone," he said rather triumphantly, and the two lads walked to the front of the bus, only to be greeted by a policeman! They didn't say a word; they just turned around, walked to the back of the bus and sat down in the aisle.

"You can't stay on here," the bus charge said.

"Well, we're not going with *him*," they replied.

Another triumph for British and, perhaps more importantly, Liverpool policing. The police had been appalling, and as for the best behaved supporters in the land, well, we all found out what a right load of bollocks that really was. I seem to remember that we did take our two extra passengers back to Chesterfield.

Several of the people on our bus boarded with only one shoe or a bloody nose and an empty pocket. As one person remarked: "It wouldn't have been so bad if they'd just beat you up."

As we were leaving Liverpool the coaches came under attack from all sorts of debris. Anything the scousers couldn't sell was used as ammunition and thrown. Consequently, a 14 year old boy was hit by a missile launched through a bus window and had to spend the night in a hospital in St Helens with concussion. And just to finish off the drama, on the way home one of the coaches in our little lot ran into a horse! I nearly put 'ran over' but you most definitely *run into* them!

The following day I saw a friend of mine who had travelled by train.

"What was it like, John?" I said.

"Fuckin' murder," was his short and seemingly accurate reply.

His recollection was a wonderful yarn of uncaring police, mad Liverpool fans and no transport to the station. He seemed to have spent most of the evening being chased around Liverpool. He said he'd had no idea where he was running, he just ran: up streets, over gardens, down alleyways.

Despite having taken two special trains to Liverpool that night, we only brought back one. The rest of the supporters came back on buses; otherwise, as far as I know, some of them may still be running around Liverpool, in which case they'll have gone feral by now!

The most ironic thing about my mate being chased all over Liverpool is that he was actually a Liverpool fan, a point I had tremendous fun making. It sounded like the original nightmare and I'm only too pleased I didn't have to go through it. To this day I don't know why I didn't go by train because I had done for most of Town's away trips that season. I enjoyed travelling by train: it was relatively safe as you were surrounded by hooligans, which is always a plus. But I'm bloody glad I didn't on this occasion.

Back in Chesterfield I was all fuelled-up to write to Liverpool and tell them what a bunch of wankers their supporters were and what a load of shit they were for only opening one gate. I was also set to write to the scouse police and tell them what I thought of them, too. But in the end I did nothing.

The local paper, the *Derbyshire Times*, did question them, however, and their General Secretary, Peter Robinson, when asked about the shambles, replied: *"We are obviously used to handling big crowds and we don't normally experience turnstile problems. We understand that quite a lot of Chesterfield supporters were late arriving. There were also delays caused by hooliganism in that area."*

Basically, this was the biggest load of rubbish anyone had ever come out with. Ninety percent of the fans were there on time and the hooliganism was afterwards, not before the game. However, the point he failed to mention was that any hooliganism that occurred that night was started by his bunch of idiots! But, as had been pointed out by the policeman earlier, we weren't Man United, we weren't a big team and, so, we didn't get their full respect. The fact that we frightened the crap out of them on the pitch makes me smile somewhat but it in no way compensates.

I suppose this is why Liverpool, its fans and everything associated with the dump are deeply despised by me, even today! I must say, getting that tremendous 4–4 draw there a few years ago has helped a little. The press gave them a working over no football hooligan ever could. Waking up to that news as a Liverpool fan must have been worse than a kick in the guts. So, in a way, revenge has been quite sweet – but it was a long time in coming and, do you know, IT'S STILL NOT SWEET ENOUGH!

Another Famous Chesterfield Cup Run

FA Cup First Round

November 24th, 1979 Grimsby 1 v 1 Chesterfield

Oh, to be on the march with Cox's army; a march to a first round FA Cup tie in Cleethorpes, the home of Grimsby Town FC. Admittedly, an away tie at Grimsby might not immediately conjure up the magic and romance of the Cup. In fact, a puked up curry by the side of the road has a little more magic to it than a journey to Cleethorpes. But the Mariners went on to win the Third Division this season and were among the front runners when we played them in the Cup, so we knew it was going to be a tough game against a reasonable outfit. It was also no surprise that this supposedly 'ordinary' fixture between two Third Division teams attracted a whopping attendance of 8,406. (Oh, for such first round attendances now!)

We geared up for this match by beating Mansfield 2–0 at home in the league and cracking a fair few skulls into the bargain, if memory serves me correctly. And there were several arrests for incidents which ranged from swearing at someone to punching them to the ground and kicking them. (I know which offence I'd prefer to be on the end of!) We also stuck seven past a demoralised Reading, which was incredibly funny. Not often you hear chants of, "We want 8!" at Saltergate.

I think I made the journey to Grimsby by special train – in fact, I'm almost sure I did – but now I've said that someone will undoubtedly inform me that British Rail didn't run a football special to this one. The reasons I think I went by train are twofold: firstly, I was in the unfortunate position of having the not-so-beloved Goody with me, a lad you would not choose to travel with to away matches if you could help it at all; and, secondly, I do seem to remember a rather long walk to the ground, which would also account for a journey by train.

The Friday before this game I was sitting at home, cramming my tea down me before going out to play football, when there was a knock at the door. I cursed, dragged myself away from the table and opened the door to a smiling, orange orb. The bottom half of this 'thing' was definitely Goody. You couldn't miss that because he had this annoying habit of bouncing around on the balls of his feet like a demented *Andrex* puppy. However, his thick black hair had been replaced by a translucent orange glow which made him resemble a space hopper.

"Ayup," he said, smiling, obviously waiting for me to comment on his wonderful hair-do but, to be honest, I was momentarily struck dumb. I was speechless!

"Like the hair? It's Californian Blonde!" he said.

"No, it's not," I replied. "It's fuckin' bright orange!"

"No, no, Californian Blonde always looks like this," he assured me.

"Fuck off, ya knob. It's orange. They saw you coming and no mistake!"

Now, I'm no expert on hair and the many colours one can achieve through the process of dying but, equally, I'm not colour blind either and I do know orange when I see it, especially the kind of orange that would blind someone with a sight impairment if they were exposed to it for too long. And, yet, here he was, as bold as highly polished brass, at my door, looking for all the world like... like... a boy with a satsuma for a head! I mean, he'd travelled up from Aston with his hair that colour! You've got to give him his due, he certainly had some bottle – even if he didn't have any sense of colour!

"So, what are you doing this weekend?" he asked, desperately moving the subject away from his nuclear fall-out hair.

"Oh, I'm off to Grimsby tomorrow to watch Town. Special train." I said this with a degree of comfort as I was sure Goody wouldn't be interested in attending. "But I'll be out later."

"Okay," he said, "I'll see you later." And with that he was gone, his orange head bobbing through the gloom till he resembled nothing more than a mobile street lamp.

Goody wasn't the sort of person you arranged to do anything with really, not if you could help it and certainly not once he had orange hair. And I know I didn't arrange to travel to the Grimsby game with him, therefore it came as something of a surprise when I ran into him in Chesterfield, both of us on our way to the station.

During the journey Goody spent most of the trip telling me how wonderful his time at university was, how it was a mixture of drinking and women, although I presumed you could add 'dying your hair ridiculous colours' to that list. If he hadn't spent so much of his time trying to impress everyone, I think he might have been a half-decent youth (I stress the word 'half'). But that was his problem. Now, don't get me wrong, I have nothing against universities; they are fine places – and if that's your bag then that's great. But they aren't the be-all and end-all of life and I hated the fact that Goody looked down his nose at me just because I worked for a living. This attitude did get him close to a thumping on more than one occasion but usually I would tell him to 'fuck off' and then walk away. It wasn't that I was scared of Goody; in fact, he was one of the few people who really didn't concern me in that way. He was about as threatening and dangerous as a mild skin rash. His line in conversation, however, could be lethal! We're talking about a lad who had a line of conversation that would have frightened the Kray twins. Of course, this was 1979. *Now*, Goody will be pumping iron, no doubt, and so I'd better tread carefully!

I would imagine that many are screaming, *'Then why travel with him?'* and, believe me, I've asked myself that question on more than one occasion. However, this memory does inevitably lead me to assume that I did travel to this game by train because I definitely remember 'bumping' into Goody on the way down to the station.

The journey to Cleethorpes was incredibly boring and, much as I'd like to, I really can't blame all that at the feet of my travelling companion. It was just a boring journey. However, once we were off the train and out of the station, it was the usual cacophony of clapping, singing, shouting and gesticulating at anyone close enough. You might call it 'instant atmosphere.' The police were still having problems with handling large amounts of youths descending on their towns for a punch-up and, so, it was no surprise when the first group out of the station ran past the police cordon to confront a group of Grimsby fans watching from a not-so-safe distance. A fairly decent scuffle took place while the rest of us jostled for a safe position to watch it all from. Those three or four seasons under Cox and Barlow were brilliant as the travelling support was awesome and we seemed to cause more trouble than we really should have done for a Third Division side. Don't get me wrong, we were no Millwall or Cardiff – but we had our moments. And the main thing was, from my perspective at least, I always felt safe. For me, football violence was a bit like *watching* a game before the actual game; it was just another spectator sport. For some, well, they liked to *play* a game before watching one... and that's when the trouble started!

The match itself was excellent. If I was some dumb commentator on the television (are you listening, Mr Motson?) I would be bleating on about what a fantastic advert this was for the Third Division and how a draw was a fair result, given the standard of play, etc. But I'm not, so you'll just have to work it all out for yourselves.

Grimsby scored first and, despite singing our hearts out for 90 minutes, it looked like being yet another exit from the Cup. I was trying to reconcile myself to a galling defeat when, before I could utter the words, *'Well, at least we can concentrate on the league now,'* up popped Phil Walker to equalise. Mental? I should bloomin' well cocoa! In fact, 'absolutely fuckin' mental' would be a much more accurate description of my reaction and also that of the 2,000 or so crammed into the away end. The eruption of the travelling fans seemed to suck the very air out of the place. It was unconfined joy everywhere; the type where you just lose yourself in that moment and become oblivious to everything else. When we scored, I left the floor somewhere near the front of the away end, to the right of the goal; when I finally gained my senses (some might argue that still hasn't happened) I was near the back and far more central. (All-seater stadiums have put paid to that sort of unconfined joy, haven't they?)

Normally, had I been travelling alone, I would have stayed where I was. We were deep into injury time and it wasn't worth moving but, as I figured Goody might be searching for me, I pushed my way back to where I'd left him. He was still there. Goody wasn't really a football fan. Well, he couldn't have been: he said he supported Liverpool. But, more than that, he had absolutely no idea how important that goal was. He was, quite literally, a spectator; he just happened to live in Chesterfield. I had a smile so wide it was in danger of meeting at the back of my head, but Goody seemed impervious to it all.

The game ended to massive cheers at our end and lots of disgruntled Grimsby fans marching sullenly away. The guy on the public address system announced that we should stay where we were so the police could escort us back to the station. This was met with the usual chorus of derisive remarks and, like a red rag to a bull, the Chesterfield fans marched with a degree of purpose towards the exit gates.

When I got there, so many people were lending their collective shoulder to the gates that they were bellowing out under the strain. *"Someone's going to get hurt if they give way,"* I thought, *"and if they don't give way someone's going to get crushed."* Either way, it wasn't going to be me, so I grabbed Goody by the shoulder and pulled him towards the back of the crowd. As an adult, Goody could do just what he liked. He didn't need to be mothered by me, although I did notice how easily he allowed himself to be lead backwards, especially when he saw the dustbin come flying over the gates and smash down amongst the Town fans.

The sounds that could be heard now were those of Grimsby fans standing on the other side of the gates, loading up dustbins with assorted masonry and lobbing them over the gates and wall. I was safe. They would have needed the combined talents of an Olympic shot-putter on huge doses of steroids to get anywhere close to me and, as I didn't think Grimsby had such a person, I stayed where I was.

The Mariners hadn't exactly endeared themselves to the Chesterfield fans by these actions and there were one or two disgruntled Spireites so eager to get out of the ground that some of them looked as if they would have eaten their way through the gates – they were like rabid dogs. For me, this was where it got tricky. It was no good staying at the back because you were more than likely to get picked off by some stray Mariner looking for a Town shit-bag to clobber. Equally, you didn't want to be at the front because that was for the Chesterfield fans who wanted to stand and slug it out with a bunch of hairy-arsed dockers. So I grabbed Goody and, as the crowd burst out, muscled my way into the middle of the pack and shot off down the road like a lame hare. The Chesterfield fans wanting to do a bit of chasing did just that – and I do believe there was a bit of a set-to behind me – but I just kept walking forward briskly. The problem was... I'd lost Goody! Now, after all I've said, you might think I would have been well pleased with this outcome but I'm just not that big a bastard. I mean, where was he? I didn't want to think he'd got a kicking and, so, against my better judgement, I walked tentatively back to the ground. Maybe I had him all wrong. Maybe he was a hard fucker. He certainly wasn't with scaredy-pants me. I had awful visions of a tortuous journey home with Goody telling me of his exploits wading into Grimsby's finest; but when I got back to the ground there was nothing. I turned to walk back down the road, as the stewards started to shut the bent gates to the away end, when I heard a voice behind me shout: "Hang on." And there he was, just emerging from the toilet. Not the greatest hiding place, I'm sure you'll agree, but it was probably appropriate. I think I would have found it much funnier had they actually locked him in but, then, we had a train to catch, so perhaps not.

"Fuck me," he said, "they were going mad back there. I thought I was going to get my head kicked in."

In many ways he did the right thing. At least he managed to avoid a kicking but, I must admit, I did wear the inner smile of *'I told you so'* all the way home.

Three days later and we had the replay. Goody was back at university and Saltergate bustled with 7,820 spectators. The atmosphere inside the ground literally crackled with expectancy. This wasn't our biggest gate of the season by any means but I guess it was up there. We played like a dream and it wasn't long before Bill Green and then Geoff Salmons put us 2–0 up and seemingly on our way to Round Two, which was virtually uncharted territory for Chesterfield fans at the time. With a little more luck it could have been 5; we were strolling it. And so, in the second half, that was exactly what we did (stroll) and before you had chance to say, 'Wonder who we'll get in Round Two,' Grimsby had sneaked into a 3–2 lead and went on to win without us troubling their goal again.

I was devastated, numb. I couldn't believe how we could have thrown such a comfortable lead away, but we had! Somehow we'd contrived to fashion the most amazing defeat from the jaws of victory! I was numb, bloody numb.

I wasn't even interested in the various scraps taking place in the Town Hall car park! We had a contingent of supporters who were distinctly naughty. They would come to Saltergate late, not because they'd been in the pub but because they'd been in the pub and then spent 15 minutes checking out the cars in the car park searching for the ones with stickers in them such as 'I bought my car from Bloggs of Cleethorpes.' The ones that went as far as having a 'Grimsby Town' sticker in the back window, well, they were just asking for trouble. Once they knew where the cars were, then pinpointing the fans became that much easier. This 'naughty' bunch of lads would then leave the ground early and hang around the car park, usually around the car next to the one they'd eyed up as if they were, perhaps, waiting for the driver (although how they expected anyone to believe that 15 of them were being transported in one vehicle is anyone's guess). But they knew that eventually four happy Grimsby fans would come strolling along, thinking about how easy it had all been, and then WALLOP! Mr and Mrs Jones, little Tommy, Grandpa and the poodle would head out of Chesterfield with one headlight, seven black eyes, four bloody noses and more than their fair share of loose teeth. Not exactly fair, I grant you, but *you picks your car and you takes your chance.* Let's face it, they could have picked a car owned by five seventeen-stone skinheads with pick-axe handles and a rottweiler and the chances are some of them actually did because, knowing Grimsby, they aren't short of naughty supporters themselves. But, tonight, I didn't care because, tonight, I was numb.

I left the chants of *"Spireite Aggro"* behind in the car park. A car with its headlights missing, and only one rear light working, juddered past me with three Chesterfield youths chasing it, trying desperately to re-model the bodywork into a more condensed version of the original vehicle. They thumped on the windows and threatened murder. The two youths inside stuck up two-fingered salutes from the safety of their battered shell. It was going to be a long way home for them but you could see from the smiles on their faces that winning meant an awful lot more than a dented car – and so it should.

But I was numb. I walked down towards Beetwell Street and could hear the distant shouts as Chesterfield fans accompanied their counterparts to the station. There would be fighting: Church Walk, Holywell Cross – that was my guess. But I didn't care because I was numb.

I got to my bus bay and waited. I had about 15 minutes before the bus arrived and no doubt I would be joined, eventually, by other sorry-for-themselves Chesterfield fans. I hoped so; I needed to grieve. Where was Goody when you needed the twat?

Now, I hadn't really noticed it at first – or, rather, I hadn't paid it much attention – but parked in the top bay of the bus station was a coach. It was all blacked-out when I got there and I didn't really pay it any attention at all until the lights flickered on and people started to climb aboard, not in big numbers but a couple would arrive and then, two minutes later, another few would get on and so on. It wasn't until I noticed the black and white scarf draped around the neck of one of the blokes that I realised these were Grimsby fans. By now the number of Town fans at my bus bay amounted to about five, none of whom you would depend upon if it came to a game of fisticuffs with the enemy. Mind you, I was also pretty fast on my feet in those days and so, if things did get ugly, I reckoned I could soon run myself clear of any danger.

Because of the scoreline and because one or two of the Grimsby lads had taken a smack on their way down to the coach, we started to get a fair amount of stick. It started off with harmless reminders about what the score had been. But it was after one such reminder that a Chesterfield fan at my bay responded with, "Fuck off, ya wanker!" Not the brightest thing to say, given the circumstances, but I silently and wholeheartedly agreed with the sentiment. Trouble was, *that* was when it turned a little more scary. About half a dozen Grimsby fans were standing around the entrance to the coach, talking. It looked as if they were plotting. It might seem paranoid but I'd seen enough violence to know when things were going a little pear-shaped. A couple of them started to make their way down the steps, and I was getting ready to run. Fortunately, however, a Grimsby fan, who obviously wanted to get his bus full and back to Grimsby in one piece, came forward and pushed them all back onto the bus, giving them a good talking to in the process.

As the Grimsby bus waited for its final few passengers, those on board took it in turns to rub salt into our wounds. It was harmless but it hurt. It's the situation where you think, *'I wish I was big and hard and fearless cos I'd punch your lights out, you dickhead. But, as it is, I'm small and weedy and a coward so I'll keep me gob shut.'*

As it turned out I didn't need to be big and hard that night because walking down behind the coach was this enormous Town fan, someone who resembled a yeti wearing a donkey jacket. He was huge! His neck was so thick his scarf wouldn't meet at the front; it just lay there on his shoulders – too scared to move, no doubt. He didn't look as if he was there for any trouble; he just looked like someone on his way home from the game. He'd paid the coach absolutely no attention whatsoever and was about three paces past the end of it when a Grimsby fan came to the door and screamed, "AGGGHHH, FUCK OFF, YER CHESTERFIELD WANKER!!" I don't think the Grimsby fan was addressing this big guy who was walking past. In fact, I'm sure he was aiming his remark at someone who had delivered a V sign to him as he boarded the coach.

But it was certainly the most idiotic thing he'd ever shouted in his life. I was so pleased. The Chesterfield giant stopped in his tracks, turned slowly to see who had been shouting at him and then he stood and watched the Grimsby fan walk back up the aisle of the bus, laughing to his mates before regaining his seat. With a determined and deliberate stride our hero made his way towards the bus. I thought he might just issue a warning from the doorway, a little bit of petty threatening. I certainly didn't expect him to climb aboard. But he did! He took the steps two at a time and walked with a purposeful 'Clint Eastwood' type stride down the middle of the bus, pulled the youth from his seat and SPLATT!! Funny? I'll bloody say so. The few of us at the bus stop were now cheering him on. One or two on the bus tried to help the youth out but he just splatted them as well as he headed back towards the door. All the lads at the bus stop were now singing *'Spireite Aggro,'* although I wasn't because it could have still gone wrong and I was numb, not at having lost the game anymore but because I was totally in awe of this massive youth who had answered my prayer. He walked off the bus, as unscathed as when he walked on, and disappeared into the evening.

The final Grimsby fan arrived, sporting a bloody nose, and the bus closed its doors and departed in a rather hurried fashion. We waved them away with all manner of gesticulations. Perhaps I shouldn't say this but I would be telling fibs if I didn't say that I've never been so pleased to see a bunch of supporters get clobbered in all my life. To the huge man who did it, thank you – whoever you are!

Entertaining The Blades

January 5th, 1980 Chesterfield 2 v 1 Sheffield United

In the January of 1980 we were set to play Sheffield United at home and there were 800 police on duty for that game. I knew it was going to be a tasty fixture when a Sheff Urinal fan approached me in the car park and threatened to do incredibly awful things to me; things that I ignored and hoped one of the attending 800 policemen would manage to prevent.

As I got to the ground they were already fighting outside the turnstiles at the Saltergate end and I'm not sure where the 800 police were but they weren't doing a great deal about it. And once the game started, well, let's just say we handed out one of the footballing lessons of the season. We were 2–0 up inside six minutes and, although we ended up winning 2–1, it was never really that close. After the game I stepped out jubilantly into the middle of a pitched battle that raged along Saltergate and down Soresby Street. However, being skilled at avoiding these skirmishes by now, I managed to get back to the bus station unscathed. The crowd that night was 13,887 and General Manager Arthur Sutherland said he was disappointed at the turn-out.

Later that month, a Chesterfield fan appeared in court for his part in the disturbances and commented that football matches were 'the bane of his life.' *"I always seem to end up in trouble,"* he said, no doubt with a degree of exasperation.

Weddings, Winning And Broken Legs

March 14th, 1980 Oxford 1 v 2 Chesterfield

Wynnie's Tours were now a thing of the past and Wynnie himself had long since tendered his resignation from even attending football matches, never mind having his own travel company. Because of this, we had to consider alternative travel arrangements. With the *East Midlands* also opting out of taking football specials, we were left with travelling by supporters' club coaches. It wasn't ideal – but it was that or nothing.

I was accompanied to Oxford by a fine selection of Chesterfield cowards: Higgy (Paul Higginbottom), John (John Day) and Chip (Pete Chappell) – we were nothing if not imaginative with our nicknames. Young Higgy's mother had provided him with a rather yummy selection of sandwiches for the journey down; not that young Higgy ever found out how yummy they were because the three of us scoffed the lot while he was taking a quick nap. Boy, if his mother was going to provide this fare for every away game then he could come again!

Once we reached Oxford, however, we were faced with the dilemma of how to find out whether a pub was safe to enter or not.

"I know," some smart arse said. "Why doesn't just one of us go into an ordinary looking pub while the other three wait outside? Then, if it looks a bit rough, they can have half, drink up, come out and we can go somewhere else. But if it looks okay they can get a pint and come outside and fetch the rest of us."

"*Mmmmm,*" I thought, "*that sounds like a reasonable idea... but why is everyone looking at me and smiling...?*" "You bastards!"

They laughed but it was the sort of laugh that meant I had been chosen by popular demand. So, we set off in search of this so-called desirable pub. We walked away from the ground and down a lane which looked for all the world like we were entering a different county. The sun was shining, the birds were singing and you would have thought we were in the middle of rural Suffolk rather than half a mile from the Manor Ground.

At last, we came upon a hostelry and decided that this looked as good a place as anywhere, although I think we were all just ready to plonk our weary backsides on a bench by this time. So, in I went while the other three cowardly swine stood outside, knowing that if I came out through the front window rather than the door, then it probably wasn't a suitable place for four Town fans to grab a drink. Once inside, I was surprised at how quiet it was. The pub seemed idyllic. In fact, I was about the only person in the bar, although there did seem to be an awful lot of activity in the beer garden out the back. Some kids were dancing out there and everyone seemed to be having a really good knees-up. There was no doubt about it: this pub was safe. Eventually, the landlord approached and asked me which of the five hand-pulled beers I would like. Five!! Boy, I was in real-ale heaven! I made my selection (can't remember what but I certainly tried more than one of them) and, then, suddenly became aware of someone standing at my shoulder. I turned to see this rather large bloke smiling at me, dressed in a suit, with his tie removed for comfort.

"All right, mate?" he said. "You aren't from round here, are you?"

"No," I replied. "That obvious, eh? I'm from Chesterfield. I've come to the football match."

"Fuck me, you must be desperate for entertainment to come and watch them play Oxford!"

I laughed with him and asked what he was doing dressed in his best suit on a Saturday afternoon. It transpired that he was attending a wedding and the reception buffet was being held in the pub's beer garden; a reception buffet to which he invited me!

"How cool is this?" I thought, and completely forgot about my three companions standing outside!

I'm still not quite sure why and when they entered the pub: whether they thought I'd been killed and, so, it was their duty to collect my scattered limbs and take them back home on the bus; or whether they just got so fed up waiting for me that they decided to risk it anyway. Whatever, you can imagine how disgruntled they were when they found me slurping down a bought-for pint of ale and scoffing my way through a range of exceptionally tasty sandwiches (and I thought Higgy's mum's were nice).

Despite having a cracking time and despite not really wanting to leave, we eventually decided that we really ought to. It would have been wrong to go all that way just to attend a wedding of someone we didn't even know. So we said goodbye to our new friends and left for the ground. After all, the fixture we were supposed to be attending might only be going to last 90 minutes but it was more important to us than the fixture between the bride and groom!

As we got up to the ground there was an awful atmosphere and it was apparent that there had been some serious clashes between rival fans. We were even threatened by a group of Town fans who didn't know us. John Day was quick to point out their error and they apologised and moved off in search of someone local to smack.

I can't remember that much about the game: I know we won 2–1 with goals by Green and Walker but I don't remember much else. What I do remember is that there was fighting after the game as well. Being on the supporters' club coach was a blessing for once as we were fairly quickly escorted onto it and out of town. But one Town fan was not so lucky: he was attacked by around 30 Oxford fans as he walked back to his car. The clobbering they gave him was so almighty that they broke his right leg in two places. The police reckoned that one of his attackers had been wearing steel toe-capped boots (no shit, Sherlock!). Now, that may be bad enough on its own but when the poor unfortunate got to Accident and Emergency, he found that his first visitors were two of the original group who had set about him in Oxford! They threatened him again and, had it not been for the intervention of some hospital staff, he might have got his left leg broken to match. I mean, I've heard of ambulance chasers but that's ridiculous! The lad's friends managed to escape serious injury, which probably means they could run quicker, but the thugs did kick seven bells out of his car, too. The police in Oxford arrested six people in connection with the incident. The lad spent nine days in hospital in Oxford where the club's directors presented him with a basket of fruit and a card. I'll bet that cheered him up no end! Still, it was probably more than he got from Chesterfield's directors.

Nevertheless, the promotion push was officially on!

Train Dancing

March 29th, 1980 Reading 2 v 2 Chesterfield

Before Reading moved to the opulence of the Madejski Stadium, they played in a run-down shit-tip called Elm Park. With Cox's side riding high in Division 3, this was just another one of those games you couldn't afford to miss.

A special train had been laid on and tickets for this had sold out easily. I always thought that if the club organised a special train to every away game then they would fill it. Travelling by train was always a little bit more of an adventure – or it felt like it to me, at least. The usual mob I travelled with had equipped themselves with tickets and we were looking forward to a day 'daaan sarf.'

When we boarded the train on the morning of the 29th, it looked at first like any other football special: carriages specially vandalised for the occasion. But this one was slightly different in that towards the front of the train there were a couple of those old 1950's carriages where you walk down the side of the carriage and peer into separate compartments, all shut off with their own sliding door. We were somewhat surprised to find one of these compartments vacant and, so, four of us took advantage of this unexpected and, yet, more than welcome splendour.

The train had its usual complement of travelling coppers and, so, we weren't expecting anything out of the ordinary to happen. In fact, it was quite a peaceful journey. Even the police were walking about smiling, so we could only deduce that things throughout the rest of the train were running smoothly, too.

Of course, it couldn't last. As we approached London, or were within a few miles of it, the train began to slow. At first, we thought we were pulling into the station but I checked my watch and realised that if we were we had probably just broken the land speed record for this particular journey. There didn't appear to be any reason for the train slowing, so, being the nosy one, I left the compartment, pulled down the window in the door and got the shock of my life. As I looked towards the rear of the train, I could see a crowd of Town fans on the roof! Yes, that's right. Some were actually on the roof of the train, dancing and singing, while others were now attempting to climb out of the windows to join them. I took a step back inside and thought about it for a minute or two... No, I must have been seeing things. But, just to make sure I wasn't hallucinating, I stuck my head back out of the window to take another look... I wasn't!

I turned around and looked at this copper who had come up behind me to tell me, I assume, not to look out of the window but, on reflection, he may well have been thinking that I was about to join the fans on the roof and, so, perhaps, he was trying to deter me. He needn't have worried: you wouldn't have got me on that roof even if the train had been stationary, never mind moving!

"There's..." I said, pointing and giving my best impression of a goldfish, ever, "... on the roof!"

"I know," he replied. "Just go and sit down."

I pulled the window up and looked at my hands. They were covered in oil. But before I had chance to speak the officer said, "Something wrong with the engine," and he held up his dirty, oil-covered hands in sympathy.

I went to the toilet to try to wash the oil off but the only water in those toilets was down the bog itself and I certainly wasn't dipping my hands down there! Looking in the mirror, I got the shock of my life: I looked like a dalmatian! Big globs of oil covered my face. I cursed several times and if there had been a cat handy I feel sure I would have kicked it. I got out my hanky and just about rubbed my skin off trying to remove the bloody stuff. As I stepped out of the toilet, another policeman walked past. He, too, had been looking out of the window and looked like someone going to audition for the George Mitchell Minstrels (for the younger readers, ask your dads or granddads about them). We may well have been sitting in a *carriage* that came out of the 1950's but from the amount of shit coming from the engine it would be fair to say that the *engine* itself might have come from that era also. God knows what the youths on top of the train looked like because they were in the direct line of all the gunk that was flying about!

So, without the basic convenience of running water, I took my hanky and a big chunk of bog roll back to our compartment to try to get the worst of it off. I was, of course, ripe for people taking the piss – and who could blame them? I would have done exactly the same! What with my dalmatian appearance and my news of fans on the train roof, I soon had everyone bent double with laughter and I'm not sure that everyone really believed me. I did encourage one lad to stick his head out of the compartment window just to confirm my story. Secretly, I wanted nothing more than for someone else to get an oil covering. As I expected, he could do no more than agree that there were, indeed, Town fans on the roof and then he called me a few choice words as we laughed at his black-spotted face.

Now, whether the train was going slowly because it was breaking down or because there were fans on the roof, I really couldn't say. My guess, and it is only a guess, is that the train slowed because it was starting to break down and this enabled the supporters to climb out onto the roof. But you have to be seriously pissed up to try a stunt like that and, if you are seriously pissed up, then it isn't a stunt you want to be trying. How no one was killed I will never know and, although it still remains one of the most incredulous things I've ever seen, it somehow didn't concern me. I was shocked, admittedly; but, then, once I'd realised I'd got oil all over my hands and face, I didn't really give a shit either way.

As a result of the train running so slowly, we were late getting into Reading which was, perhaps, a good thing. We had been on this dilapidated excuse for transport for over three hours and people were getting a little stir-crazy. You could sense that if there hadn't been a football match with an imminent kick-off, then there would certainly have been a trashed boozer. We were half escorted, half let loose, as we all chased up the road in order to make the kick-off.

Town played well. Earlier that season we had drubbed Reading 7–1 at Saltergate and they were reminded about this at regular intervals. For their part, you could see there was a degree of pride at stake. I can't remember how the scoring went but Ridley and Bonneyman got the Chesterfield goals and we had to settle for a 2–2 draw. It had been an entertaining game; a little one-sided, perhaps, as we dominated proceedings throughout but couldn't get that vital third goal. However, it wasn't the end of the world just yet. There were still plenty of points left to play for.

As we made our way back along the high street to the station it all kicked off. Once again, this was a very one-sided affair. The Reading fans hadn't been expecting any trouble, I don't think, but suddenly there was a roar from behind me and all at once people were scattering everywhere. I continued to walk at the same pace towards the station. I was pretty certain that it was the Chesterfield fans who were causing the trouble but to be seen running at this stage could get you mistaken for a Reading fan, and I didn't want that to happen!

All around me fans were being chased up alleyways, over gardens and into shops. The two youths in front of me looked very uneasy and, as one of the Town heavies stood in the road looking around him, they couldn't resist the temptation to try to run off. I say 'try' because they had moved but 5 yards when one of them disappeared into a pile of dustbins, with the help of a well-placed Chesterfield fist! His mate did what any decent mate would do: he tried to run away. But his big mistake was thinking that sanctuary could be found inside a chip shop. I did think it was a strange move at the time and I stood and watched through the window as he talked with a degree of agitation to the bloke behind the counter. My guess is he wasn't ordering cod and chips! Before the bloke, who I assumed was the owner, could offer him the back door (if, indeed, he had been going to do that), the Town fan ran into the chip shop and chinned the Reading fan where he stood. The youth went down rather easily and stayed down when a well-placed Doc Mart curled into his midriff.

The Town fan stood for a minute or two looking at the other people in the chip shop queue who all suddenly found really interesting things to examine hiding in their loose change. He said a few words to the bloke behind the counter, wagged a finger in his general direction and then ran out, back onto the street. What he didn't see was the guy in the chip shop waving one of those things you use for sharpening knives at him as he left the building. Now, I'd seen hundreds of people get hit at football matches and, yet, watching one get hit in a shop while I was looking through the front window was really bizarre. It's a hell of a window display and I couldn't help but think that if shopkeepers employed moving displays like that in their windows then they would get a hell of a lot more people stopping to take a look and, who knows, they might even get people coming in to buy. I mean, I'd seen someone beaten up and, yet, suddenly, I really wanted to go into the shop and order fish and chips. If I hadn't been worried about missing the train or being mistaken for someone with a mysterious polka-dot disease, I dare say I would have done. Ahh, the power of advertising!

The police who had come down on the train with us were running around trying to maintain a degree of law and order and, more importantly, attempting to get everyone back to the station but, with the violence being scattered along the length of the main street, it was difficult to get anyone to do anything. Perhaps one of the reasons why they found it so difficult to maintain any law and order was because of the relationship they had with the Town hard cases. In some respects it was a very friendly one: they all seemed to be on first name terms. However, while I'm sure this was part of trying to treat individuals with respect and, hopefully, preventing them from causing trouble, it resulted in the police finding it hard to stop the violence when it did break out.

I first noticed this relationship on the way back from Rotherham earlier that season. We had lost 2–0 and, so, there were a lot of angry Town fans at the railway station. We hadn't gone far out of Rotherham when the train started to slow quite alarmingly and it transpired that some Rotherham fans had put a railway sleeper across the lines in the hope of derailing the train. Before the train had stopped, those Town fans who could see the culprits were piling out of the doors at the back of the train and giving chase. There were some general instructions to the police, like, "Don't worry; we'll get them for you," and I dare say they would have, too, but the Rotherham fans were young and quick – and no doubt crapping themselves – and they were gone in an instant. The police on the train shepherded the Town fans back on board with smiles and pats on their backs, and I remember thinking then that a very cosy little relationship seemed to have developed.

Here in Reading, I had proof that this cosy relationship only lasted while ever the Town fans wanted it to. But I didn't mind. Once again, I had managed to avoid any trouble whatsoever and looked forward to my private little compartment all the way back to Chesterfield. Disappointingly, although I managed to plant my backside down in the seat, it only stayed there for about 30 seconds before a couple of coppers came in and told us to 'fuck off to the cheap seats.' Charming! They were commandeering our compartment for the journey back. They looked tired and fed up and a couple of them looked distinctly oily. And I didn't see one member of Her Majesty's police force for the rest of the journey home.

April 29th, 1980 Sheff Utd 0 v 2 Chesterfield

When we travelled to Sheffield to play the Urinals we still had an outside chance of promotion – a very outside chance. *If* fourth-from-bottom Bury managed to beat Blackburn *and* we managed to beat Sheff United, then we could do it. It would go to the wire. And, although we turned up in our numbers and watched as we slaughtered them 2–0, Bury couldn't even do the one little favour that we'd asked of them. Having said that, I don't think anyone really expected them to – but we lived in hope! Hey, we were Chesterfield fans; we always lived in hope. We went on and thumped Exeter 3–0 in our final home game of the season. And that was that. Well, almost. It was certainly everything on the pitch finished with.

But, despite a decent finale to the season, we missed out on promotion yet again, by one solitary point. As I mentioned in the 'Wednesday' chapter, the Owls finished above us. And then the League had the gall to change the points system to 3 points for a win for the 80/81 season. Had they thought about this one season earlier, it would have been us rather than the Owls that were promoted and Division 2 would have been ours!

June 1980

Fame waited briefly when I was playing cricket for Wingerworth that season: I was picked to play in the Second XI alongside Colin Tartt – or should that be Colin Tartt was picked to play alongside me? After all, I'd been playing for them for years. Whatever, Colin was a Chesterfield hero and an all round nice bloke. I think I was so awestruck that I never spoke to him. His wife was gorgeous, too!

But, back at Saltergate, Chairman Ian Gaunt had at last got the news he was waiting for: planning permission had finally been granted to modernise the ground. They had tried to get planning permission the previous season when they had wanted to build a covered staircase from the back of the stand down into a bungalow that was owned by Chesterfield FC and to turn the bungalow into an executive club, but it never happened. The residents committee, which for some reason was led by some old scrote who lived about a mile away from the ground, managed to get the application turned down. However, this time things were different and the *Derbyshire Times* went with the following blockbusting headline and article:

"Soccer Club scores with new look for the 80's

"*Chesterfield FC has at last won approval from the Borough Council for its ground improvement plans. Planning permission has been given for a new office complex on pillars at the main entrance to the Saltergate ground. It will extend 20 feet onto the forecourt leaving room for car parking underneath. The club has also won the go ahead to build a vice-president's lounge under the main stand. A permanent stand for TV cameras is also to be built on the Compton Street side of the ground. Work has already started on the TV platform and it should be ready for the start of the new season. However planning permission for the new office complex came too late for the club to start and Chairman Ian Gaunt said, 'We'll have to wait until the end of next season.'*"

Now, you don't need me to tell you that this never actually happened. Well, okay, we probably built the vice-president's lounge/shed and the TV gantry but the new offices and major refurbishment remained a dream, which is a real shame as the plans that were printed in the newspaper looked quite impressive. Who knows, maybe they would have led to a whole host of ground improvements... But, then again, maybe not!

Chairman Ian Gaunt took a lot of stick for his handling of the Chesterfield finances (and, in some respects, I suppose I can understand why Gaunt faced the criticism he did) but anyone who watched Chesterfield during these few seasons saw, without doubt, the best football that had ever been produced by a Chesterfield side – and that's some boast. Promotion would have made Gaunt a hero and saved the club. But promotion was needed – and it was needed fast!

Magnificent turn out at Anfield in 79/80 as Chesterfield fans eventually manage to get through the one turnstyle opened for them.

Chesterfield fans celebrate Birch's stunning free kick in the 3-1 defeat at Anfield in 79/80. However all is not well, some town fans and even the police (bottom left) are already turning to see that a right royal ruck has kicked off at the back of the terrace. Liverpool eh – best behaved supporters in the land my arris!

The travelling fans are happy as Chesterfield ease to a 2-1 victory at Exeter in 79/80. That will have made the journey home a little less painful.

Girl Power
SEASON 80/81

No sooner had season 79/80 finished than season 80/81 was starting. Over the years, I feel that the gap between the end of one season and the start of another has diminished and I'm not quite sure why that is. The restructuring of the leagues and the added pressure placed on the game by television are, I'm sure, contributing factors. However, it could also be something as mind-numbingly simple as the fact that time does seem to fly by at an alarming rate as you get older. This particular season, though, the gap really was minute as we'd been entered into the Anglo-Scottish Cup. What little pre-season we'd had seemed to have been taken up with Cox splashing out even more money, in particular the £100,000 for bargain of the century Danny Wilson from Bury. So, what little close season there had been was something of a blur.

I can't say that everyone was that enthralled by the Anglo-Scottish Cup; in fact, very few people knew anything about it! The competition itself had replaced the Texaco Cup in 75/76 and had included such notable winners as Middlesbrough, Forest, Bristol City, Burnley and St Mirren. In fact, St Mirren were the only Scottish club ever to appear in a final – and they managed it twice, winning one and losing one. So that gives you an indication of either how seriously the competition was viewed north of the border or that Scottish teams, by and large, are shit! But let's not travel down that particular road.

The Cup itself wasn't a simple knock-out trophy. To begin with, it had a qualifying group and drawn alongside Chesterfield were Sheffield United, Grimsby and Hull City. While I doubt that anyone ever dreamt we'd actually win the bloody thing, there was much salivating at the prospect of sticking one up those whingeing Blades yet again. With the group stages for this competition set for pre-season, it was July 31st, 1980 when we hung them out to dry at Saltergate, with Bonneyman scoring the only goal. So, as you can see, it wasn't just my imagination: this season really did come around quickly.

For a clash with the Blades it wasn't the biggest attendance but, then again, you weren't going to complain at 7,693 for what was, in many respects, a pre-season friendly. But it was fun to see that Dee-Dah tartan army shuffle back home with nothing to show for their troubles. A 3–3 draw at Grimsby meant we only needed to draw with Hull to qualify. An Alan Birch penalty gave us the 1–1 scoreline needed to book our passage into the quarter final and a two-legged tie with the famous Glasgow Rangers. (This could be the closest we ever got to playing in Europe!) But that wasn't until October and, so, it gave all the shopkeepers and landlords two months to shit themselves at the prospect. For the rest of us it was business as usual and back to the league.

In effect, while the gap between the seasons may have diminished, it transpired that the gap in the hooligan calendar didn't abate at all; in fact, it just continued on into the cricket season with a right old scuffle with Somerset supporters. According to the press, *"Somerset's notorious travelling fans"* made a lot of noise at a cricket match in Queen's Park. However, it was a group of 30 or more Chesterfield supporters that were guilty of the worst excesses: not only were they encouraged by this 'notorious' bunch of cricketing followers, they also showed them the true meaning of the word 'notorious.' Everyone was used to football violence at football grounds but when it crossed over onto cricket, well, it just wasn't 'cricket,' if you know what I mean. Also, for some strange reason, it wasn't classed as 'cricket violence.' Oh no, this was football violence crossing over to cricket; and the media, as expected, took great delight in telling us how football supporters really were almost out of control. To be honest, I don't entirely go along with the notion. Let's face it, violence *was* extremely prevalent in society back in the late 70's and early 80's. You only have to glance at the headlines in the *Derbyshire Times* to see that violence and hooliganism were by no means isolated to sporting venues and, in particular, football. *"Man Struck Neighbour With Garden Spade," "Vandals Vandalise Vandal-Proof Lights," "Boy Admitted Kicking Cat," "Woman Head-Butted By Brother-in-law," "Accused of Stabbing Man Outside Pub," "Stole Shotgun From Man He Didn't Like"* (fuck knows what he would have done if he'd hated him) are just a few of the random things that were making the local press back then. Don't believe me? Go see for yourself: there are hundreds, nay, thousands, all of a similar nature.

Personally, I blame Thatcher but, then again, I do tend to blame her for everything, from the decline of the mining industry to the bubonic plague, so that in itself is hardly surprising. However, this was a time of great unrest and, while I don't want to get too deeply involved in the political angle (mainly because there isn't one, really), I'm sure it all played a part in the melting pot that was society as we knew it back then.

The season proper started on August 16th when Huddersfield rolled into town and wrecked the place. No one really expected it. This was Huddersfield. I'd seen more trouble with the local girls' choir than I had with Huddersfield; so this was something of a surprise. Once again, the *Derbyshire Times* sprang into action with:

"Soccer Hooligans Wreck Pub

"Soccer hooligans wrecked a town centre pub before Chesterfield's first league game of the season against Huddersfield Town. More than 100 Huddersfield Town fans entered 'The Painted Wagon' on Cavendish Street on Saturday. After 25 minutes a fight broke out and damage estimated at £600 was caused. The Huddersfield fans came into Chesterfield on an earlier train than police anticipated and threw escort plans out of step."

Now, don't get me wrong, I'm sure trying to police football supporters every Saturday was a bit of a bind – certainly not something I would want to do myself – but if all it takes to cause you grief is for the expected masses to turn up on an earlier train, then you're in for some very long Saturdays indeed. It does make one wonder, though, how the police actually planned for the arrival of visiting supporters. Did they just get a train timetable and think, *'Well, I'd come on this one'?* Surely the police had learned enough by now to know that football hooligans don't really operate to normal timetables. Well, obviously not. Town centre landlords were certainly getting restless (again) but who could blame them? If a bunch of raggedy-arsed tykes can cause so much disruption simply by coming into town earlier than anticipated, what was going to happen when a hoard of hairy-arsed, caber-wielding jocks come piling over the border for the Anglo-Scottish Cup game? I think the landlords had every right to feel worried, don't you?

But October was months away. I couldn't understand what all the fuss was about. We had to go to United for a league game before then.

There's Something About South Yorkshire
August 19th, 1980 Sheffield Utd 2 v 0 Chesterfield

Ahhhh, South Yorkshire... you can't help but hate it, can you? I must admit, the place has changed considerably. Today, when you get off the train at Sheffield, you're met with a plethora of fountains and water features, all there to make you feel as if you're in the land of culture. Walking up from the station, there is even a 300ft poem on the side of a building. All of this is a massive improvement from the Sheffield of 1980. That Sheffield was dreadful. In fact, it was worse than dreadful: it was as if someone had built the perfect city to condemn. It was so bad we used to call it 'the place the dustbin men delivered.' The place was nothing more than a glorified landfill site. I mean, in 1980, if someone had given me the choice of going to Sheffield or drowning my favourite pet cat in flaming petrol, then I would have chosen the latter. The place stunk. I'm sorry, it has to be said: it was a dump. It was, as they say, a shit hole. But I didn't have a pet cat and so I didn't have a real excuse for not attending this game. As for today, well, actually, I quite like Sheffield. The people still talk funny and they are mostly Yorkshire folk, which is always going to be something of a hindrance, but, that aside, the Sheffield of today is a hundred times better than that of 20 years ago. (And, yes, one could aim the same criticism at the Chesterfield of 20 years ago – but, then, why should I?)

So, with Sheffield being the huge mountain of crap that I've tried to describe, why six of us should decide to get the 11.30am train into that God-forsaken hell hole is a mystery, especially as the game itself didn't kick off until 7.30pm! Yes, that's right: we gave ourselves just about seven hours to walk from the station to the ground! I can't remember whose idea it was, and I can't imagine why I decided it would be a good idea, but I took a day off work (unpaid) and off we trotted. I really was an idiot; this game cost me a fortune!

The first thing we did was hit a *Ward's* pub just up from the station. Now, for those of you too young to remember what *Ward's* actually tasted like, well, the following tasting notes might be useful to you: 'Exceptionally malty beer, with a light, hoppy finish and if you need a damn good clear out, then this is the potion for you!' While I may not be the world's biggest consumer of alcohol, I do enjoy the odd pint or three. But I had no intention of getting legless on this trip, so, after we had finished in the pub, I literally had no idea what we were going to do. Somewhere along the line we split up and the six of us became three: myself, Tim Wilson and Richard (Spiney) Norman. It wasn't as if we had anything planned. I think we went into *John Lewis* at one point and lounged about on their settees – only because we were tired and wanted a rest. But three lads looking at living room furniture doesn't cut it with the staff, so we were soon shown the door!

At some point during the afternoon, eggs came into the equation and I can only assume that someone had decided that buying six eggs would be a good thing. I know it wasn't me but I can't think for one minute that we would have bought them in advance and hung on to them for this long. After a few rib-tickling ideas about what one might do with said eggs, we decided to go to the top of a multi-storey car park and drop them on people. Great idea! They were, after all, only eggs. It never crossed my mind that an egg hitting you on the skull from a few hundred feet above may as well be a block of granite! We waited patiently atop that car park... and we waited... and we waited... and were just about to give up when our first target walked by. We missed! By about 300 feet! In fact, we were so far off they didn't even realise anything had been despatched in their direction. However, with each passing citizen our eggs got closer and closer until, finally, with only two eggs remaining, we hit someone on the shoulder. We stood there, laughing and pointing, expecting him to shake his angry fist skywards and scream something along the lines of, *'I'll get you for that, you young scallywag!'* What he actually did was take one look up at us and rush into the entrance of the car park. We looked at each other and our laughter was now that of the nervous condemned man. We had two options: run down the stairs or run down the ramps where the cars come up. Figuring he'd go for the quickest route, we ran round the car track and, thankfully, saw neither hide nor hair of him. He probably only pretended to run into the car park. I have no idea, but this set the tone for the whole evening and had us giggling like fools at everything else that happened.

Later that evening we ran into the other three from our party. Whether this was pre-arranged or just coincidental I can't say, and honestly don't remember, but we had one more pint and set off for the match. None of us were particularly legless but we were somewhat lightheaded on a mixture of alcohol and high expectations and consequently were all rather foolish.

All of this was supposed to be a seamless link into the stupidity of the South Yorkshire Constabulary but, as you can see, it hasn't quite worked, so I'm going to have to take a more direct approach: I HATE SOUTH YORKSHIRE POLICE! They are, without doubt, the most unyielding, unhelpful, bitter, twisted, sad, misogynistic, misologistic, humour-crippling individuals it has ever been my misfortune to come across. I've had two-week-old dog shit on my shoe with more personality than half the bastards assigned to this particular police force. Of course, they were all there outside Bramhall Lane, searching us either for concealed weapons or just simply trying to feel us up, I really cannot say. What I do know is that, on seeing this bunch of charmless nerks outside the ground, I felt I ought to bring some joviality to the proceedings. I hate the tension that exists between fans and policemen – there is no need for it – and so, as the police officer felt me up and down, I came out with the old classic, "And you didn't even buy me a drink!"

The copper looked at me, grunted, muttered something under his breath and then asked if I was carrying any sharp implements.

"Only my wit," I responded.

Yes, and some of it really did fall on stony ground. Okay, they may not be the funniest and most original gags one has ever heard but I was only trying to make light of the situation. Instead, I was simply pushed towards the turnstile by some jack-booted official who had had enough of this smart aleck from Derbyshire.

There were nearly 18,500 there that night, which included a huge following from Chesterfield that filled the away end. In 1980, the away end at Sheffield was awful. The terraced area was compact and positioned under the stand behind the goal. The view was crap; there were large pillars every so often, so unless you were 6ft tall and built like a brick shithouse, then finding a decent viewing position could be difficult. I ended up at the back and could see most of what I needed to see – for ten minutes, at least. That was when two very friendly Sheffield policemen came and stood directly in front of me. I tried desperately to look around them, over them, under them... but all to no avail. All I could see was a wall of dark blue.

Feeling somewhat pissed off, I tapped one of them on the shoulder and said, "Excuse me, would you mind moving? I can't see."

I thought it a reasonable request: I couldn't see and I had paid. But the boys in blue looked at me as if I'd just asked if it was possible for me to nip back to theirs and screw their wives. I suppose the look was enough. It didn't need an answer but I got one anyway.

"No, we can't," one of them said in a voice so gruff it sounded as if he'd been taking special 'gruff' lessons!

The upshot was that I had to spend most of the first half scurrying about like a ferret trying to find a decent vantage point. In the end, I wished I hadn't bothered as we went down 2–0. We were just two games into the season and Sheffield United fans considered they were as good as promoted already. Oh, how they bleated. But 'he who laughs last, laughs longest' and I pissed myself for days when they got relegated.

Cox Out

A set-back against Sheffield United wasn't anything to be concerned about, though. What was a worry, even at this stage of the season, was that every time a manager's position became vacant, Arthur Cox was linked to the job. It was to be expected, I suppose: we were a great side and only misfortune had kept us in this God-forsaken division.

It was of no surprise, therefore, to hear in September that Newcastle were taking quite a shine to our manager. The rumours never went away and, come October, he was gone. The club said goodbye to Mr Cox by nipping down to Oxford and thumping them 3–0. Some said it was the players' way of saying goodbye; others said the players didn't really like him so they were just showing him they could manage without him. Frank Barlow, who was Cox's No 2 (should I rephrase that?), was handed the Chesterfield job immediately and I just hoped that he would prove to be as a good a manager as Cox had been and get us the success we craved. Frank Barlow was a genuine good bloke. I had a lot of time for him and he certainly didn't appear to be overawed by the responsibility.

While Chesterfield supporters craved success and dreamed of playing some of the bigger clubs in the country, the town's landlords must have hoped we would go out of business as they were getting pretty tired of having their pubs trashed. As I said earlier, it is understandable. It wasn't as if pubs were being smashed up infrequently; if anything, it was quite the opposite! I saw it regularly on my travels and, while I may not have frequented the hostelries where it happened in Chesterfield, I was well aware that it *was* happening. It was hardly surprising, therefore, to read the following headline and article in the *Derbyshire Times*:

"Scared Landlords Vow – 'We'll Shut Out Rangers Fans'

"A meeting of town centre landlords has voted unanimously to close for the day during the Rangers – Chesterfield clash. The landlords have been told that a number of shops intend to support their efforts to make it a dry town by refusing to sell drink on the day. Mr Tony Wood, landlord of The Welbeck, said, 'None of my customers will be coming in – so all you are going to be opening up for is yobs!'"

All this, of course, was agreed months before the so-called yobs came to town and it was one of the biggest knee-jerk reactions the town had ever invoked. Let's face it, no one knew whether the jocks would be a scurrilous bunch of ragamuffins or a few nice lads in kilts wanting a glass of single malt before they went to watch the match. It was purely a case of misdiagnosed 'big-match' syndrome. For instance, I don't remember the landlords getting together to demand that Chesterfield be a temperance town when the Sheffield Wednesday bandwagon rode into town and, yet, *they were* a club that had previous, especially in Chesterfield! I can't remember any club coming and causing quite as much mayhem during the 70's as Wednesday did; and, equally, I can't remember the pubs closing for any other club either. They were more than happy to take their money. Perhaps it was the Scottish currency they feared?

But the Rangers match was more than a month away and a lot could happen in a month; like the two Scabs fans travelling back from an away game who launched an unprovoked attack on a Town fan (Mr Wilkinson) whilst making an unscheduled stop just outside Chesterfield. (You can see this is a really dated piece by the fact that Mansfield were actually taking a coach-load of fans to an away game somewhere other than Chesterfield.) Their coach was later stopped by police on its way back to Mansfield and a Mr Ian Bull was arrested. The court heard that Ian Bull, who was 6ft-6ins tall and weighed 19 stones, asked Mr Wilkinson which team he supported and when he replied, "Chesterfield," he hit him. When asked why he had done it, Mr Bull replied that three years previously he himself had received some fist in Chesterfield. They were fined about £600 for the attack – which, today, would probably buy their football club! But I guess Mr Bull thought that revenge was sweet, if not a little late in coming.

At the beginning of October 1980, Chesterfield FC itself took a bit of a punching when it announced that the club's losses were a quarter of a million. This news was issued with the rider that, *"If the supporters do not back the club then they may be forced to sell."* You always knew it was going to be our fault somehow! But these were heavy debts. Let's face it, in today's money you'd be straight into administration. But, back then, we shrugged and thought it would all go away. Well, I did anyway.

On the field, things were progressing well. In the league, we had five wins out of six games, including demolishing Carlisle 6–2 away from home, and we were handily placed. We beat Hull at home 1–0 before heading north to Glasgow to play Rangers. I have to hold my hands up at this point and say that I didn't go. No, I too had been bewitched by those evil news reports that depicted everything north of the border as overtly ginger and violent. However, some of my friends who did go came back with tales of great spirit: how they had been welcomed into the drinking establishments and how a good time had generally been had by all. Now, they may have been treating us this way because they thought they were going to beat us easily but could just as easily have thought that this was a decent way to treat a bunch of lads supporting a side they might never play again in their history. Either way, we got a commendable 1–1 draw in the first leg of the tie and this set up the second leg very nicely indeed.

As I have stated, I didn't go: mostly because I was apprehensive but also because I was going to Reading on the Saturday and wasn't sure if my meagre salary would stretch that far. The Reading game wasn't half as much fun as the previous season's game. Very little happened but we did win 3–2, which made me very happy indeed.

October 25th, 1980 Chesterfield 1 v 2 Walsall

We warmed up for our big outing against the Jocksters with another bunch of enemies from the Midlands, Walsall. I say 'enemies' but that's mainly because we never seemed to beat the buggers and they were considered a bogey side. As everyone really expected, we lost the game 2–1; but it was a notable game as Walsall kicked seven shades of turquoise out of us on the pitch and had two men sent off in the process. Back then two sendings-off in one game was very rare but this was becoming something of a regular occurrence with sides playing Chesterfield: if they couldn't beat us, then they would kick us into submission. Today, sides would never get away with it.

As the second Walsall player headed for the changing room the visiting fans ran down the terracing, enraged at the referee's decision. They were gesticulating and generally unhappy about how their team was being treated. The police got involved and a bit of rough and tumble took place. Quite how much I wasn't aware of until I read the local paper which said: ***"Girl Soccer Fan Denies Attack on Policeman."*** The article outlined the case against the young girl and how she had allegedly jumped on the back of a police officer, grabbed him by the throat and pulled his hair. The officer's helmet was knocked off and his tie ripped from his neck. His whistle and chain were pulled from his tunic and his pocket ripped open. The officer claimed he was also hit on the back of the head and kicked on the leg. The article went on to say: *"The alleged assault on PC John Dudley occurred when he tried to arrest a youth who was seen to run down the terrace directing abuse towards the ref. The youth was followed by a large number of Walsall fans, including the girl who was his girlfriend. As the officer tried to arrest the youth, the two of them fell to the floor and it was at this point that the girl jumped on his back. Eventually, the pair were taken from the ground, struggling and shouting."*

There had been a number of other incidents during the game but this was by far the worst. The girl pleaded not guilty to the charge of assaulting a police officer in the execution of his duty. The court was told that the youth had pleaded guilty to the charge at a previous hearing and had been fined £200 with costs. However, the girl was eventually found guilty and ordered to pay £264. The court said it would have been a much higher fine had it not been for the fact that she had received glowing character references and that this incident could also damage her career, being employed by Walsall in their supporters' club. It's hardly a career that you'd be worried about damaging but, having read the case through, I couldn't help but feel a bit sorry for her. Most hooligans accepted their fate; very few pleaded not guilty. In her defence, the girl said she had tried to part the policeman and her boyfriend and had grabbed the policeman by the arm. In fairness, her account seemed a lot more plausible than that of the police officer but as a supporter you were on a hiding to nothing.

After the game, a Chesterfield fan was arrested for shouting, "Come on, you bastards, you're going to die," at which point a crowd of Walsall fans lunged towards him. He was probably glad he got arrested!

Anglo-Scottish Cup Quarter Final

October 28th, 1980 Chesterfield 3 v 0 Rangers

I must admit to feeling quite nervous on the day of the game, not just because it was the quarter final, which sounded rather glamorous in itself, but more so because of the possible mayhem that was supposed to be breaking out in the town centre. As it happened, I had no reason to worry: Chesterfield had virtually closed for the day. A few pubs did stay open but very few. Some of them had Scottish connections so felt it their duty to stay open, but most were locked. I remember going down to *The Badger* with some friends for a drink. It was far enough outside of town not to attract wandering Rangers fans but, as I seem to remember, there was still a nervy atmosphere.

Having read the press build-up and then being fuelled by urban myths about what would happen on the night, I think I had good reason to be nervous. But, like so many things in life, reality seldom lives up to the hype. This game was a fantastic case in point. The Rangers fans had spent the day in a closed-down Chesterfield, wet and cold and with nowhere to hide away until kick-off time. Then, just to rub salt into their already tired and frozen wounds, we stuffed them 3–0. If I recall this correctly, Phil Bonneyman was made captain against his old club and he led the rout with a couple of goals. Ernie got the other; and, to be honest, there could have been a lot more. Rangers were dreadful and we dominated proceedings from start to finish.

As for the Tartan Army, well, they supported their team and left, and you couldn't help but think that we had done them a great injustice. In two weeks' time we were due to play Sheffield United at home and you could bet your life the landlords in Chesterfield would be opening their pubs for that game; after all, they did have a living to make. The following week, people wrote into the *Derbyshire Times* saying how ashamed we should be for the way we had treated the folk from Scotland. And they were right: we *had* done them an injustice.

But the league goes on and, after a couple of decent away draws at Fulham and Rotherham and then a home victory over Brentford, we were more than ready for Sheffield United – again. And, once again, we sent them packing, beating them 1–0 with Bonneyman scoring the only goal. I can recall a few skirmishes on Saltergate before the match but don't really remember it kicking off big style. Perhaps they were so worn down by us continually beating them. Who can say? But a crowd of just over 15,000 watched as we moved up to second in the league. I bet 'Praise and Grumble' would have been fun to listen to that night, if it existed back then.

Second in the league! Surely everyone would be going to Leeds Road to watch us play Huddersfield.

This One's For The Ladies

November 15th, 1980 Huddersfield 2 v 0 Chesterfield

I rejected my usual form of transport for this game (which had been supporters' club coaches this season) and accepted a lift with my sister and brother-in-law. We stopped at a couple of nice pubs before heading off to a wind-swept and rain-lashed Leeds Road. (This was pre-big-fancy-stadium.) Because the weather was so foul we opted to sit down, rather than stand up on the uncovered terrace and get soaked. I'm quite glad we did because: (a) I didn't have a mack so would have got soaked; and, (b) I had a rather good view of the goings-on behind the goal where the Chesterfield fans were congregated. After a while I got the impression that some of the supporters were very cold because it wasn't long before they were running around in circles chasing each other! Yes, you've guessed it: it all kicked off. Sitting in the stand wasn't the best place to see just who had the upper hand but I did see about half a dozen Chesterfield fans being ejected. But, come that week's *Derbyshire Times*, I was amazed at the headline which confronted me: ***"Girl Fans Arrested."*** It went on to say:

"Three Chesterfield girl football supporters were arrested following trouble on the terraces at Huddersfield on Saturday. The girls, aged 17 and 18, were charged with public order offences and will appear in court at Huddersfield next Wednesday. Scuffles broke out on the terraces behind the goal where the Chesterfield fans were gathered."

Obviously, there was a great deal more to this story and on the 28th another headline of a similar nature told the whole sordid episode – and quite enthralling it is, too [names withheld as I don't want them or their husbands coming after me]:

"Girl Fans In Soccer Violence

"Soccer violence which flared on the terraces shocked a court on Wednesday. Magistrates at Huddersfield heard that three fans who were fighting, kicking and screaming obscenities were all girls! The girls from Chesterfield attacked two rival girl fans from Huddersfield when their teams met in a division three game at Huddersfield earlier this month. Police had to rescue the two Huddersfield girls from a large group of Chesterfield fans which included the three girls, and even as one of the police officers carried one of the fans to safety 18 year old JH was trying to get at her.

"JH and JM of Chesterfield and KS of New Tupton pleaded guilty to using threatening behaviour. Each were fined £100 and bound over to be of good behaviour for 12 months. They were told by the Chairman Dr Maurice Livera, 'Your behaviour can only be described as disgusting; you could have been fined £1,000 or sent to prison for three months.'

"The trouble broke out at half-time when a large group of Chesterfield supporters, among whom were the three girls, closed in on two Huddersfield girls. They were chanting, 'Slags, slags, get the slags!' and JH and JM started raining blows down on them and kicking them. JH was kicking out at anyone who got in the way and was swearing and shouting: 'Let me get at the bitch!' as police carried one of the girls to safety. Soon afterwards KS was arrested after she became involved in a brawl with rival fans. She was fighting on the ground and kicking and shouting at one of the girls, 'I'll kill you, you bitch.' KS told police that the two Huddersfield girls started the trouble and while she denied kicking them she admitted hitting one in the mouth."

I don't know why but that last sentence makes me howl with laughter every time I read it. It's as if kicking someone is a really terrible thing to do but punching someone in the mouth, well, that's okay really, isn't it?

Now, the press got really carried away with this story; so much so that it attracted headlines from such major tabloids as the *Daily Express* and the *Daily Star*. (Well, Diana hadn't died yet, so they had to talk about something.) While I found it quite amusing to see pictures of Town girl thugs in a national daily paper, we weren't the first exponent of the 'girl hooligan' by any stretch of the imagination. These girls were, perhaps, just the first ones to get caught and, for a while, they were the closest thing we had to local celebrities. Given the right management I'm sure they could have made a fortune opening supermarkets. Who needs scissors when you can kick the doors open with your monkey boots? The articles made interesting reading but, for the life of me, I haven't been able to find a copy of them to include here. However, I do remember them saying that they loved their club so much they even went and watched the Reserves! Now, that's what you call passion.

But, for all their passion and 'skull-thuggery,' Town went down 2–0 at Huddersfield; a result that put a dent in the promotion push – just as every bad result did – but there was still a long way to go. We could do this, we could. We really could.

So, while the girls were keeping a cell warm in Huddersfield nick, three Town fans came back to Chesterfield and broke into their own club! They had obviously been out on the piss as they eventually fell asleep in the press box. On waking, they put on some kit from the changing rooms to keep themselves warm. One was given a three-month prison sentence, suspended for two months, while the other two were fined £75 each for stealing tracksuit tops. The fines did seem a little steep; nowadays they would probably land their own survival show on TV for demonstrating such aptitude.

FA Cup First Round

November 22nd, 1980 Wigan 2 v 2 Chesterfield

According to the *DT*, over 4,000 Town fans made the trip to the grassy knoll that was Wigan Athletic. Now, I know a large number went but 4,000 seems a lot, even taking into account the over-zealous reporting of the *Derbyshire Times*, but I could be wrong. Wigan's tiny little muck heap really was bursting at the seams and it did kick off, especially when Alan Birch made a two-fingered salute to the home supporters. They didn't find it amusing. We did. And the rest is history. The game was drawn 2–2 in front of nearly 9,000, so perhaps the *DT* wasn't so far out after all. Let's face it, Wigan struggle to get crowds like that now they are in the Premier League. The replay, which was held mid-week after the original fixture, was won comfortably by Town 2–0 and we strolled into Round 2 where we would play none other than Sheffield United.

I think someone somewhere hated Sheffield United; someone apart from me, that is. That year we played them twice in the league, twice in the FA Cup and once in the Anglo-Scottish Cup. In those five meetings they beat us once, drew once and got hammered the rest of the time.

Anglo-Scottish Cup Update

On December 2nd we went to Bury and won 2–1 in the semi-final of the Anglo-Scottish Cup first leg. The attendance was a miserly 3,720. Heavens above! I know it wasn't exactly the FA Cup but this *was* a semi-final! Surely, any semi-final is worth supporting. A week later, at Saltergate, 6,440 (lower than our average league attendance) turned out to watch us consolidate with a 1–1 draw and book our place in the first final the club had ever been in. Well, it was to my knowledge. In that final we would play that well-known Scottish outfit, Second Division Notts McCounty. Being one whole division higher than us, Notts must have really fancied their chances but we didn't care: we were good, we were certs for promotion and, anyhow, we didn't play them till March – that was ages away.

The games were coming thick and fast now. In November and December we played 16 games, which boils down to Saturday and mid-week every week. I was happy enough, I was getting to see more football, but the players must have been blowing out of their arses trying to keep up with it all.

December 6th, 1980 Chesterfield 3 v 0 Millwall

In between the two Bury semi-finals we had the dubious pleasure of entertaining Millwall. I can't honestly remember a great deal happening during the game but there was certainly plenty happening in and around town. Millwall might not have brought that many supporters but the ones that did travel could always be relied upon to assist if you were desperately inclined towards a punch-up. As it happened, someone was. Once again, for fear of my own safety and also not wanting to tarnish what might now be a wonderful human being, I won't name the person to whom the following article relates. It's boring, I know, but once a coward always a coward.

The local paper rolled out its now customary headline for incidents such as this: **"Mayhem Broke Out Among Fans In Pub,"** and the article said:

"Although he had never been to a football match in his life, a Chesterfield man got himself mixed up with a group of Millwall supporters one lunch-time, a court heard. Thinking he was going to be involved in a violent scene, he threatened them and started a disturbance in The Buck Inn, Holywell Street. Chesterfield magistrates sentenced him to 3 months in prison suspended for 2 years. He admitted using threatening behaviour and was ordered to pay £25 costs. The Chesterfield man was mixed up in a disturbance with Millwall fans and several glasses were thrown and the landlady was hit by a piece of broken glass. He was not responsible for her injury but it was his action which started the trouble, as his manner was both threatening and abusive towards the Millwall fans.

"In his defence he said he had never been to a football match before and the other supporters were singing, laughing and chanting and looking in his direction. He was frightened of becoming involved in a scene so he threatened the other youths and mayhem broke out. The Chesterfield man was surprised at the way in which the football fans reacted so quickly to his comments."

Now, don't get me wrong, far be it from me to cast aspersions on an individual, especially when they are a Chesterfield fan/man/bloke at a bar, but if you think for one minute that 'looking in your direction' is a pre-curser to a scuffle, then you are seriously deranged. As far as excuses go, this has to be the lamest example I have ever come across. I'm sorry, Chesterfield man, while I admire your bottle for getting stuck into a bunch of Millwall louts, I think you could have shown a little more imagination with your defence. *'They came at me with a broken bottle, guvnor,'* would have sounded a little more plausible and, against Millwall, would also have been believable!

December 26th, 1980 Chesterfield 0 v 0 Barnsley

Before we became bogged down with Health & Safety it was possible to get quite a few people into Saltergate and this game was one of those that proved it. A crowd of 17,169 packed into the ground to see two teams, battling for promotion, hammer out a 0–0 draw; a scoreline that was about as predictable as the aggro that accompanied the game. I managed to get a ticket in the enclosure. For those of you too young to know, Chesterfield had a wonderful little viewing area below the main stand called the 'enclosure.' In effect, it was nothing more than a tiny terrace but it afforded a wonderful view and you could hear every grunt and thwack as players came into contact with each other. The atmosphere in there always seemed to be reasonably friendly but, then again, it's hard not to be friends with people when they are pretty much standing in your pocket. The enclosure gave you the security of sitting in the stand while at the same time being able to stand up – something that couldn't be guaranteed anywhere else in the ground. Alas, the enclosure was a victim of Health & Safety itself as it disappeared when we had to have steps built down from the stand to the pitch.

As I remember, trouble began relatively early on in the game and most of it was in and around the Cross Street end. I can't pretend to know who was doing what to whom but they all seemed to be enjoying it!

Something and Nothing - January 1981

1981 started without any real shocks. I didn't make the New Year's honours list again but, after creaming Sheffield United in an FA Cup second round replay, I was at last going to watch Town in a third round FA Cup tie – something which didn't happen that often. We were drawn away at Peterborough. Another 8,000+ crowd saw us very nearly go through, thanks to an Alan Crawford goal, but Robbie Cook did what he always did against Town: he scored to make sure the game went to a replay. Despite the home advantage, despite being the better side, despite everything, we managed to do what we have always done in FA Cup replays... we lost!

So, in this year's FA Cup we'd actually played six games (more than most Premier League teams have to play to win it) and we'd been knocked out in the third round! (Add on the six games we'd played in the League Cup and the seven we'd played so far in the Anglo-Scottish Cup and you could say the games were beginning to mount up.)

Years later, I ended up playing cricket with Robbie Cooke's cousin (it's not a claim to fame, just a fact) and he told me how much Robbie Cooke enjoyed playing against Chesterfield as he always seemed to score. I told my cricketing colleague how much I hated his cousin and how I'd never forgiven him for the goal at Peterborough. He laughed. I didn't.

January 31st, 1981 Chesterfield 3 v 0 Burnley

Let's face it, Burnley fans aren't very nice. I've been there a couple of times since and I doubt I'll be going back again in a hurry. My last journey to Burnley was in 95/96 by car with my brother and his friends, and we only just made it out of the car park alive as a group of Burnley fans were patrolling the car park armed with a baseball bat and checking the registration plates. Those cars showing that they'd been sold by the Ford dealership in Chesterfield were having their back window and lights destroyed. The Burnley fans were about five cars away when we scrambled into ours and zoomed out of the car park with more than a distinct smell of shit emanating from our trousers! Of course, when I agreed to go to Burnley with my brother and his friends in 95/96, I had forgotten all about the happenings that took place at Saltergate at the end of January 1981.

By our standards it wasn't a massive crowd, only 7,637, but there was more than enough trouble — and this was one of those games where you just didn't expect it. Yes, there might be the odd scuffle between rival fans outside the ground but there seemed to be trouble throughout this game and I don't think it was helped by the fact that we stuffed them 3–0. It was greeted in the *Derbyshire Times* with: ***"Violence Flares At Soccer Match."*** (Whoever came up with their headlines was never going to make it big in journalism.) However, the article went on to tell how two teenage fans needed hospital treatment after violence had flared during the Saturday game. A 15 year old schoolboy was attacked by a group of Burnley fans and was left battered and bleeding, while a Burnley fan was badly hurt by, and I quote, *"brick-throwing vandals."*

After the game there was also a fair degree of scuffling where Burnley seemed to give more than they actually took. I'm basing this on what I can remember and a few articles I've read. I remember walking down for the bus and being scared; not as scared as when Wednesday came but scared, nonetheless. Still, beating Burnley was enough to push us up into fifth place so, despite being scared, despite people I knew getting a kicking, I was just glad that we were climbing the league.

Unfortunately, the promotion push never came. We'd win a couple, and then lose a couple. For instance, we had two decent home victories against Oxford and Carlisle before going to Newport and getting turned over 5–1. We even went to Walsall and watched Ernie Moss score a fine hat-trick yet still come away on the losing side as we went down 4–3. Perhaps that was a reaction to playing the first leg of the Anglo-Scottish Cup final just four days earlier at Saltergate. We managed 10,190 for the first leg which we won 1–0, thanks again to an Ernie Moss goal. We all wondered if it would be enough and a week later we trooped off to Meadow Lane to find out.

We'll Take The Anglo-Scottish Cup
Forever And Ever And Ever
March 31st, 1981 Notts County 1 v 1 Chesterfield (aet)

I'm not for one minute saying this game ranks up there with the FA Cup semi-final appearance (although it was probably better than the replay), and I'm not suggesting that we haven't had other famous nights as Chesterfield supporters (not that I can think of too many), but this really was special, mostly because we won the bloody thing! In 1981, I was celebrating something like 20 years of being a Chesterfield fan and in all that time I'd seen us win the Fourth Division only once. One could hardly accuse any Chesterfield supporter of being a glory-hunter so, while there was anything remotely resembling glory up for grabs, well, I reckoned I more than deserved my fair share.

Now, back then, Meadow Lane wasn't the nice, compact stadium they have today. Oh no, it was ghastly. The away end was a sprawling affair, cut up into sections and fenced off from the pitch. The view was almost non-existent; well, it was if you were a short-arse like me. The game didn't start well for us in that reserve goalkeeper Paul Gregory came in for the injured John Turner for his first start of the season. I was nervous: not, for once, because I feared for my safety but because this felt like the big one. This was a final, with a proper cup and everything. There were nearly 13,000 inside Meadow Lane and County were looking dominant. Paul Gregory was, well, awesome. The guy made some breathtaking saves and kept us in the game but disaster struck and they scored, which meant we were now level on aggregate. We played much better in the second half and took the game to them a little more but the final whistle blew with the aggregate score at 1–1. This meant 30 minutes extra time. We needed this like a hole in the head.

During that interval between the end of the game and the start of what is usually a boring 30 minutes of cat-and-mouse football, I fell in love! Yes, it happened! I turned and saw a small, blonde-haired, Chesterfield fan standing near me. I was way too shy to speak, so she broke the deadlock by asking if I could see much. I had to admit that I couldn't.

"I can't see anything," she continued. "Will you tell me if we score?"

Would I tell you?! I'd have whisked her away to a love nest and let her bear my children. Of course I'd bloody tell her! I thought it best not to mention the love nest and childbearing thing; after all, we had only just met. We chatted away and I would have been quite happy if they'd decided to cut the cup in half at that point, and then I could have carried on talking to her, but the ref decided to start the game again and my eyes were drawn back to the field of play. (I've always hated refs.)

Every now and again, throughout the extra-time period, I would turn and look at her, giving her my best smile and checking to see if she could see. If she couldn't, I would try and keep her informed, which wasn't easy as half the time I wanted to shout things like, 'Oooooo, that was a foul, you dirty County bastard!' which I doubted was a great way to impress someone. So, mostly, I just said things like "Free kick, Town" or "Corner, them." They may not be chat-up lines but they stopped me putting my foot well and truly in my mouth.

As the clock clicked down towards the end of the 30 minutes, we launched what must surely be the last attack. Phil Walker controlled the ball, rolled the defender and crossed into the box. It was slightly behind Alan Crawford but, somehow, he managed the cutest little back-flick to put the ball past the County keeper and send all the Chesterfield fans delirious. I never actually saw the ball enter the net. I saw the cross, I knew Crawford was close, and then it all went barmy. Suddenly, a tidal wave of blue and white bounced haphazardly around the away terrace, not caring who it fell over or bumped into. People were hugging people they didn't even know, which was a great excuse for me to grab this beautiful, blonde-haired girl, hug her and dance with delight. I was in heaven. Yes, we had won the Cup!

This story would be all the more fitting if I could say that I met the girl several times after that game and we finally fell in love and had children, all of whom are season tickets holders. But, sadly, love is cruel and on this occasion it wasn't to be. We enjoyed the moment, we rushed to the fencing together as the players brought the cup over to us to celebrate but, as we all filed out of the ground, I lost her. She was on one of the many coaches back to Chesterfield – as was I – but, alas, not on mine. I looked for her at other games but never saw her again. *[Sighs deeply and removes tear from cheek.]* Crazy thing is, I never even found out her name! But we had been successful; we'd won the Cup! Yes, won it! I didn't care that it was a bunch of no-marks like Notts County making up the opposition. You can only beat what is put in front of you and, on this occasion, we'd done 'em all. The Anglo-Scottish Cup, in its very last outing, was ours. Yes, and it still is!

We could have stopped with the Anglo-Scottish Cup but, no, that wasn't enough anymore. We had a taste for silverware now and so the reserves gave us another special night by winning the North Midland's League Cup. The trophy cabinet at Chesterfield would be bursting at the seams if the club continued its quest for glory like this. How we hoped they would!

Regrettably, back in the league, it all went horribly wrong. Home draws to Fulham and Swindon before losing away at Brentford saw us slip back and virtually destroy whatever chance we had. Despite winning our last three games, we finished fifth. Our last game that season was a 1–0 home victory over Exeter – and I left Saltergate with my spirits lower than a dwarf's scrotum.

"Will I ever see us get out of this fucking division?" I screamed at anyone who would listen. But no one answered; probably because they were all feeling as pissed off as I was.

In hindsight, which, as we all know, is a wonderful thing, the number of games we played probably cost us our promotion. In the 80/81 season we played 65 games and 30 minutes extra time, which must have been fairly tiring, and I think we only had a squad of around 22 players.

Off the pitch, the club's debts were spiralling. Chairman Ian Gaunt said he had been concerned for some time about the communication between the public and the club and steps would be taken to rectify this. "Relations," he said, "could also be helped if some people would rid themselves of this ridiculous notion that Chesterfield FC do not want promotion."

In fairness to Mr Gaunt, he had given us some of the most attractive football to watch that I'd ever seen. Yes, it had just about bankrupted the club but it had been enjoyable, nonetheless. In fact, looking back now, I still doubt that we've had a side comparable to the one Cox, and then Barlow, assembled.

The only thing wrong with Mr Gaunt's plan was that he had gambled on promotion. It was one of those 'shit or bust' throws of the dice. Alas, we had bust. If we'd got promotion, well, who knows? Gaunt would have been a legend in his own lunch-time. As it turned out, he was just another chairman who was very quick to blame the public when things didn't really pan out. For instance, one of his usual come-backs was that the town didn't support the football club in great enough numbers (something we've heard from other chairmen on an all too frequent basis over the years) but, looking at the home games for the 80/81 season, we had a reasonable attendance – and one the club would give its right arm for now! The average home attendance was 7,331 in the league, with an average of 10,431 in the FA Cup, 4,672 in the League Cup and 8,636 in the Anglo-Scottish Cup – and these are just the home games. Basically, people were coming out to watch Chesterfield more than they ever had before and so it was, perhaps, unfair to lay the blame at the door of the fans.

By the end of May one sensed a shift in the mood. Bonneyman announced that he was unsettled and joined Colin Tartt, Gary Simpson and John Stirk on the 'open to offers' list. Striker Keith Walwyn also rejected new terms, along with Ernie Moss who promptly signed for Port Vale for £15,000. Alan Birch had been on the radar of many clubs for some time and his old boss at Newcastle, Arthur Cox, tabled a bid of £150,000 for him. We refused. Derby offered a similar amount and, at one point, we were all resigned to losing him to the Sheep-shaggers (which would have been terrible for me as I worked with a bunch of the muppets) but, at the eleventh hour, Wolves weighed in with a bid of £200,000 and we accepted. Again with the benefit of hindsight, this was a huge mistake as we got royally shafted by the bastards who, it turned out, actuality had little more than a pot to piss in. Simpson went to Chester for £6,000 and, eventually, Tartt moved to Port Vale for £150,000. You now began to wonder who would actually be left once the clear-out had finished. One thing was certain: we were going to be short of quite a few players come the following season.

From the left Tartt, Bonneyman and Walker celebrate as we cruise to a 6-2 victory at Carlisle in 80/81 (and doesn't the Carlisle player look like Peter Beardsley). The Chesterfield fans go wild in the corner and one town fan (far left) is already over the advertising hoardings!

A Chesterfield fan throws a smoke bomb in the net at Bramhall Lane (circa 1980) And yet everyone looks so innocent! "Who me officer?" I wonder how many times that was said that afternoon?

Mark Kendall – and he looks as if he's come out to play with his frisbee! But keepers always seemed to take to the field with a clutch-bag in those days. As for the cap, well I can't say I ever remember him playing in one like that so can only assume it was a gift from the young scallywags just disappearing back into the crowd

Third Time Lucky?
SEASON 81/82

Over the last few seasons Chesterfield and Sheffield United had been inexplicably joined at the hip when it came down to fixtures, and so it was of no surprise to find ourselves pitted against them once more in the all new Football League Group Cup. After a couple of dismal defeats away at Grimsby and Doncaster, we entertained Sheffield Urinal and drew 1–1. It wasn't a massive crowd compared to what we usually got for the games against them but 4,900 isn't to be sniffed at and it was still enough to make sure the evening went off with something approaching a bang.

The trouble started in the town centre at about 5pm and was still going on when I got there about 7pm. It was the usual story; running battles and smashed-up pubs were the order of the day. Inside the ground, segregation had limited the amount of trouble but it still took place.

It could never be said that the *Derbyshire Times* was a sensationalist newspaper but they did like to 'up the ante' when it came to football violence. I guess there was nothing wrong in them spelling it out. How else could you get the message out that this kind of behaviour wasn't acceptable unless it was printed in foot high letters in the newspaper? Anyway, they gave over the usual column inches for a hell of a night in Chesterfield and they led with the headline: *"Cup Tie Fans On Rampage In Chesterfield Pubs."* The article went something like this:

"Rampaging football hooligans caused damage valued at over £500 to a Chesterfield town centre pub before Friday night's derby cup game with Sheffield United in the Football Group Cup. The landlord at Ye Olde Crooked Spire and his wife were so sickened by the wanton vandalism they are considering moving out of town.

"The trouble started in the Red Lion on Vicar Lane not long after the pub opened at 5.30pm. There was also unruly behaviour in the nearby Hare and Greyhound. They then congregated in the Crooked Spire boasting of their previous exploits. Sensing trouble Mr Hall dialled 999

and awaited police. It was then that trouble flared with glasses smashed and tables turned over and cigarettes, wine and spirits stolen. They even stole four charity boxes; these were found in the toilet where they had been covered in excreta.

"There was some misbehaviour during the game with 2 policemen being assaulted."

Now, forgive me for being cynical but it comes to something when the covering of charity boxes in poo gets more of a write-up than two policemen being assaulted. But, then again, perhaps when you cover football violence it does become a bit samey after a while and having something new to focus on must be viewed as something of a bonus. Having said that, what I can't quite get my head around is why, if you were one of the fans who had stolen the said charity boxes, you would think it a good idea to nip into the toilet and shit on them! I always thought Sheffield United fans were a bit weird and this just confirms it really. Anyone who would nick a blind box with 38p in and then have a dump on it has, in my opinion, a serious mental condition. And, if that's what passes as fun in South Yorkshire then I'm glad I live in Chesterfield where we tend to leave the money in the poor box, take a shit in the toilet and wipe our arses afterwards. Man, we live on the edge!

But the Spireites had a good September, managing to remain unbeaten throughout that month. In fact, our loss at Newport on the opening day of the season was beginning to look like a bit of a blip, and when we went to Reading on October 8th we were seven games unbeaten.

Running From Home

October 10th, 1981 Reading 0 v 2 Chesterfield

My previous journeys to Reading had always proved entertaining for a variety of reasons but this season, apart from winning 2–0 with goals from Crawford and Windridge, it was a pretty tame affair. For once, I had gone to an average football match: off the coach, in the ground, back on the coach, home.

However, it wasn't quite like that for one Chesterfield fan. As he and several of his mates were travelling by car, they decided to stop off in Brackley (near Northampton) for a pint. Feeling pretty good because his team had won, and obviously feeling a little brave because of the beer consumed, the said Spireite approached two women in the pub and started to chat them up. Now, so far, I don't think he's done anything wrong but one of the locals decided that the girls didn't want his company (although, according to the paper, they seemed more than happy with the attention they were receiving). Then, said local, James Green, decided to talk to the girls himself with the intention of drawing them away. The Town fan wasn't amused by his actions and stormed out of the pub but came back moments later, grabbed Green by the pullover and pulled him outside. Mr Green, apparently, tried to restrain the Town fan but still found himself outside. The Chesterfield fan then launched a savage attack on Green who, in an attempt to defend himself, accidently put his arm through a window and severed an artery. At this, the Chesterfield fan grabbed Green and started to bang his head against the door and window.

Green was taken to hospital where he was treated for a severed artery and numerous other cuts and bruises. And the Chesterfield fan fled the scene to a chorus of jubilant cheers from his mates – although perhaps the ones who were supposed to be in his car weren't cheering that loudly. Having made his getaway, the Town fan was picked up by police near Towcester later that evening and charged. However, before he was due to appear in court, he jumped bail and fled to America and wasn't re-arrested until he returned to Britain in August, some ten months later! TEN MONTHS!!! Honestly, the lengths some people will go to to avoid watching Chesterfield!

In his defence (which I'm surprised they allowed him to have) he said he was drunk at the time and had not intended to hurt the man. He also said he'd stopped going to football matches and was attempting to mend his ways. (Of course he'd stopped going to football games: he'd been out of the country for ten months!) If you were playing devil's advocate, then you might say the guy who was beaten up was asking for trouble. I mean, would you go up and vie for the attention of a couple of women if they were already chatting to someone else? I know I wouldn't. It's seen as pretty bad form, to be fair, even these days, but to try that on with a drunken football supporter back in the 80's... Well, you pretty much get what you ask for in those circumstances.

Back on the football pitch, any self-respecting, pessimistic Town fan (is there any other kind?) knew that our enterprising start wouldn't last. We hoped it would but, I suppose, deep down we knew it wouldn't. This side wasn't half as good as the one we'd had in the last two seasons and, after countless years of disappointment, we knew it was all too good to be true. Even an eight-game, unbeaten run wasn't enough to make us think that we had what it took. The bubble was bound to burst at some point. Wasn't it? Yes, of course it was. But, as we entered January, and with 19 games gone, we still had the top spot. This was awful: we were starting to believe; daring to hope.

I didn't make many journeys away from home that season but one game I wanted to go to – mainly because it was a new ground for me – was the away game at Fulham and I'd be able to see for myself whether we were flattering to deceive or real promotion candidates. So, on that cool January day, I boarded the coach to London. It was interesting, to say the least.

A Little Bit Of Cottaging

January 30th, 1982 Fulham 1 v 0 Chesterfield

Before anyone says anything, this is still the same book. I have not changed sexual persuasion or hobbies but I am at a loss as to how to describe my trip to Craven Cottage. This was one of those games that we knew would be tight; but a win would really make us look like we were actual promotion candidates yet again because, as things stood, we still seemed to be in a bit of a false position.

I made the journey down to Fulham with my usual travelling companions at that time: John Day, Pete Chappell and Paul Higginbottom. (We had to invite Higgy because it was *his* mum who made such good sandwiches.) We arrived there nice and early and tried desperately to find something resembling a safe and hospitable hostelry with decent beer but we drew a blank and ended up just ambling up and down by the side of the River Thames on a cold January day.

The game was fairly even, although we created very little in the way of scoring chances. Having said that, we weren't exactly put under a great deal of pressure either. It had all the hallmarks of a very predictable 0–0 draw, right up until the point that John Turner rushed out of his goal to collect a ball he could never reach. It was also a ball their striker couldn't have done much with; well, not unless the idiot goalie you're playing against comes streaking out of goal in order to make life that much easier for you! That really was about the sum of it, as I remember. Their striker stroked the ball home from an acute angle, made less difficult by the fact that the goal was empty, and suddenly the 0–0 draw would have been very welcome indeed.

Afterwards, cursing John Turner for such a catastrophic error, we trooped out of the ground, back to the buses, expecting nothing more than a long and tedious journey back to Derbyshire. Again, that would actually have been very welcome. Instead, we were met in the car park by a gang of Fulham hoodlums. I paid them no attention; there were more of them than us and they looked a lot more aggressive than we were (which wasn't difficult). I was also in such a crap mood that I just wanted to get on the bus and sulk, which is exactly what I did.

Finding my seat on the bus, I stared out into the blank wasteland of the car park, wondering what that one piece of goalkeeping madness would do to our season. The seats around me started to fill up quickly but I paid little attention until my reverie was shattered by a brick coming through the window with more than an alarming smash! There was a moment of stunned, shocked silence as we all spat out pieces of glass and tried to shake it out of our hair. (I actually had hair in those days!) And then it happened. I'm still not quite sure why but I suddenly acted totally out of character: I screamed at the Fulham supporters congregating around our now missing window, leapt from my seat and headed for the door, issuing all manner of threats. Things like, "I'm going to kill you, you bastards," were clearly audible to others. Apparently, I was like some kind of rabid dog, with spittle and foam spewing out of my mouth, and, according to my friends, had to be literally dragged back to my seat, which I think was a good and sensible thing as that bunch of wild animals outside would have torn me limb from limb!

To this day I cannot account for my actions during this minor altercation. My memory of it is vivid but it's as if scenes are missing. I remember getting out of my seat but, *me*, threaten other fans? I think not. Well, not usually, but it just shows what can happen when your goalkeeper makes a huge error.

The *Derbyshire Times* did comment on the incident. The report said:

"Bricks and cans were thrown when rampaging Fulham supporters clashed with 3 coach-loads of Chesterfield fans after Saturday's game at Craven Cottage. One coach from Branson's of Brampton had a side

window smashed and another had the emergency door forced open. The incident happened immediately outside the ground where the coaches were parked. No one was injured but Chesterfield fan Dave Radford acted like a prize dick." (That last bit might be made up!)

I do remember it being a very cold journey going up the M1 back home and all we could do to stop the blast of cold air from freezing our gonads off was to hang a large Chesterfield Union Jack flag over the window. It did very little, in fairness, but the thought was there. Once in town, we settled in the *Fleece* and had a couple of single malts to warm us up before getting the bus home. Come to think of it, I don't think Higgy ever did get his round in!

Club In Turmoil

Around the time of the Fulham trip, the club announced losses of £345,000 over the previous two years. Once again, Chairman Ian Gaunt said that the town needed to back the club or they would be forced to sell, and I quote, "star players." Someone who called himself 'Ex-Fan' responded admirably to this statement when he asked, in a letter to the *Derbyshire Times*, "just who these star players are."

Attendances were down despite the club being top and so the *Derbyshire Times* decided to ask the supporters what *they* thought. They probably wished they hadn't bothered because while most people recognised we were top, they also recognised it wouldn't last because we were, quite simply, awful.

In February we dropped to third after a defeat at Carlisle and, apart from getting 'mullered' 5–1 in our following game at Portsmouth, the only thing of note that month was the goal by Alan Crawford in the 2–2 home draw with Plymouth. We kicked off the second half at 1–1 and Crawford beat what seemed to be the entire Plymouth side from the kick-off before chipping exquisitely into the net. In fact, I think he beat perhaps three or four of them but it was a stunning run and goal, and worthy of all the points. But, once again, we couldn't hang on to claim all 3 points.

Despite Bonneyman being unsettled at the start of the season, he'd managed to be ever present during the season. This couldn't be said of Geoff Salmons who'd been ordered by doctors to take a three-week rest from playing football. Because of this, Geoff thought it was unfair that the club should pay his wages during this period of inactivity and so he asked not to be paid! Can you imagine that happening now? What a legend that man was.

In March I travelled to Brentford, mainly because someone had told me there was a pub on every corner and I was eager to try all four. As it happened, I managed to try just one, a great little *Fullers* pub, and the beer was delicious. In retrospect, I wish I'd stayed there because, from a Chesterfield perspective, the match was dire. We lost 2–0 in the March sunshine and the best bit was the banter with some local girls. Oh, how we laughed when one of them fell off the stanchion she was sitting on. Oh, how *they* laughed when we lost! I would have fallen off a stanchion quite happily had it meant we could win the game but, alas, it doesn't work like that. However, come the end of March, results in other games meant we were still third. We still had a chance. Never had a side so certain to miss out on promotion hung on for so long.

Unfortunately, defeats to Lincoln, Gillingham and Burnley left us in sixth place and suddenly we were soccer's 'nearly men' once again. Supporters were now rueing a fairly miserable hat-trick of near misses. It was, quite simply, a case of 'close but no cigar.' The *Derbyshire Times*, like vampires eager to suck on our misery, swung into action conducting street polls of the club's supporters and the general consensus was that we weren't as hungry for success as our rivals. Even before the season had ended, the *DT* appeared to be championing the removal of Ian Gaunt as chairman. They ran with the headline, **"Blues Fans Go All Out For Change,"** and it was made to sound like they had the opinion of the 4,000 who turned up week in, week out. In actual fact, this was the opinion of just two Chesterfield supporters. One of them, Peter Stockton, said: *"All the fans I have spoken to are disgusted at the way the club is being run. The Board have no vision and no idea how to raise money. Mr Gaunt should step down in favour of Mike Watterson, he is a Chesterfield supporter and always has been. If he could organise the world of snooker, he could organise Chesterfield from top to bottom."*

It was an interesting concept, I suppose, but there were holes in Mr Stockton's argument. To say the club had no vision, after allowing Arthur Cox to break the club's transfer record on more than one occasion, was a slight over-reaction. Admittedly, the Board may well have been clueless when it came to raising extra revenue but that point could be made about every board of directors that has ever been in charge at

Saltergate. This fan's criticism of the Board and, indeed, of Mr Gaunt was, perhaps, a knee-jerk reaction to yet another failed promotion attempt. I'd been a Chesterfield fan for 20 short years and thought I'd suffered enough pain in those years than it was fair to inflict on anyone at any time. (If only I'd known how much more was to follow!)

The only person who seemed to talk any sense at the end of it all was the manager, Frank Barlow. He openly admitted that he'd failed and he knew that many saw him as a weak manager. Personally, I thought there was something about Frank Barlow that you couldn't help but like. He was a genuinely nice bloke. I always remember seeing Frank walking his dog near where I used to play football on a Sunday morning. He would stop and watch for a while and I would always allow myself to dream of him stopping me and saying, *"You're just the kind of right back I'm looking for."* But he never did. He watched, probably realised that however bad it got in his job it was never going to be this bad, and then his dog would eventually drag him away.

The sports post-bag in the *Derbyshire Times* was crammed with letters from all manner of disgusted and disgruntled Town fans. One, from a bunch of Centre Stand season ticket holders, suggested that all directors should retire at 65 and make way for young, successful businessmen who had played the game and desperately wanted the club to succeed. (Bit of a tall order, I thought.) But they continued, saying that anyone sitting in the directors' box should pay £250 for the privilege – that would get rid of the hangers-on. And I can agree with that.

The odd thing, though, was that the week after being tipped to be Chesterfield's new supremo, Mike Watterson went into press, hitting out at Chesterfield's "fair-weather fans" for not supporting the club. He went on to say that he fully supported Mr Gaunt. Now, there was a dagger in the back if ever I've seen one.

We ended the season with chants of, *"Sack the Board,"* and a letter in the *Derbyshire Times* saying, *"Everyone is to blame."* (Well, it would have been churlish to miss anyone out, wouldn't it?)

It's Hard Going Up, Son,
But Twice As Hard Coming Down
SEASON 82/83

Season 82/83 started with an off-the-field wrangle that was pretty similar to how the previous season had finished really, the only difference being that this was a different wrangle. I suppose that if there was a prize for off-field wrangling then we would have been promoted and cup winners twice over! Instead, we were just headline fodder.

This particular off-field controversy involved Wolves, Derek Dougan and Alan Birch (and not necessarily in that order). Basically, we'd been stitched up by Wolves. Out of the promised £200,000 transfer fee for Alan Birch we were still owed around £80,000 and they had made a verbal agreement to pay the outstanding amount in full. However, they then denied to the Football League they had made this agreement with us, and they obviously believed them, and we remained one of their creditors. As we still owed money to Leicester City, we were now prevented by the League from signing anyone.

Wolves were currently under the mismanagement of a board of directors led by their old striker and resident ugly bastard, Derek Dougan. Now, I've never particularly liked Dougan; didn't *like* him as a 'footballer' (and I use the word loosely to describe the hopeless, inept lump) and now he'd actually given me reason to *hate* him! Hating him was really easy, if not essential. He was an arrogant, self-assured, big, ugly, bug-eyed twat of a man who had all the charm of five-year-old chip fat. To be fair, his consortium didn't stop at trying to stitch up small clubs like Chesterfield. Oh no. Mr Dougan was out to stitch up as many football clubs as he possibly could. He'd even managed to pull one over near neighbours Birmingham City, which must have gone down really well. I can't say I'll forget Mr Dougan in a hurry, and if someone is reading this to you, you illiterate bag of shite, just remember you'll never be welcome in these parts. And if I ever see you in Chesterfield High Street then you can rest assured the chances are I'll take something out of your begging bowl rather than put something in! (Phew! I've waited 28 years to get that off my chest. Perhaps I can move on now.)

On the field, Bonneyman, Ridley, Crawford, Hunter and Salmons had all gone; and with Phil Walker saying he wanted to go, too, the future didn't look bright. In our first seven games of the season we won just one and managed two 0–0 draws. We were anchored to the bottom of the league. It was of no surprise, therefore, that attendances had slipped to an all-time low. The *Derbyshire Times*, seemingly aware that last year's attempts at slagging off the Board hadn't met with much success, came at this particular crisis from a different angle. Suddenly they wanted to know where all the stay-away fans had gone and pleaded with them to write in and let them know why they no longer attended. They must have been expecting a bumper crop of letters which they could then use against the club but, since they printed just three of them, one of which supported the club during this hard time, it would appear that most of Saltergate's missing fans must also have been missing a pen!

But the club rallied, despite having a nothing side, and moved clear of the relegation positions. We even managed our ritual humiliation of Sheffield United, hammering them 3–1 on December 27th, which was about the best Christmas present you could have given me at the time. However, it didn't last and our form slipped alarmingly. Come the end of January, we found ourselves sixth from the bottom. Most Chesterfield supporters knew that this season was going to end disastrously. We looked like a relegated side most of the time but there was the odd bright moment, like being 3–0 down at Doncaster and then coming back to draw 3–3. But the writing had been on the wall from the start of the season, really.

Because of his exploits in the loan market and his ability to cobble together a side from the cast-offs of other clubs, the *Derbyshire Times* dubbed Frank Barlow *"The Loan Arranger"* which was a pretty smart and nifty play on words, even for them. According to Stuart Basson's club history, we used 28 players that season which was unheard of at the time. It was a ridiculous amount of players to bring into the side on a short-term basis and expect them to form any sort of rapport. Having said that, by some managerial standards 28 is a drop in the ocean!

Mike Watterson, who had been tipped by many and heralded as the man most likely to step in and save us from the current board of directors, took over total control of Derby County, instead. So much for him being a Chesterfield fan, then. But, from my perspective, they were welcome to him – and he was welcome to them. Just because you can organise a snooker match doesn't mean you know how to run a football club. Look at Darren Brown, Chesterfield's ex-chairman. By all accounts he was a great photocopier salesman but it turns out he knew jack-shit about running a business. (Well, knew jack-shit about running one properly. If you want to run one crookedly, then he's your man!)

By March we were fourth from the bottom and staring relegation quite squarely in the mush. As if facing relegation with crippling debts wasn't bad enough, Cardiff came to town on April 30th and ran amok. This was the second time this band of slavering savages had kicked off in Chesterfield, to my recollection. The difference was that the first time there was an unruly mob of Chesterfield fans all ready to fight back but this time there was very little resistance indeed. In fact, it was so one-sided that some Cardiff fans took to turning over empty market stalls! It seemed rather surreal at the time – almost as if they were at a loss for something to do. I remember walking carefully by and thinking how foolish it all looked. (But, then, you could say that about any football violence, really.) However, according to the paper, the violence wasn't quite so frivolous in other areas of town. On Stevenson's Place, for instance, one teenager was smacked in the face without provocation because, as the Cardiff fan said in court, the boy had been looking at him. WOW!!! Poor kid hadn't even been to the bloody game. But windows were smashed, cars were damaged and, in total, the rampaging mob was fined over £2,000. On top of this, the defeat sealed our relegation. Could things really have got any worse?

The *Derbyshire Times*, who had been guilty of kicking the club when they were staggering, I thought, decided that now they were down they'd offer them a crutch and, for once, were fully behind the club as we entered the last game of the season – at home to Millwall. The paper issued a rallying call to all supporters, urging them to show the board of directors they really did care and really did want a football club in the town. The paper argued that, with the club relegated, then a crowd of around 1,500 would be expected; anything in excess of that would prove to the directors that the club was worth saving. Personally, I didn't think the directors should need proof: they were partly to blame for the situation and had seen supporters turn up in their thousands over the last three years. Having said that, when I checked out Stuart Basson's history of the club, I was amazed and very proud to see that a total of

4,500 had turned up for the game. *"Good old Town fans,"* I thought... until I read the *DT* which said that some 3,000 supporters had come up from Millwall!

It was a strange Saturday. Violence kicked off early when 50 Man United fans broke their journey to Nottingham with a punch-up in Chesterfield. (Hadn't we suffered enough?) According to the police, they clashed with both Chesterfield and Millwall fans, although my guess is that they got more action from the latter. If memory serves me correctly, Millwall still had an outside chance of going down but, by beating us in that final game, it meant that all their worries were washed away. To celebrate staying up, they invaded the pitch and then got into all kinds of ghastly mischief after the final whistle.

But it mattered not one jot to me. I left the ground feeling thoroughly deflated. Another season was done and dusted and, yet, I couldn't shake off that awful feeling of dread that accompanies the drop. It was made somewhat worse by the fact that we'd gained just 2 points from our last nine games and had surrendered our Division 3 status with a whimper rather than having gone out kicking and screaming as we should have done. The club's debts were now so large they were making front page news, in the *Derbyshire Times* at least. Tough times lay ahead.

Relegation is horrible. It is one of the worst feelings in the world. All the time and effort you've invested in the club you love seems wasted. But football is a capricious mistress and as quickly as she takes all hope away, she gives you fresh hope with the start of a new season. If only women were like that!

We Started Out With Nothing And We Still Had Most Of It Left
SEASON 83/84

Last season was a disaster: we'd dropped from Division 3 like a stone attached to an anvil and it was going to need something pretty amazing to turn things around. Players were released and Barlow was expected to have just seven professionals available for the start of the season. There were rumours that various people were interested in buying the club but nothing happened. Then, just when all seemed lost, the club was bought by that famous Arab zillionaire, Sheik Ya Moneymaker. He promised to put squillions of his own money into the club, and we would be in Division 1 inside four seasons, and we would be champions of Europe in five... and then I woke up. Yes, it had all been a dream. Or had it?

On June 10th the club was taken over by *Transworld Publications* and one Sheik Barry Hubbard would be chairman. Baz was a printing magnet from Brimington (by that I don't mean you could stick him to fridge doors) and he said he wanted the club to have better association with the supporters. (Mmmm, I'm saying nowt, as they say.) There was some speculation – and a degree of panic from supporters – that Emlyn Hughes, who had just been sacked by Rotherscum, would be the new boss but, in the end, a certain John Duncan, "a promising young manager" who had recently left Scunthorpe, got the job. Although Frank Barlow was offered a position as Duncan's number two, he turned it down as he thought the club deserved a clean break. He was also concerned that his entire back room staff had been sacked and, so, to take on the job would have felt wrong. As I said earlier, Frank Barlow was, at the very least, a thoroughly decent bloke.

Duncan's first signing was John Clayton, and he followed this up by putting in a £4,000 bid for Steve Spooner from Halifax Town. They laughed at such a derisory figure, claiming Spooner was worth ten times that amount. Eventually, a tribunal decided he was worth £11,500 and Halifax huffed and puffed but, ultimately, couldn't do a thing about it. Utility man Brian Scrimgeour came from Dundee and JD entered into talks with Steve Baines at Scunthorpe regarding the position of player/coach with Chesterfield. There were also rumours about a return for Les Hunter.

There were also comings and not so many goings on the director front. Mike Watterson became a director in the July, along with Danny Kelly who had a plant hire business in Nether Handley. Now, as we currently rent our business premises from the latter and as he's just put our rent up by over 50%, I have no intention of incurring his wrath and saying anything derogatory about him in here. Mike Watterson, on the other hand, well, where does one start? Many had wanted him as 'chair' for a couple of seasons, obviously believing that being able to promote a snooker tournament made him just the man for the job. Big Baz clearly believed Watterson could do some kind of job – and he came to Chesterfield at last. To say Mike Watterson's credentials as a director were capricious is something of an understatement. He'd started out as a director of Sheffield United and had lasted just five months! After that, he packed his snooker case and became chairman at Derby, a role he managed to hang on to for eight months. However, he said that he did intend to be vice chair of Chesterfield FC for a little longer. Oh, well, that's alright then. For a minute I thought you were just in it for the kudos.

Early in July we completed the signing of Steve Baines and Steve Waddington and a midfielder called John Black who I don't think ever actually pulled on a blue shirt in anger. For me, however, July was dominated by a tale of split lips and broken teeth. I'd actually forgotten all about this until reading through some back issues of the *Derbyshire Times* but, when I saw one particular article, I actually cringed as I recalled the pain and, most of all, the cost. The headline in the sports section read: ***"Brave Dave Is Cricket Club Hero."*** In short, I had an altercation with a cricket ball which left me with multiple stitches in my lips and a wobbly front tooth. (This was in the day when cricketers were men and wearing a helmet was frowned upon; in fact, I doubt they'd been invented. Oh, no. Why bother with a helmet when you can have brain damage!) The hero bit was because, on my return to the cricket match after leaving the hospital, I took seven wickets, all without appealing as my mouth was still frozen from the anaesthetic I'd had for the stitches. The *Derbyshire Times* ended the report with the fabulous line: *"Dave returned to sew up victory."* Brilliant! Anyhow, despite career-best bowling figures (up to that point, anyway) and a write-up in the *DT*, I was more concerned about my front tooth which my dentist eventually informed me would have to come out.

As we moved into August, my wobbly tooth was replaced by a temporary denture and, bit by bit, my scars started to heal. I still wasn't happy at having to pay out hundreds of pounds for dental work, though, and thought the tight bastards at Wingerworth Cricket Club could have had some form of insurance, at least, to cover my ass. But they didn't, so I put my pads in my bag and decided I'd play for a team that did have such insurance in place. I suppose the words 'stable,' 'horse' and 'bolted' spring to mind here but, then, a broken man has to do what a broken man has to do. Nevertheless, apart from my temporary denture, I was feeling good again and starting to think about football.

According to the press, Duncan was eager to sign former Chesterfield favourite Alan Birch who was now at Barnsley. They had apparently turned down an offer of £40,000 but eventually caved in when we offered £45,000. Duncan also signed midfielder Brian Klug from Ipswich on a month's loan but he hoped it would become a permanent deal. To top it off, we also signed Winston White! "Who?!" was the collective shout from more or less every Chesterfield fan at the time. To complete the off-field dealings, Kevin Randall was recruited as coach and Barry Watson, Chesterfield's very own potato king, was appointed to the Board. This was viewed with raised eyebrows but was also seen as a shrewd move as Barry Watson was a well-known Chesterfield fan and a proper fan at that, the 'stands-on-the-terraces-and-sings-songs' type of fan. For Chesterfield, getting someone like Barry onto the Board was seen as something of a breakthrough in Board/supporter relations.

It was obvious that a major rebuilding and restructuring operation was going on at Saltergate; bigger by far than the one the dentist was going to have to do on my shattered mouth. I just hoped that both the directors and dentist would perform as well as they had promised.

And so it was that on August 27th we kicked off and beat Swindon 1–0, with Alan Birch doing the honours. I mention this, not because we were brilliant – in fact, we were far from it – but because this is where the story of my temporary denture and how I came by it meets up with football. Well, kind of. I was still getting used to this single tooth on a plate in the bottom of my mouth. It moved around and tipped up if you bit into anything. I also had an annoying habit of pushing my tongue under it if ever I was nervous, tilting the tooth forward in my mouth. (Sounds disgusting, doesn't it?) Now, to be fair, I'm always nervous when I'm watching Chesterfield and, with my tongue under the plate as we attacked the Swindon goal during the first game, Birch scored. I leapt into the air with my customary celebration yell of 'YEEEEAAAAAA!!!' and watched in horror as my temporary denture shot from my mouth and hit the bloke in front of me on the back of the head. I then spent five minutes scrabbling around on my hands and knees looking for one white tooth on a pink plastic plate! On finding it I was then faced with the dilemma of whether to put it in my pocket or slip it nonchalantly back into my mouth. I wasn't sure which was worse: the thought of the germs it had picked up on its travels around Saltergate or what people might have thought of me with a gap where a tooth should have been. In the end, vanity prevailed and I slipped the offending article back into my mouth. Both the points and my tooth were safe – but only because we never looked like scoring again.

However, just to show that the result wasn't a fluke, in the midweek we went and played Middlesbrough in the League Cup First Leg and won 1–0 at Ayresome Park with Steve Baines giving us that all-important win. With Middlesbrough being a division higher, this gave everyone a massive lift. Perhaps this really was *the* season?

Nothing ever happens at Crewe.........

Well, it doesn't, does it? You go there, usually get hammered by a good footballing side and then come home. There has never, ever, ever, been any trouble at Crewe. Well, not until September 3rd, 1983 that is. Yes, we got beat, as was expected, but quite what happened to the Chesterfield fans that day I can't tell you. Needless to say, although segregated from the home supporters by a good-sized fence, the Chesterfield fans did all they could to break it down. At half-time Hubbard and Watterson had to come onto the terraces and appeal for calm, such was the rabid mood among the masses. The thought of Hubbard strolling through a bunch of Town hoodlums – like Jesus attempting to pour oil on troubled waters – still makes me giggle. But, all in all, it was a completely farcical day and I have to say that, apart from that one time, I have still never known anything happening at Crewe.

We were a team possessed, though. Not only were the crowds up but we also managed our first penalty shoot-out success; it came in the second leg of the League Cup at Saltergate. Middlesbrough beat us 1–0, sending the game into extra time and then penalties. Klug, Bellamy, Bell and O'Neill (scoring his first goal in eight seasons) put us 4–3 up. Brown waited nervously in goal and then pulled off a fantastic save to his right in front of the Kop. All Alan Birch had to do was score (let's face it, scripts like this were written for the little man) and he managed it so convincingly, sending us through to a two-legged tie with Everton in the next round.

.........or at Northampton

Now, I've been to Northampton many times and never felt in the slightest bit worried by the events unfolding in front of me. And so it was on October 1st, 1983. There was a goodly following of Chesterfield fans on the steep, open away end (this was when they played at the rather fabulous, three-sided cricket ground). However, soon after the start of the game it became noticeable that all was not well on the home end and quite a ruck had broken out. According to the press, about 25 Chesterfield fans had gone onto the Hotel End (Northampton kop) and confronted the home fans. A policeman was punched in the face, twice, as he tried to separate rival fans. The ringleader was led away with the assistance of several other officers. In court, the Town fan said in his defence that he'd been directed to the wrong end of the ground; it was the first time he'd been to Northampton so he didn't know which end was for the away fans. (Perhaps he didn't notice the massive signs saying 'Home fans only.') He apologised for what he'd done but said he was simply trying to protect himself. Back in Chesterfield there were unconfirmed reports that someone from Northampton had been stabbed that day but there was nothing in the papers about it and I feel that something like that might just have made the headlines. The game finished 1–1 thanks to an Alan Birch goal and just three days later we were due to entertain Everton in the Football League Milk Cup.

The Everton fixture drew over 10,000 to Saltergate and, to be fair, they got a bit of a fright. Yes, they beat us 1–0 but they weren't that good and we could see that an upset really would have been possible if only we'd carried more of a threat up front. Clayton was okay but we weren't scoring enough goals and we needed someone who would stick the ball in from 6 yards. Duncan must have been having similar thoughts because, before we even went to Everton, he nipped in and signed the legend that is Bob Newton from Port Vale. In fairness, he cost next to nothing as we somehow managed to convince Port Vale that Henderson was a decent striker so they agreed to take him and £10,000 and everyone was happy – particularly Bob who was a local lad returning to play for his local team.

I remember Bob's debut away at Rochdale as if it were yesterday. There were only 1,700 at the game but it appeared as if most of them were from Chesterfield. Bob plundered two majestic goals before racing over to the bank of Chesterfield fans and standing before us with his arms outstretched as if he was our saviour. It was quite a divine moment and, at that point, I think we would all have gladly followed him to the ends of the earth, which says more about us as success-starved fans than it does about 'The Newt.' By the end of October we were sixth. Things were looking good.

Truncheoned

Football League Cup Second Round, Second Leg

November 4th, 1983 Everton 2 v 2 Chesterfield

I hate Everton. I said that to my mate Richard once and he replied, "Mate, you hate every fucker. Is there one other football club that you can honestly say you like?"

I thought hard about this and eventually said, "Well, I don't have any really bad feelings about West Brom but that's only because we've never played them and I've never been chased, threatened or beaten up by their fans. But, as for the rest, I just hate 'em!"

He laughed. But the thing is: it *is* true. So, this is the story of how and why I hate Everton.

Despite being impressive in our home leg of this match against what was, at the time, a very poor Everton side, no one ever thought we really had a chance in this one. A good following of Chesterfield fans made the journey, mostly because they wanted to go to a ground they hadn't been to before coupled with the fact that this was also a great opportunity to take the piss out of their diminutive striker, Adrian Heath. What other incentives could you possibly want?

We travelled to Merseyside by supporters' club coach. The journey itself was surreal as a bunch of us from Wingerworth went up with a lad who, although being an Everton fan, had decided to support the Spireites on this occasion. Now, Nige wasn't just an Everton fan by name, he used to go and watch them every week; so it was quite something for him to nail his colours to *our* mast for the evening. And, for some reason, as well as being an Everton fan and part-time Chesterfield fan, Nige took a great interest in the 'old firm' derbies in Scotland. Apparently, Merseyside was as split in its allegiance to these clubs as it was to their own, and Nigel had come down heavily on the Rangers side. So, as we made our way north-west that evening, Nigel kept us entertained with stories of the encounters he'd seen north of the border. He also started to teach us the outrageously bigoted songs that both sets of fans would taunt each other with during the game. So we spent a bizarre and somewhat surreal journey singing songs I neither knew nor understood (and, to be honest, never wanted to understand).

As we got off the coach in Everton we were met by those friendly Scouse bobbies as well as some not so friendly ones on horseback. It was odd. When 70 coach-loads of us turned up at Liverpool a few seasons back the police were conspicuous by their absence but, here, there were about 800 of us and anyone would have thought a mafia war was about to kick off! Talk about getting it wrong. In many ways it showed that there were still inconsistencies in the policing of football matches. Yes, there was still trouble but you always got the feeling that the police would eventually get it under control. So, by and large, things were a whole lot better. Tonight, for example, didn't need a great deal of policing: show us the turnstiles, let us in and sit back and enjoy the evening. It should have been that simple but, then, some people like to make sure it never is.

As we walked along the road, all laughing and joking and daring to conjure up images of Town turning Everton over, no one would have guessed it was a football match. We were just happy travellers, glad to be off the coach and pleased to be heading in the general direction of the football ground. However, a policeman on horseback quite near to me kept barking out orders for us to stay on the pavement. In some respects there was nothing wrong with that request; nothing at all, if it's a wide pavement and you're all being given enough room to walk on it.

But, unfortunately, it wasn't and the police weren't. They had us all crammed up so tight that something was always going to give.

People were stepping on one another's heels and trying desperately to make the best of a bad situation. I slipped off the edge of the pavement a couple of times before thinking it would be much easier to walk on the road rather than risk torn ankle ligaments. I know I wasn't physically on the pavement as instructed but, then, neither was I running around Everton with my dick out shouting, *"Come and 'ave a go if you think yer 'ard enough!"* I was more or less in the gutter and honestly thought I was being sensible. It was then that the copper on the horse hit me. Perhaps 'hit' is something of an understatement as the moron (and I apologise but there is no other word for this) twatted me with his truncheon! It wasn't your ordinary, short, bulbous number; it was a long one, specially made so policemen on horseback could crack out beatings without having to dismount. He literally pulled it back and smashed me round the head with said stick and screamed, "I said get on the fuckin' pavement!" Only he said it in scouse so it sounded nothing like that. In my head I said, *"Why don't you die, you fat fuck."* I had tears in my eyes, genuine tears, because of the terrifying pain this weapon had brought down upon my skull. And, with that, I quickly got back on the pavement as instructed, the side of my head ringing as a result of the crack that had just been so severely dealt to me. My ear was burning so ferociously because of the pain that I thought it was going to self-combust. If I'd been any trouble before the smack with the truncheon then, let me assure you, I was a hell of a lot less trouble afterwards.

What an idiot that policeman was, though. Seriously, what an absolute jerk. He's probably dead by now or, at least, I can but hope he is. He probably tossed himself to sleep that night thinking about how he'd battered some defenceless idiot from Chesterfield round the head with the big stick the nice man at the station had given him. (Believe me, writing about this is like therapy: you wouldn't believe how quickly and angrily I've written this last piece.) And I suppose it was situations like this that made you question if anyone who policed football matches actually knew what they were doing at all.

So, with face ablaze, they let me and the rest of the Chesterfield contingent into the away end. Unlike the Liverpool debacle, we actually had a collection of turnstiles to choose from and we were all well positioned for the kick-off. We were expecting a rousing Town performance but that started to look a million miles away when Adrian Heath put them up about five minutes into the game. It's always the case, isn't it? You want to take the piss out of someone but before you get started he goes and scores a goal, which kind of makes your taunts all seem quite stupid, doesn't it? However, not being ones to bow down to any form of convention, we decided to take the piss out of him anyway and, in a rather camp, limp-wristed voice (if you can have such a thing), we all began to sing, *"Adrian, Adrian, Adrian,"* while simultaneously drooping our wrists in an overly emphatic, gay manner. It was hilarious! About 500 of us all chanting the name 'Adrian' as if we were on a gay pride march rather than being at a football match. It was a very surreal evening, indeed.

Before you could blink, though, we were 2–0 down and the rousing come-back was now just a dream. But, just as we were resigning ourselves to another cup exit, Brian Scrimgeour lashed the ball home from the edge of the box to give us something at least to cheer. And, no sooner had we settled our voices than someone was up-ended in the box and Birch stepped up to make it 2–2 on the night. With about ten minutes to go, this could be one hell of a come-back. Unfortunately, Everton held out as we swarmed all over them for the final ten minutes of the game. They managed to go through in front of what I believe was their lowest-ever crowd and they were booed off, too, while we cheered and sung as if we'd won! I suppose we had the moral victory.

Fortunately, however, my journey back to the bus was uninterrupted by policemen or their weapons. But I shall never forget the miserable fuck who decided to smash me round the head just for walking!

Into 1984

After what had been an exceptionally bright start to the season, we had slipped to 19th in the table with a steady stream of indifferent performances. We desperately needed a win to keep us away from the arse end of the division.

Second Time Around

February 4th, 1984 Chesterfield 2 v 1 Northampton

God, this was an odd one and no mistake. It should have been one of those regulation games. You know, the ones where you walk up to the ground, have a laugh with your mates, cheer at the result and then walk home with a smile. No one really expected anything else. The crowd was a less than enthusiastic 3,250 but, given our current form and the team we were playing, it was as good as we could have hoped for.

So, there I am, standing in the Kop, chatting to friends, all of us minding our own business, when all hell breaks loose. Suddenly, there's boots and fists flying everywhere and general panic sets in among everyone. I wanted to run but, as usual, wasn't sure where to go and so, consequently, stood still and watched as it all unfolded in front of me. To me, it looked as if a mob of Northampton fans had invaded the Kop, couldn't find many people to fight, so started on the police instead. A WPC went down in a heap on the pitch and I swear I saw someone wielding a toilet chain. Eventually, the Northampton fans were pushed away from the Kop by the police and we were left with the very startling image of a prone and motionless woman constable. St John's Ambulance were quick to assist, as were Chesterfield fans to be honest, and the WPC was stretchered out of the ground.

Quite what sparked this off, no one knew. Was it revenge for what had happened earlier in the season? Again, there didn't appear to be any real answers, although the *Derbyshire Times* did cover the carnage in full:

"WPC Kicked Unconscious In Pitch Battle

"*A policewoman was kicked unconscious by rioting football hooligans at Saltergate, minutes before the start of the match between Chesterfield and Northampton. WPC Tart was beaten senseless by a 100 strong gang of rampaging thugs as she tried bravely to stop the pitch invasion before the start of the 4th division game. Her policeman husband Jeff, who was on duty outside the ground, knew nothing of the attack until he saw his unconscious wife being taken away on a stretcher. Four other policemen received injuries as rival fans fought running battles on the pitch.*"

The latter part is, perhaps, the only bit I'd take issue with in the *Derbyshire Times*. I didn't see it as running battles between rival fans. To me, it looked very one-sided indeed – and that side wasn't us. I'd been watching Chesterfield FC for long enough and, more importantly, I'd been watching the behaviour of the club's supporters to feel I could say with a degree of confidence that if they *had been* there then they would have been only too pleased to have got involved. On this occasion, though, it appeared to be the Northampton thugs against the police. There *was* scuffling between fans but I would have called it minimal rather than 'running battles.'

The report in the *Derbyshire Times* went on to say:

"WPC Tart (27) regained consciousness 20 minutes later in Chesterfield Royal Hospital where she was detained for head and chest injuries. Twenty seven fans – all but one from Northampton – were arrested. The rioters left a trail of devastation in their wake and caused damage totalling several hundred pounds to the Chesterfield ground.

"Trouble erupted again in the 83rd minute and the game had to be stopped when another gang of supporters invaded the pitch. Chesterfield FC secretary Bob Pepper said, 'These are not football fans – they didn't come to watch the game. We do not want them to come to Saltergate again.' Chairman Barry Hubbard said it was a mystery why Northampton fans arrived at Saltergate in such large numbers. Northampton expected one coach load of supporters and about ten cars to come to Chesterfield, which is normal for their away games. But coaches arrived from Peterborough, Corby and Milton Keynes, and Northampton were as surprised as anyone.

"The chairman praised the Saltergate regulars for their behaviour and for not responding. [Oh, Barry, it was nothing; trust me, I found it very easy.] *The players held a dressing room collection and the directors and management also had a collection and each sent a bouquet of flowers and a basket of fruit to WPC Tart.*

"Some time later a Northampton Town fan was jailed for his part in the violence that day. The fork lift truck driver told Derby Crown Court that he and 60 other fans invaded the pitch before the start of the game to fight with Chesterfield fans. He said he lashed out with his fists and WPC Tart stepped into his path and was hit in the face. The policewoman then fell to the ground and was savagely kicked by several other hooligans. He pleaded guilty to actual bodily harm but said he had not kicked the policewoman and that he had actually caught her on the shoulder and not in the face. 'I was trying to hit a Chesterfield fan,' he said. He was sentenced to 4 days in prison." (To be honest, if you manage to knock someone out for 20 minutes by hitting them on the shoulder then you pack one hell of a punch!)

One of the other Northampton fans appearing before the court pleaded guilty to criminal damage and using threatening behaviour. He was arrested after he pulled down an advertising hoarding. The police said that he was definitely one of the ringleaders and his actions were some of the worst they'd ever seen. (And these coppers had seen us play Wednesday!) Parsons was fined £300 with £95 compensation and £25 costs. And he wept throughout the hearing. Now, how funny is that? Some Neanderthal lopes into the ground, beats up a few Town fans, rips down some advertising hoardings, threatens a few policemen and then, in court, has the audacity to cry! If you can summon up tears in such a situation, then you have *really* missed your calling. You shouldn't have been a hooligan; you should have been a Shakespearian actor (darlink). I'm not sure if the people chairing the bench having to listen to these stories were ever convinced by such theatrics or not but one can only assume it was possible.

The only Chesterfield fan to be arrested that day was found guilty for repeatedly punching a Northampton fan in the face but at least he didn't cry when he was handed his £150 fine. I think the fact that only one Chesterfield fan was arrested tells you all you need to know about the goings-on that day.

And that was more or less that. A fairly decent March and a half-decent April saw us climb to safety and finish a respectable 13th. It wasn't what we'd hoped for but it would have to do. After all, there was always next season!

Goodbye To All That
SEASON 84/85

We didn't exactly set the transfer market on fire during the closed season. Bryan Klug wanted to leave because we couldn't guarantee him first team football; Ernie Moss wanted to return; but perhaps the most significant signing was midfielder John Matthews. We also offered a contract to a young keeper who had been making an impression in the reserves, Chris Marples.

Like every season, we started out with enthusiasm, hope and dreams but in our cynical Chesterfield hearts we probably expected very little. However, a fine victory on the opening day of the season and then thumping Northampton 3–1 away in the second game were a good start. After the mauling and brawling that had taken place at Chesterfield with the aforementioned club the previous season, many went there, including me, expecting to see Chesterfield fans carry out some terrible retribution. And yet, apart from the three goals we scored, the game was quieter than a church mouse's funeral! We then beat Southend at home and were looking for four straight wins away at Scunthorpe. We turned out in rather large numbers.

Anyway, Anyhow, Anywhere
September 15th, 1984 Scunthorpe 2 v 4 Chesterfield

We may have started the season hardly daring to hope but three straight wins do tend to provide one with a little optimism and, to be fair, in the games we'd seen so far we had looked a decent side. Matthews had been particularly impressive in midfield and 'Mossy' and 'The Newt'[5] looked a threat up front.

I'd travelled to Northampton by supporters' club coach but was getting tired of this mode of transport. Alas, I was no longer able to call upon the services of Wynnie's Tours or *East Midland Travel*, so I had to persuade someone to take a car to games instead. Somehow, I'd managed to talk John Day into driving to this one. It wasn't exactly far

---

[5] Affectionate nicknames for the powerful strike force of Ernie Moss and Bob Newton.

and we had precious little alternative – especially as I couldn't (and still can't) drive. There were, if I remember correctly, four of us in the car and as we entered Scunthorpe it was apparent that the hardest thing was going to be finding a parking spot. We drove around in circles for what seemed like ages until, in exasperation and with the kick-off looming, we joined many others and drove the car into the middle of a roundabout and parked up. This wasn't a roundabout like the Holywell Cross roundabout in Chesterfield: one that has a designated car park in the middle of it. Oh, no. This was just a relatively small roundabout with, for now, a nice covering of grass and a flowery border. In all honesty, none of us really cared what happened to the car, or the roundabout come to that; this was a football match we were attending and if Scunthorpe couldn't provide adequate parking facilities then that was their look out.

We made the kick-off with seconds to spare and had just rested our arms on a convenient stanchion when Scunthorpe took the lead.

"Fuck me!" John Day said, kicking at the ground with the impetuousness of youth. "Fuckin' typical."

"It's okay," I responded. "It just gives us longer to equalise."

I can't imagine why I was being so confident and philosophical. This certainly wasn't something that watching Chesterfield had instilled in me – if anything it was quite the opposite – but for some reason I really did think we would win this one, and shipping a goal early on was of no real concern to me.

The away end at the old Scunthorpe ground was a strange affair, a bit like the whole ground really which was nothing more than a scrambled mess of terracing and stands. I believe most of the old football league grounds had something that you can't build: character. Unfortunately, Scunthorpe's ground managed to possess no character or charm at all. What is even more incredible is that when the club relocated and built one of the first new 'purpose-built' stadia in the country they impressed everyone by managing to build a brand new stadium that lacked all the charm and character that their old ground lacked.

But shortly after that first goal in '84, pockets of fighting broke out in one corner of the ground. Some of it was slightly too close for comfort and so we did a sideways move and shuffled to what we thought was a safer area. We had no sooner settled than fighting broke out around us. John moved to the front and I moved to the back and we let them get on with it. It was at times like this you really needed that third eye: a couple to watch the game and one to watch the antics of the fans so you could take evasive action if necessary. Not being thus blessed, however, meant I was trying to watch the game and the fans at the same time – and missing out on the best bits of both, no doubt.

While I was wandering around the back of this group of half-tumbling football supporters, a thin, emaciated-looking individual approached me. He looked at me for what was rather too long for comfort before saying, in a voice sounding more like that of some alien creature than a human being: "We'll get you, you know, and we'll kill you."

If he'd said this in a butch cockney accent I might have filled my pants and left; but the fact that he looked more like an emaciated hobbit than anything I'd ever seen before just made me smile. I wasn't happy standing next to this urchin; for one thing, he looked as if he could well have been diseased. And although I can't say that I took his threat seriously, I was always far too much of a coward to call his bluff. I started to walk away from him but he followed me, still talking in that horrible, whiny voice.

"We're going to get you," he repeated and gave me a smile that was neither warming nor threatening. It was somewhere in between, if that's possible.

I continued to walk along the back of the terracing and, like a bad smell, he continued to follow me. Before he had the chance to say anything else, we equalised. I punched the air in celebration, just as everyone around me did, and for a minute or two of manic celebration I completely forgot about my unwanted guest. As things settled down again, the youth looked at me with a puzzled look on his face; perhaps it had always been there.

"Look!" I said. "Why don't you just fuck off!" I didn't say it as a question and didn't expect a response, although I half expected the munchkin to supply one. But he didn't. Instead, he turned away, looking almost sad that his new-found friend had turned on him so violently and, for a split second, I felt kind of guilty. Cor, blimey! I would never have made a hooligan, would I?

The skirmishes between the real hooligans continued on and off for a little while but died away as we took complete control of the game, to a large extent the ground and, to my knowledge, one of the roundabouts outside. Chesterfield ran out 4–2 winners and our fourth straight victory was in the bag.

When we got back to the roundabout it looked amazing. It was full of vehicles, all parked higgledy-piggledy. It was as if someone had just dropped about 12 cars into the middle of the road and created a metal roundabout. Getting the car out of there was another problem as you couldn't move until other people came and moved their cars first – but as they were all Town fans, no one really minded. We were one of the last cars to pull away. The police (to their credit, in my opinion) hadn't done a thing about us parking there; they just left the cars and, presumably, left the council to clear up the mess we made as we drove away, dismantling the flower beds in the process.

Stuck In Chicken Town

October 13th, 1984 Halifax 1 v 3 Chesterfield

There was a good following making the trip to Halifax, another side that aren't exactly synonymous with football violence in the lower leagues. Having said that, though, perhaps there are supporters out there who think Chesterfield aren't. But, whatever; on this day we managed to find trouble where none should have existed. It was a fairly uneventful journey and an uneventful match, which we won 3–1. However, after the game the Town fans were like rabid dogs let loose. I can't imagine why but I do remember running very quickly to the car that had transported me there. I passed a lone, and what looked like very innocent, Halifax fan taking one in the kisser and falling in a heap but, rather than remonstrate with the Chesterfield fan who'd carried out this cowardly attack, I just kept running. I was no fool.

Afterwards, rumours circulated that a Halifax supporter had been stabbed and, while everyone assured me this was the case, the papers were exceedingly quiet about it. It could be that the papers had decided to no longer cover these extreme Saturday afternoon activities – after all, the miners' strike was in full swing and that did seem to be taking up the column inches. There was some concern, at the time, about the way football hooliganism was covered by the media, and a theory that making it headline news was simply making matters worse. The best explanation I've ever heard as to why this phenomenon became so prevalent was simply that of young football supporters having no role models with them at the ground. Previously, watching football had been something that fathers and sons did together. However, as the country was swaying towards a middle class idyll, with families being encouraged to buy their own houses and everyone suddenly feeling they were upwardly mobile, fathers stopped going to football matches and, instead, spent their Saturday afternoons pottering around garden centres or *B&Q*. This, of course, left their young, disenchanted, often unemployed children to run amok at football matches. I don't suppose anyone really knows why football violence was so rife but I don't believe for one minute that any 'would-be thug' ever thought it might be worth beating someone up just to see how it would be covered in the newspaper. But, then again, what do I know? As I write this, there could be thousands of wrinkled, old hooligans pawing gently at their old scrapbooks and purring at the mayhem they caused.

As far as Halifax was concerned, well, yes, someone did get stabbed. The *Derbyshire Times* eventually ran the story with the headline: ***"Knife Attack Fan A Disgrace To A Nation."*** It read as follows:

"A Chesterfield soccer fan who knifed a rival supporter in the back puncturing his lung was beginning a 4 year youth custody sentence this week. Passing sentence on the 18 year old, Judge Geoffrey Baker told him at Huddersfield Crown Court: 'You are a disgrace to the Chesterfield supporters, to football and to the nation. This was a vicious, cowardly and wanton attack and it is one of the worst cases of unprovoked violence I have ever heard.'

"The 18 year old had pleaded not guilty to wounding the 20 year old Halifax fan with intent to cause him grievous bodily harm, but on the 4th day of the trial he changed his plea to guilty. Mr Lionel Scott, prosecuting, said the Halifax fan had been walking near the Halifax Town ground with his girlfriend when he was set upon by four Chesterfield fans. They punched and kicked him; one of them had him in a headlock so that he was helpless. The Chesterfield fan, who was nearby, joined in the attack and plunged a Stanley knife into his back.

"The Halifax Town supporter was taken to hospital with a collapsed lung and detained for a week. Mr Scott said that the youths who first attacked the Halifax fan had not been traced but the Chesterfield

supporter who had committed the stabbing had been traced following enquiries in Chesterfield. When questioned the 18 year old Chesterfield supporter said he had drunk 7 pints of beer and blamed the alcohol for what had happened. He also told police that many fans took Stanley knives to matches. The court was told the 18 year old had previous convictions for offences of violence and had been to both borstal and a detention centre.

"In his summing up the judge said that perhaps it was time for football supporters to be screened by metal detectors before entering the ground and also it was perhaps time to ban alcohol both before and during a game."

WTC Hits The Road

October 22nd, 1984 Port Vale 0 v 0 Chesterfield

Ahh, Burslem. It's almost as romantic as Gresley. Port Vale was one of the first away grounds I ever visited. My dad took me and my sister one rainy Wednesday night after we'd pestered him all day. It was a game I remembered, mainly because the maroon Morris Oxford car we were travelling in kept breaking down every mile or so on the way home because it was overheating and my dad kept laboriously filling the radiator with water from puddles at the side of the road. Eeeeee, them were the days! But that was way back... well, a date and time I can't remember, and a scoreline that has disappeared from my brain forever.

But Monday, October 22nd, 1984 was a completely different ball game altogether as this was not just any old away game. This was the inaugural outing of the Wingerworth Travel Club, or WTC as we unofficially called ourselves. Now, living in Wingerworth – or supporting Chesterfield, come to that – was not a prerequisite for travelling with the WTC. In fact, the only thing you needed was the money to pay your share for the hired van. Obviously, your ability to protect me from a severe beating would always be a welcomed bonus but, as most of us were law-abiding citizens anyway, it wasn't really necessary.

The luxury travel for this trip was a crummy old Transit van. In fact, calling it crummy is being somewhat detrimental to the word 'crummy' as it veered more towards shite. Oh yes, it looked okay from the outside and, as the guy loaning it to us said, 'it would get us there and back.' However, one look at the insides told me it wasn't going to do it with any degree of comfort! For the three people lucky enough to be in the cockpit with the soft seats, well, their life was somewhat easier, but for the rest of us in the back the journey was painful. The back of the van had been fitted out to carry workmen and it sported fixed, wooden benches down each side. At first we thought this would be fine but after two miles the novelty had worn off and every jolt and bump reverberated up the spine. As I also travelled in a similar van to work every day, I can't really say that it was a novelty to begin with but, for some, it most definitely was. The back doors were an interesting design. One might say they had seen better days as they wouldn't stay shut unless they were held, and so a stout piece of wood had been supplied to slot down between the two door catches to keep the doors from flying open. However, it was impossible to lock them once you had climbed out of the back door. Brilliant! For our first trip we had a Transit van that would have looked more at home with Coco the Clown and friends rather than a bunch of football supporters. Yes, I think it's fair to say that this was one crap van. We did expect some teething troubles on our maiden journey, it has to be said, but this wasn't so much a case of teething troubles as a severe case of 'gingival hyperplasia' (ask your dentist!).

Our driver for the evening was Simon Moulson, otherwise known as 'Troll.' Quite why he sported such a nickname, I cannot say; he neither looked nor acted like one – but that's the beauty of nicknames, I suppose. The reason for them is usually pretty spurious at best but, for some reason, they last you a lifetime. Originally, we'd decided that drivers would be picked on a sort of rota basis, which suited me fine because, as I've already mentioned, I couldn't drive. However, in the end, I think it was just a case of whoever was willing to do it on the day. There was usually a brief argument along the lines of *'I did it last time'* but as we all wanted to get to the match, they never seemed to last long.

The core travellers with the WTC, along with myself, were the aforementioned Simon Moulson, Andrew Bond, Kev Walker, Doggy, Dave and Pete Brignall, and Nige Brown. Now, I should give you some background to these individuals because they were all quite normal. Honestly! Nothing like the 'on remand' mob that I travelled with in my early footballing days. Andrew Bond, aka Ronnie/Bondy, was like an excitable puppy after a sniff of shandy. You could throw sticks for him all day and he wouldn't chase them at all; he'd stay and jump up at you, getting his muddy paw marks all over your best coat. If Bondy was driving, though, he suddenly became incredibly serious. It was as if he was responsible for the bus or van and the contents therein. You wouldn't get a smile out of Bondy till it was all over. Having said all that, you couldn't help but like him. Troll (Simon Moulson) appeared to have a dark and deep side – and I still think he does, in a way – but, just when you thought you weren't going to get anything from him, he'd suddenly hear something funny and erupt into a great bellowing laugh. Kev Walker, or Chick, was another laconic individual who seemed to have more time than he knew what to do with but, rather like Ronnie, when he was driving he became very serious. Doggy, well, Doggy was so laid-back he was almost horizontal – and you'll hear more of him later. Dave and Pete Brignall were brothers and about as similar as chalk and cheese. Pete was the younger of the two, 6ft tall and as soft as..., while Dave was small with a nasty streak. Nige was one of my best mates at the time and I could write a book about him on his own. There were others, to be fair, but that's a flavour of the main protagonists.

But it wasn't just the aforementioned individuals who travelled to away games with the WTC; we did have the occasional terrorist, and for this game we'd picked the worst one we could possibly find in a Derby fan by the name of Chris Woods. He worked in Matlock but did actually live in Wingerworth. I have to say, I knew the youth and had no objections to him coming along: it made things cheaper for everyone. Unfortunately, you can know someone on a superficial level without actually really knowing them at all and this was how it was with Chris Woods. Knowing what I know now about the youth, I would have gladly paid him to stay at home. He was, what can only be described as, the most annoying twat I have ever travelled anywhere with in my life.

Perhaps the first trip was destined to be a disaster and, I must admit, that *is* how I remember it. We set off late. Much too late. Simon was adamant that we would do it easily. The van, despite its outward appearance, had "got quite a bit of poke," he said. To a non-driving person this meant nothing and I was still doubtful, especially as it took half an hour just to get to Matlock. I was even more sure of a late arrival when, as the van pulled up at *The Crown* roundabout, the Derby fan decided that a drink would be useful and he left the van and marched into the wine shop that used to stand on the corner there. Half a dozen of the others followed. I shook my head in dismay. At this rate we would be lucky to see injury time. Watching them walk round the wine shop, filling their arms with cans of beer and then walking out without paying was slightly funny, though. You should have seen the look on the face of the girl behind the counter. Someone even said thank you as they left, which really was taking the piss. As we set off again, I had visions of the police pulling us up and arresting us all for robbery but, fortunately, that never happened. I may have been against them going into the place but I have to admit that when the free beer was offered I took it. I may not be a villain but the words 'never look a gift-horse in the mouth' are tattooed onto the insides of my eyelids.

Despite the promises of the driver, by the time we reached the ground the game was well underway. We pulled into the car park at the back of the Port Vale kop, reversed the van into a bush – the only way we could think of locking the back doors – and went in through the nearest turnstiles. We sniggered at the thought of us actually taking the kop but this was by no means the intention. The turnstile operator informed us of the scoreless proceedings and in we walked. Our next duty was to find a policeman, which wasn't difficult. And, with a look hovering somewhere between innocence and despair, we said something along the lines of, 'Oh, I am sorry, Officer, we seem to have come in the wrong end of the ground,' and with that the police officer began to walk us round to the away end. Now, this may sound like a simple enough procedure but, at the time, the Vale fans had the same luxury that Chesterfield fans had at Saltergate: that of being able to walk out of the kop and down the side of the ground so they could get a better view of their team attacking the away team's goal. As we walked along the bottom of the terracing, it felt as if every eye had turned to see the 12 strangers who had entered together. Of course, it only felt like that. I mean, there must have been at least 30 people who couldn't care less! The fact that we were being escorted by one lone policeman also looked decidedly dodgy. Well, that's how it felt, I can tell you.

As we neared the fence between the Vale fans and the away end, the feeling of being stared at intensified. Here we were, standing like lambs for the slaughter, on view to Port Vale's hardest fans. The policeman escorting us said something to his colleague on the gate that would lead us to the safety of the visiting supporters and, as he did so, he turned and pointed at us. If this didn't happen quickly, we were going to be history. We were already being pointed at and it might have been just an illusion brought about through fear but it did seem to go really quiet. Thankfully, the copper on the gate nodded his head and started to unlock it. Chesterfield supporters in the away end started to sing, *"Spireite Aggro."* Briggy turned around and looked at the steeply-banked terrace filled with Port Vale nuclear warheads, put his hands above his head and sang, ***"CHES-TER-FIELD!"*** The terracing came tumbling down towards us like stacked dominoes after the initial shove. I shit myself. I think we all shit ourselves. I'm not a violent man and, yet, the panic instilled by those charging Vale fans had me throwing friends out of the way in an attempt to reach safety. Fortunately, we all made it. And, of course, if we hadn't, then we would have dished some serious fist out! Okay, I would have been the first human being to have jumped a 12ft fence from a standing position!

Once through the gate, we all moved as far away from the home supporters as was possible; all except Pete that is, who stood in the corner and egged them on. What an exhibitionist! For a while he got them quite riled but, eventually, they stopped trying to gob on him and just sang about him. He loved it. In the end, he had to be removed by the police – but only from the corner. They escorted him to the Chesterfield fans and then left him. (Bastards threw me out for much less than that a few years later! I hate the Staffordshire police.) Briggy Jnr was one of the nicer characters, despite being a 6ft-3ins skinhead with knee-length Doc Martens, turned-up Levi's and a leather jacket covered in studs and chains. The fact that he was a member of Her Majesty's Royal Tank Corps means very little actually but it does help to paint a picture. He was the most evil-looking youth aboard the bus – but only if you didn't know him. In reality, he was as soft as shit, and I mean that in a really kind way. The lad would do anything for you: lend you money, give you lifts, look evil... anything. When you got to know him you could see that all he ever did was laugh and smile but at first glance he really did cut a frightening figure.

As for the game, well, it was a dull first half and, as the whistle approached, I started to make my way over to the snap cabin with Nige, the Everton fan. We were both hungry but poor finances meant he was unable to buy anything.

"It's okay," I said. "Tell me what you want."

"No," he replied. "I'm okay. Just make sure you stand in the queue behind me, though."

Well, that sounded easy enough. Even someone as terrified of confrontation as I was could manage that. So, I stood behind him in the queue and, when it was his turn to be served, he smiled and asked for a meat and potato pie, cup of tea, bag of crisps...

"Blimey," I thought. *"Considering he can't afford anything, he's doing okay."*

And when he had it all in his hands, he looked the guy in the eyes and said, "Oh, and a Mars bar, please."

The lad turned around to get the Mars bar and Nigel walked calmly away from the hut, taking a bite out of his pie as he did so. When the lad turned back, he found me instead, with my money in my hand, asking for a pie. He looked at me with a rather baffled look on his face and then turned around as if the customer he thought he should be serving might be hiding behind him.

"What happened to that youth?" he asked.

"What youth?" I said, and repeated my order.

"What about...?" he said, his words floating away in the cool night air.

"What about what?" I replied, as if he was having some kind of breakdown.

"That youth who had that stuff."

"What youth? What stuff? Look! Can I have a meat and potato pie, please?"

The look of confusion on this lad's face was a joy to behold. He swore because he thought he'd been conned – but he wasn't quite sure. Eventually, he gave me my pie and made sure I paid him. And I walked off, smiling at the sheer audacity of it all. It was so easy and, yet, I wouldn't have dared to have done the trick myself. I sat down on the terracing next to Nigel and laughed, calling him a few choice names into the bargain.

"Thanks for that," he said. "I owe you a meal."

And I laughed again because I couldn't possibly see how he was ever going to afford one. But he was true to his word: one Saturday night in *McDonalds* he got me a Big Mac and large fries. He had the same. Did he pay? Did he fuck!

Anyway, that was about the most interesting thing that happened during this game. It ended up a dull 0–0 draw.

After the game, the Staffordshire police kept us inside the ground for a while for our safety, which was good of them because I wasn't looking forward to walking across their car park while they were still piling out of the ground. When we were eventually let out of the ground we made our way round to the car park and, to be honest, I doubt any of us expected to see the van still there, especially considering the back doors were open. But surprise, surprise, it was. As we walked across the car park to the van we picked up stones; it was a natural reaction. There might not have been as much violence in the 80's but there was still some and it was always worth having some ammunition on you. Personally, I thought having your pockets full of stones just slowed you down when you were running away but, then, that was the way *I* thought. Others thought having a back-up plan was good sense.

There was a group of Vale fans over in the opposite corner of the car park but they didn't look too threatening and it looked like we were going to get back to the van without any problem. However, I'd not reckoned on the Derby nutcase. He picked up a largish missile, hurled it at them and then followed it, shouting something like, "Come on, lads!" Half of the van-load were stupid enough to go with him. The rest, me included, headed for the van. We were all running in generally the same direction, the only difference being that some of our crew were picking up stones, hurling them and charging towards the Vale fans with threats of murder while the rest of us – the 'soft-as-shit five' – had slung our stones to the ground and were doing pretty reasonable impressions of Linford Christie across the car park towards the van. The reactions of the Vale fans were really quite funny. I don't know how many of them there were but they shuffled about on the corner as the 'mad seven' got even closer. One or two of them turned and ran for it but the rest just stood there, not quite knowing what to do. Eventually, though, they turned and ran, too. Perhaps they thought that the few of us heading for the van were going for our weapons – or even to give chase in the van! So maybe we weren't the cowardly bastards they thought we were, after all. But it mattered not: they ran – thank God – and we were left alone in the car park singing, *"Spireite Aggro!"* The unfortunate thing was that small confrontation actually led to the mayhem that was to follow.

We still had beer in the van and it was eagerly consumed, causing the Derby nutcase to become even more aggressive. By the time we were ten miles out of Burslem we were all thinking the same thing: *'I hope nobody asks this idiot again.'* As we cruised down some empty road, he kept on about how great it would be if we'd got some logs to throw out of the back doors at cars as they got close to us. Yeah, great idea. Let's all get locked up for murder! Of course, he went on to tell us at length that this is what Derby fans would do because they're *really* hard. We all yawned and hoped that he might just forget the idea if we didn't respond. However, he wouldn't be shaken and he continued on and on and on about it until, eventually, he stood up and demanded that we stop the van so he could have a piss. No one said a word, so he opened the doors and successfully lost the piece of wood that had been holding them shut. That was when we realised he really was serious about getting out. In fact, he looked like he was ready to jump out of the van while we were still doing 50 or so down the road and, at that particular moment, I don't think I would have been too unhappy if he'd actually gone ahead and jumped. But, being the right-minded people we were, we did try to stop him and Simon began to slow down. Before we'd managed to actually come to a stop, however, the Derby fan stepped out. He hit the ground, didn't bounce much, and rolled a couple of times, and I'm sure I wasn't the only one who thought at that moment, *'Let's just drive off; he might be dead anyway.'* And we could have just left him really. After all, he was only a Derby fan. What possible use could he be to the world of football?

Alas, he was a big lad and, so as to show how hard he was, he stood up quickly in the middle of the road, put his hands above his head and chanted, *"Der-by."* Then, he stood in the bushes, merrily pissing away and letting us all know just how big his dick was. (If it was as big as his brain: it was minute!) But we stopped, and waited, and pleaded for him to hurry up. We could hear him grunting and groaning in the undergrowth and no one really wanted to imagine what was happening back there or what animal might be suffering from his advances but, eventually, he came back with this ruddy great 8ft fence pole! I kid you not. It must have been 6ins square. It was massive. There was a collective groan when we saw him waddling towards the back of the van with a grin almost as wide as the post he was carrying. Anyone would have thought he'd just discovered gold rather than wood. Once he was close enough to the van, he summoned up every ounce of strength he had and launched this thing into the back, point first. There were two thuds, separated by an "OUCH!" The first thud was the point of the fencepost smashing into my friend's head. The 'ouch' was self-explanatory. The second thud was said friend disappearing over the front two passenger seats and crashing to the floor. In all honesty, it was a nasty injury. Nige was cut, obviously in pain, but perhaps the most distressing thing was that had it hit him two inches lower it would probably have taken his eye out; in fact, it would probably have killed him! I was really worried about my mate as he sat there, saying very little and probably only just hanging on to consciousness. For a few miles it was all apologies from the Derby fan and, in a way, it sobered the wanker up – but only for a few miles.

Ten miles further on the Derby fan forgot his error and was now looking out for a car to come up behind us so he could hurl the fencepost at it. Good old Ronnie Bond decided that his brand of serious reasoning might help and said something in an attempt to get the imbecile to behave. Unfortunately, Chris Woods had never really liked Ronnie and so he dropped-kicked him in the chest and sent him flying over the rest of the bodies in the van. It wasn't funny anymore, not that it ever had been really, but the idiot was now out of control. I don't think I've ever seen anyone out of their skull on drugs but if someone had told me that Chris Woods was that night, then I would have believed it. I don't think he was; I think he was just a dick, simple as! With Ronnie dispatched, Nige almost unconscious, Simon trying to get us home as quickly as possible and the rest of us in the van really quiet, Mr Woods turned his attention back to the fencepost. He was still adamant that we should throw it out at any car that came up behind us. To be honest, the post was that big it would have derailed a fucking train, never mind smashed up an innocent motorist, and it took us all our time to stop him from ejecting it onto the road on two occasions. Eventually, though, he grew tired of the idea. Well, almost (I can only assume the beer was wearing off) and we relented and let him kick the fencepost out onto an empty road. At least that way someone would have plenty of chance of seeing and avoiding it. And, with that, we breathed a huge sigh of relief. I was fed up. This idiot had made it a thoroughly unpleasant night indeed.

I thought the evening was over and couldn't wait to get out of the van and into my bed. The welcoming sight of Deerlands Road in Wingerworth was warming and I knew that I was now just seconds from being dropped off. If only life were that simple. But, alas, it isn't and I hadn't reckoned on the Derby fan being rejuvenated by arriving back home. In fact, he was more than rejuvenated; he went mental. For those of you who don't know it, Deerlands Road is a semi-steep road. Simon hit the accelerator to make sure the van got to the top quickly. It had been a long day and we all wanted to get home and forget it had ever happened. As we neared the top, I stood up and issued instructions to Simon as to where he could drop me but, before I had chance to say goodnight, the Derby nutcase decided that he was going to try to throw me out of the van! To this day I don't know why he did it – and he probably doesn't either. It wasn't as if this was a pretend bit of fun; this youth was strong and very serious. He was laughing like a maniac but I didn't find it that funny. He had me by the throat and was pushing me out of the back doors which, of course, were open. I clung on to the lip of the roof for grim death, my finger nails trying to push holes into the van's rusty exterior in a vain attempt to give me a little more grip; but this youth's arms were longer than mine and I could see that he was determined to achieve his aim. I'm sure he would have, too, if it had not been for Simon slamming his foot on the brake.

We stopped so fast that both the nutcase and I were slung to the front of the van. Now, if everything in life was fair, I would have landed safely atop the idiot's body, him breaking my fall and me accidentally breaking some part of his anatomy. But life is not a fairy tale and, as we both flew to the front of the van, he slid along the floor while I completely missed everything. Well, everything, that is, until my head smacked into the metal bars that ran down behind the driver's seat. Boy, did it ring. Everyone still on board laughed; except me, of course. I stumbled out of the van with an egg-sized lump starting to form on the top of my head, but also with the satisfaction of knowing that the Derby bastard would never be allowed to darken a WTC journey again. And, do you know what? He never did.

Born To Be Wild?

October 27th, 1984 Chester 1 v 1 Chesterfield

I'm still not quite sure how I managed to persuade Dean Newman (now one of our esteemed sponsors) to take me to this one in his car. I hadn't known Dean that long. I'd met him as I played for the same Sunday side as he did and, then, over the following few months, I introduced him to several of the people that I travelled with to watch Chesterfield. He was a likeable character. He had a car and would occasionally ferry us to some of the closer away matches.

Now, it would be wrong to assume that Chester is a hot bed of football violence, because it isn't. I've lost count of the number of times I've been there and nothing, I repeat, nothing, has ever happened. As my mother was very keen to remind me, "There's always a first time, son." And, guess what. This was it!

Wingerworth Travel Club had decided against having an excursion of its own. After the previous Monday night with the Port Vale match, I don't think anybody could face it but, more to the point, there were plenty of other ways to travel to this game. The Supporters' Club had numerous coaches running and there were, of course, the private and more 'specialised' coaches (and you can read into that what you will). Last but by no means least, there was a special train. It had been a long time since a train had been organised for a Chesterfield game and I'm surprised I didn't use it for my own travelling requirements. Now, this all makes me think that I didn't have to work too hard to persuade Dean to take me; in fact, it could well be that he offered. I honestly can't remember. What I do remember, quite well as it happened, was trying to persuade Dean during our journey to go on the Chester kop. I'd heard from several people how anyone who was anyone was going to be on there and I didn't want us to be left out of the party. After all, we all knew nothing would happen so it was going to be alright. Right? I constantly reminded Dean how it would be more of a giggle than any serious implication on our part to get involved in anything dodgy. We laughed at how, in years to come, we would regale our children with tales of how we took the Chester kop single-handedly; it was such fun.

We arrived in Chester, parked the car and, with more than a little 'Oh, shall we? Shan't we?' from both sides, we decided to pay our money and stride manfully onto the Chester home end. Ah, the sight that greeted us! Chesterfield FC already on the pitch waiting to kick off and all the Town fans standing down one side of the ground. This certainly wasn't in the planning brochure. We said nothing and started to quietly make our way down to the front of the pitch, with Dean whispering to me out of the side of his mouth rather like someone who's had a stroke but isn't aware of the fact. I couldn't make out everything he said but I was getting a cheekful of saliva into the bargain. And my guess was that he was only whispering out loud what I was thinking inside: something along the lines of, *'What do we do now?'* On the other hand, he may well have been saying something along the lines of, *'Why did you bring me on here, you prick?!'* and, if that *was* what he was saying, I could hardly have blamed him because I was beginning to have similar thoughts myself. All I could think of was pulling a similar stunt to the one we'd pulled just less than a week earlier at Port Vale: that is, to apologise profusely to a nice, kind policeman and let him know that you've accidently come into the wrong end of the ground and could you please join your own fans in the correct part. As I was rehearsing this speech, Kendall smashed in a great goal to put us 1–0 up. *'The idiot,'* I thought as I semi-cheered, *'he could have waited ten minutes.'*

The game was just four minutes old. What a start! As I said, we celebrated (sort of) and then we realised we weren't actually the only Chesterfield fans on there. Okay, there wasn't the army of hooligans that had been promised but what they lacked in actual numbers, they more than made up for in enthusiasm. I wondered, briefly, if it was worth joining them. The chances were that we would all be escorted round to the main batch of Chesterfield fans anyway. I glanced back at the pitch and saw that it was just full of Town fans! But why they decided to invade was anyone's guess. If it was simply high spirits then fair enough but I got the feeling that there was much more behind it than that. Whatever it was, the game had to be stopped while the fans were ushered back to the side and I realised that this was our chance. I quickly climbed over the wall onto the side of the pitch and went up to a rather flummoxed-looking PC. He wasn't sure whether he should be in the crowd sorting out the hooligans from Chesterfield, on the pitch clearing it of hooligans from Chesterfield or deciding that he really needed to go to the toilet before he did anything. (The latter looked a distinct possibility.) Anyway, I grabbed his arm, shouted over the din that we'd come in at the wrong end and could we go over the pitch, and before he had the chance to reply I grabbed Dean, shouted, "Thanks," and we legged it across three-quarters of the Sealand Road pitch. We weren't exactly greeted like conquering heroes, mainly because anyone who knew anything about football violence knew that we were just two lads in the wrong end, and Dean and I were safely tucked up in our away end before the police had managed to clear the pitch of the marauding Town fans, so our little dalliance was nothing really.

Unfortunately, the game didn't go to plan: Chester equalised and we had to settle for one point. After the game, the police attempted to keep the 600 or so travelling fans inside the ground until everyone else had cleared. But the Town fans had other ideas that day and managed to force down a large, iron gate before tearing off into Chester for what I could only imagine was a bit of a rough-and-tumble. Dean and I walked slowly back to the car, ruminating on what might have been and how three points would have helped tremendously. I didn't know, until reading the *Derbyshire Times* the following Thursday, the full extent of the trouble at Chester that day. It read:

"Blues Fans In Chester Violence

"One man was arrested after dozens of Chesterfield fans went on the rampage at Chester City's football ground during the fourth division match on Saturday. Trouble flared just after the game started when Chesterfield's Steve Kendall put the blues into the lead. About 50 of Chesterfield's 600 travelling fans invaded the Sealand Road pitch which had to be cleared by police before the match restarted.

"One disabled supporter, who was sitting in a wheelchair at the edge of the pitch, had to be taken to hospital after being struck in the face by an empty whisky bottle thrown by a Chesterfield supporter. [The odd thing about this one is that the disabled supporter, who was smacked on the bonce and ended up in hospital, was actually a Chesterfield fan.] Another fan was carried from the ground on a stretcher by Red Cross volunteers. After the match, which ended 1–1, Chesterfield fans smashed down a large iron gate at the ground before rampaging into town. A special train which took 250 Blues fans to the game had to be stopped and boarded by railway police in Manchester after reports of light bulbs being smashed and tables being thrown out of railway carriage windows. Chesterfield chairman Barry Hubbard said the vast majority of Blues fans were well behaved and that the trouble was caused by no more than 20 youths."

Well, no offence, Barry, but I was in the crowd and I'd have to disagree. But what really amuses me is that the railway police boarded the train as 'tables were being thrown out of carriage windows.' I've been on many special trains, I've seen light bulbs smashed and thrown out of windows, I've seen carriages more or less demolished, but to this day I've never seen a table being thrown out of a window! And, by my reckoning, you'd need to take the window out first to do that. Perhaps there was something the Derbyshire Times wasn't telling us?

Holidays In Winter

FA Cup First Round

November 17th, 1984 Whitby 1 v 3 Chesterfield

Being drawn away to a non-league side would normally be seen as something of a plus. However, when you have the worst FA Cup record in the country, then it's just another hurdle you might fail to clear. You know you should win easily... but this is Chesterfield FC we're talking about and having a good run in the Cup usually amounted to little more than taking the other side to a replay. In order to boost our chances of a big money pay day further down the line our genial chairman requested that this tie be switched to Saltergate as the numbers travelling from Chesterfield would be significant and, so, holding the game at a larger venue would invariably give more people the chance to see such an intriguing fixture. (They are my words, not his.) It would also give Whitby a chance of eking a bit more money out of this affair; not a lot, it has to be said, but a bit. It was good thinking, which is not something I've accused the chairman of many times, but his suggestions fell on stony ground and I can't help but admit that a cold, uneasy shiver ran through my heart when they turned us down flat, with the additional statement of: "We won't bundle Chesterfield out of the FA Cup, we'll beat them by pure skill." Playing against an upstart, non-league team is one thing; playing against one with a grudge, well, that just makes life so much harder.

We went into the game on the back of a ten-game unbeaten run, so we were feeling slightly confident and, had we wanted it, I'm sure the WTC could have fashioned a van or minibus and filled it quite easily. But this was a day at the seaside and, so, those of us who wanted to found lifts with various people. I had my first offer of a lift from my brother-in-law and sister, who were going to go to the game via Robin Hood's Bay to sample some of the quality ale on offer in the town, but I decided against it and my brother went with them instead. I could also have got there with my mum and dad who were going over to Whitby for the weekend. My dad loved Whitby and usually came home with a crate of smoked kippers which my mother would then cook for him over the next six months. However, I didn't want to stay the night, so I took the lift offered to me by the one and only Dean Newman. Along with Dean and myself, there were Pete Chappell, Higgy and John Day, and we all quite happily squeezed ourselves into the confines of whatever Dean Newman was driving in those days. It was a relatively long journey but we sang and laughed, making it a mostly pleasurable one.

The night before the game I'd been engrossed in *The Good Beer Guide* along with my brother who wanted to know the places to go for a decent ale in Robin Hood's Bay while I wanted to know the good ones in Whitby. Having run my discerning eye over the list of bars/pubs, I subjected them to memory and dreamt of a first round cup win and some quality beverages. It never crossed my mind that any sort of hooliganistic act would take place in this snug, little, seaside town. I mean, this was the seaside: they didn't do hooligans, did they?

It was, therefore, something of a surprise to be greeted by just that the moment we set foot out of the car. I remember being aware of some kind of skirmish about 500 yards away at the other side of the car park. We moved rapidly away from it and headed towards the town centre which would be full of day trippers, Town fans and police, so we thought we'd be fairly safe. The first thing I saw was my mum and dad eating fish and chips from the paper. My dad was wearing a suit and tie and highly polished, handmade, brown leather brogues and, yet, there he was scoffing chips from the paper! What an image. (You might take the man out of Stonebroom but you can't take Stonebroom out of the man!) We chatted with them for a while and when we were sure that everything had settled down I questioned my dad on the whereabouts of a decent pub. After receiving directions, we bade them farewell and set off.

However, we didn't get that far before we found ourselves running with some Town fans away from supposed Whitby fans. These weren't just any old hooligans, though; these were hooligans with weapons. One of them had a pickaxe handle or baseball bat (hard to say which when all you can see is a well-shaped piece of wood, and certainly not worth hanging around to see if you can get a better look at it for the sake of an article you might write about the event some 20 years later). Another was carrying a mediaeval mace, and I'm not talking ye olde man-repellent pepper spray here, I'm talking large, metal ball attached to a chain. The group of fans chasing us seemed to remain the same in terms of number while the group of Chesterfield fans would grow in number and then some would disappear up a different road, seemingly to freedom. Eventually, we took a gamble, made a quick turn up a side road and breathed a huge sigh of relief as the chasing mob continued down the road we'd just been on and disappeared. We gave each other a look, one that meant, *'It wasn't supposed to be like this,'* and walked as calmly as we could along a few side streets before stumbling upon a little pub and deciding that this was as safe a place as anywhere to get a drink.

I can't say I was impressed by the array of ales. In fact, if truth be known, I would rather have sampled my own piss! However, after being chased around Whitby, it didn't really seem apt to insist on leaving this particular bar in search of the 'Dog's Scrotum' or whatever pubs I'd committed to memory the night before. Thinking back, the bar we were in probably had a little more in common with that particular appendage but, as they say, beggars can't be choosers. No, this wasn't a salubrious watering hole but it did appear to be safe.

We were in a small room that had no actual bar of its own, just a hatch that you went to and ordered your drinks through. It looked as if the real opening to the pub and, indeed, the public bar was off another street altogether. Anyway, we ordered the gassy wazzzz that was on sale and started to settle down, quietly discussing the events of the morning thus far. However, ten minutes later our discussion came to an abrupt halt as the door to the public bar opened and, upon sight of the mace, I threw myself up against the dividing wall and pointed to the other room. My fellow travellers looked at me with some degree of suspicion but one glance into the other room had them quickly following suit. I don't think I've ever downed a pint of ale so quickly in all my life! It didn't touch my mouth; just splashed into my stomach as if someone had put a funnel down my throat and emptied the glass. We all did the same, actually, and then, with my eyes watering as they are wont to do when you've drunk something like that far too quickly for your own good, we crept silently out of the pub.

I think, in the end, we did manage a decent pint of ale in a pub called *The Dolphin*, or something equally obscure; something you certainly weren't going to see on that neck of the coastline, anyway. Mind you, on saying that, I hadn't expected to see a mediaeval mace and a baseball bat, so perhaps *The Dolphin* is extremely plausible after all. Tales were now reaching us that the assorted miscreants causing all the trouble were, in fact, Middlesbrough fans who had journeyed down/across (*delete as appropriate* – geography not my strong point) to Whitby for some Saturday afternoon knuckling. Whether they had or not it's hard to say but if they were locals, then, boy, the non-league must have been dishing up some right aggro on a Saturday afternoon!

The police (and heaven alone knows which constabulary governed that area) had been conspicuous by their absence all afternoon. Little scraps were breaking out all over the place and this really was something that no one had bargained for. However, it added a fair degree of spice to what, on paper, looked like a fairly ordinary first round cup tie.

Eventually, after avoiding all the little fights developing around the town, we started to make our way up to the ground. We thought this bit would be easy and uneventful, especially as all of a sudden the police appeared to be on every corner of every street and most of the people heading up to the tiny ground were locals who were of little or no threat. We were a little more relaxed now and were laughing and joking about the possibility of a great Chesterfield victory and who we'd like to come up against in the second and third round. I'm sure you've all had similar conversations on first round day. It's the anticipation that does it, the chance that it *could* happen.

Suddenly, a girl behind us started on about what a set of wankers we were. We said nothing and laughed amongst ourselves as this girl then went on to unleash a never-ending stream of garbage. You couldn't even call it vitriol as it was, even by my standards, extremely tame. In fact, apart from the first swear-word, I don't think she swore at all and she certainly said nothing that carried a threat or was in any way harmful. She didn't curse my parents or grandparents; she simply went on and on, at length, *ad nauseum*. Just mind-bogglingly boring and superfluous crap. On and on and on and on she went. I'm sure you all heard the vuvuzelas during the World Cup in South Africa, how they've added that mind-numbing yet somehow enchanting drone to football games? Well, this girl was like a vuvuzela but without the charisma. The words 'bland' and 'rattle' were invented for just such a member of the human race. She couldn't have been much more than 15, and her friends – of whom there were approximately half a dozen – were of a similar age but didn't have the muscular jaw that she seemed to possess. This girl was obviously in charge of her peer group. You could tell by the way they laughed at the things she said and how, when they encouraged her, they did so by looking at their feet. But this young girl had a future. She must have already topped her class at spouting bullshit and was probably on her way to an honours degree in the subject!

I don't know. Perhaps we should be more forgiving of those with less life experience than ourselves but, then again, perhaps we should just twat them and have done with it. That was certainly what I felt like doing. But we continued to walk up the road and the girl continued to talk and talk and talk and talk behind us. At first it was banter: they say a few things, you say a few things back and then, hopefully, they'll go away. But it was now starting to get on everyone's nerves and, eventually, his patience having worn thin, Pete Chappell, who was probably the most mild-mannered one amongst us, turned to the girl and said rather sternly and in quite a loud voice, too: "Why don't you shut the fuck up?!"

They were words we'd all been thinking, sentiments we echoed silently, and I must admit I believed, rather misguidedly, that she actually might just comply. Alas, telling her to shut up was like dangling a red rag to a bull and she just continued to open her mouth and carry on in pretty much the same way as she had been doing before, only this time she started to throw in the occasional threat like, "And what are you going to do if I don't shut up, eh?"

Again we laughed because I'm sure we were all thinking of throwing her under the nearest car, perhaps, or stuffing her Whitby scarf as far down her throat as we could get it! Once again, though, Farmer Chappell had the answer. He turned, said something to her and, then, with one swift movement, picked her up and threw her through a very large privet hedge. As you will have guessed, Pete was a farmer and was used to throwing bales of straw and the occasional pig around in the farmyard, so, let's face it, a 15-year-old schoolgirl stood very little chance indeed. The sight of her floundering in the hedge, struggling to get out, her legs and feet waggling helplessly in the air, was one of the funniest things we'd seen all day and, after what had been quite a stressful morning, proved to be just the tonic we needed. Considering how nervy we'd been in the town centre, this fantastic piece of light-heartedness was a blessed relief for everyone. Well, everyone except the girl, that is, who was now being quite literally pulled from the hedge backwards. She was extremely red-faced when she landed back on the pavement, with twigs of privet sticking out of her hair and mouth, and when she saw us laughing she let off a volley of real, proper abuse. But that just made us laugh even more! I rather hoped that Pete would repeat his hedge trick but, instead, *he* turned away and *she* disappeared – obviously one hedge ducking was more than enough!

After that, the match was a doddle. Despite going behind early on, goals from Kendal, Brown and Newton gave us an FA Cup victory, something that was as rare as rocking-horse poo. There were a few slight altercations after the game but nothing like we'd seen before. And, who cared now? We were in the second round of the Cup! We could keep on dreaming!

WTC Goes Large

November 24th, 1984 Torquay 0 v 1 Chesterfield

Ahh, the south coast. How could we miss this one? Seven days ago I was on the north-east coast watching Town, so I could hardly pass up the opportunity of watching them on the English Riviera. I've always found long haul coach journeys pretty dull, no matter who you travel with, and they've never really been my cup of tea. Occasionally, though, a good journey would arise out of an unexpected one but, for the most part, they were long, boring journeys that were to be avoided if at all possible.

I revelled in the atmosphere of Wynnie's Tours because of their sheer unpredictability. *East Midland's (Hooligan) Transport* had to be travelled on to be believed but if you're going to go from one end of the country to the other, what better way to go than by train? At least it affords you a freedom of movement that you don't get on the bus. Also, if you haven't travelled by special train, then you haven't really travelled, and never really lived!

This season, however, was the season of the Wingerworth Travel Club and I quite enjoyed the few journeys we made. Most of the WTC trips were small, minibus or Transit van affairs but when Torquay came around, well, it was obvious that these modes of transport were never going to be sufficient. No one fancied being crammed, sightless, into the back of a van or simply being crammed into a minibus for the best part of half a day. Organising a bus can be a painstaking and miserable affair, especially if no one turns up. I know; I've done it (and failed).

Now, I'd never been to Torquay before, so when my good friend Nige, the Everton fan I spoke of earlier, declared that he was going to organise a bus (all 52 glorious seats of it) to Torquay, I was more than a little surprised. Running a bus to Torquay is an expensive trip. Nige knew he had perhaps 12 to 15 regulars but also knew he needed to double that number if he was to at least break even on the cost of the coach. So Nige and his henchman Dave Brignall (the older and more menacing one of the Brignall brothers) started the greatest sales pitch ever, and it went something like this:

> 'Right, we're hiring an executive coach: toilets, TV, video, reclining seats, coffee-making facilities, the lot. There's free sandwiches and free beer for everyone, and we're stopping off at several pubs on the way down and on the way back. We're going to have a full day. And it's yours, all for just £10.

He tried this speech out on the usual travellers and received the same disbelief from us all. Basically, as we thrust the £10 into his hand, we wanted to know just one thing: "What time do we leave?" However, such a sales pitch might be okay for your friends – if you didn't deliver the promises, then it was no big deal – but when you were attempting to coax people who hadn't been to a football match before, never mind a Chesterfield one, then the details were crucial. These were the things that could make or break a trip. It was, as the saying goes, all in the detail. As things stood, Nige needed to land about 15 more fish. Most of the people he was trying to land just laughed when they were sober but after they'd had a few pints Nige could have told them we were staying in a brothel for the week and they would have believed him! And it was this economy of truth which meant that by Thursday evening the bus wasn't exactly full but would be travelling.

Nige phoned me and told me to be at Wingerworth Lido around 6am, I think, and, somewhat warily, I decided that an early night on Friday might be a good idea. We chatted for a while and Nige thought it would be a great idea to get hold of a 'Player of the Year' award from one of the trophy shops in town and run onto the pitch at Torquay to present it to Bob Newton. In fact, we spent far too long discussing how we might make this happen. But how we were going to get hold of a trophy at such short notice was anyone's guess. I knew I wasn't buying it!

So, come Friday, November 23rd, our hero is relaxing in the *Barley Mow* with the knowledge that he'd just scraped enough money together, once everyone had paid up, to pay for the coach – or should I say, *a* coach? But, as those last few drops of that last pint slipped satisfyingly down his throat, a particularly miserable scroat, whose name escapes me but someone I do remember I wasn't particularly fond of, walked up and told Nigel that, while he was sorry and all that, he wouldn't be making the trip after all. He wasn't half as sorry as he was going to be!

'Furious' is a very good word. 'Annoyed' would also fit the bill. Suffice to say, the ever-peaceful Everton fan went bloody berserk! His mate, Briggy Snr, grabbed the youth by the collar and smacked him back into the wall. There was talk of pool cues being brandished (although I think this was just in the fairy tale version) but one thing that everyone who witnessed the incident unanimously agreed was the look of fear on said youth's face. To be honest, I'm only sad I missed it. The following day I walked down to the bus and made everyone present at the incident recount the story. Oh, how I laughed! But on the Friday evening it wasn't so funny; well, not for said let-down at any rate.

Nige recovered his calm amid this crisis, dragged Dave off the youth and simply said that as the money was obviously payable in advance, it was unfortunate but he couldn't possibly give any refunds at such a late date. The youth smiled a sickly smile and mentioned, in an 'ought-I-to-be-saying-this' kind of way, that he had yet to pay. Nige dropped his smile and reiterated, rather firmly, that the money was "payable in advance!" Dave growled his 'I've-got-a-baseball-bat-in-my-pocket' growl and the youth coughed up his £10!

"I was always going to pay you," he lied, and sloped off, £10 lighter, into the best room.

Being £10 short wouldn't have been a problem really; a whip-round on the bus would have soon made up the shortfall. But, for Nige, it was "the principle of the thing."

Although I went to bed early for the 6am start, I have to admit that I did have visions of me standing at the bus stop the next day, nervously tapping my feet and anxiously checking my watch while looking up the road wondering if the bus would materialise. However, on Saturday morning when I checked my watch at the Lido, looked up the road and saw this big, beautiful bus trundling down the hill, I left my pessimism at that bus-stop. (I collected it again about three years later when a particular love failed to show up on the eve of my birthday!) Now, while I say 'beautiful,' what I actually mean is that it was a bus, from a proper bus company, the wheels went round, it had a full complement of seats, *and* it had proper drivers! It wasn't the executive, luxury cruiser that had been suggested but we hadn't been expecting that anyway, at any time of the week.

For the first hour I slept – or tried to, at least. When I eventually dragged myself awake, I was confronted with the unusual sight of Nige and Dave making cheese sandwiches on the back seat. It presented every element a dream is made of: ridiculous things happening in ridiculous surroundings. In my search for sleep I'd found nothing as crazy as this. In fact, now I come to think about it, I doubt if I've ever had a dream so ludicrous, so you can perhaps imagine what the real thing must have looked like. No one really expected free sandwiches or free beer, and most of us had been sensible enough to bring our own. However, a desperate need to be able to point to some part of his sales pitch as being the truth meant that at 9am Nige was sitting on the back seat with about five loaves of bread, a tub of marg and an assortment of cheeses. In the back corner seat there stood a mountain of beer cans, at this moment still full. Now, I am of an inquisitive nature and it did puzzle me as to how he'd afforded these items. I'd quizzed Nige earlier in the week and he'd been adamant that food *would* be available, but I didn't believe him. Well, who would? So, now, I needed to know the story. How had he come by all this?

The story he told me was that he and Dave had nipped into *Gateway* on the Friday, stacked a trolley with bread and cheese and a few cans of beer, and then legged it out of the door. I know it sounds a bit far-fetched but, then, I knew the pair of them, so believing it was easy. And, so, there they sat; one of them buttering bread, the other cutting huge lumps of cheese with a knife that he'd swiped out of his mother's kitchen drawer that morning. The sandwiches looked disgusting: nogs of cheese poking through the bread at awkward angles. And there were enough to go around. Enough to go around twice, I think, as most people took one look at them and turned the offer down. It wasn't that I had a problem with stolen goods; I just had a problem with consuming something that looked so awful! The beer, however, was a different matter. Sitting in the front portion of the bus, I simply waited for it to arrive. What a fool! The closest I came to consuming stolen beer was when an empty can whizzed over my head, hitting the youth in front of me on his occipital lobe!

Now, it doesn't matter how comfortable the surroundings, Torquay is a bloody long way. By coach it's a two-driver distance away, and our two drivers, back in '84, were bloody good. We stopped early on so they could make use of the free breakfasts they were allowed. I nipped into the toilets and then went up to the almost empty snack bar where I thought I might have a cup of coffee. I guessed it would be the only thing I could afford, especially if I wanted to grab a bite to eat in Torquay. However, I couldn't see anyone in there, so figured that everyone must have gone back to the bus. I was just about to turn round and walk out when I heard someone shout, "Oi, Dave, get yersen some food, mate." I turned on my heels to see 20 or so youths from the bus sitting around the tables in the dining area lashing down full English breakfasts and they were the fullest English breakfasts I've ever seen. I walked over to have a closer look and smiled, and said something particularly dumb like, "How did you afford that?" They all laughed and explained that they couldn't afford it. They'd walked casually down the 'serve yourself' aisle, served themselves and then walked nonchalantly past the poor girl on the till as if she didn't exist. Payment never entered into it. I couldn't quite believe how they dared do it. And I think that also went for the girl on the till, who was looking on in shock. If she was waiting for payment, then she was going to have a bloody long wait! One or two of them urged me to get a breakfast myself, almost as if it was 'on the house,' but, as nice as it looked and smelled, and as much as I wanted to drop my face into a full English breakfast, I just didn't possess the bare-faced cheek to walk up the aisle, help myself to bacon and eggs and a pot of coffee and then walk straight past the women on the tills as if they didn't exist. So, instead, I bought a cup of coffee and sat down with the crowd, while they were enjoying eating their hearty breakfasts, and felt thoroughly miserable. It wouldn't have been so bad if someone had come up and asked them to pay, but no one did a thing. We weren't troubled at all by the staff and we left with ease. It has to go down as one of the most amazing breakfast scenes *ever*. Surely, only Jesus has fed more people for less money – although I must admit that Nige had a bloody good go at it with his cheese sandwiches on the bus!

A few hours later we stopped again, this time just for a half-hour toilet break. Some of them tried to pull a similar stunt to the one they'd pulled for breakfast but, as the service station only really had a gift shop and sandwiches, it was never going to happen. A stop intended primarily to empty bladders soon became one to fill pockets. A 'certain person' on the bus had remembered (a little late!) his mother's birthday and was now in pursuit of a present of gargantuan proportions. Nige waited until everyone had left the gift shop with their 'gifts' and then started to look around it himself. I watched him through the glass door as he picked up the most enormous box of chocolates and tried to fit it inside his jacket. It didn't matter which way he turned it, a huge corner stuck up ridiculously in his face. Even if the girl on the till had been blind, she would have noticed it! The chances are she would have tripped over it! Eventually, he removed it from inside his jacket and sighed. Then he looked around to see who was looking and saw me. He smiled and shook his head. I smiled and shook mine back, then went into the gift shop myself.

"I was just going to break the fucker in half!" he said, and we laughed. "I'll *have* to get her *something*."

And with that I made my exit. And Nige's mum got a lovely carriage clock for her birthday!

There usually comes a point in a journey when you think you're almost there; when you think the greatest part of the land mass has been covered and in just a few short minutes you'll be dipping your toes in the briny. That's often the time when you realise you're less than half-way there and, in fact, you have the longest slog still ahead. We'd reached that point and were becoming a right restless bunch. Eventually, however, we hit Torquay with still about three hours to spare. The drivers, I think, had realised we were in danger of going stir crazy, so they dropped us off at the nearest pub they found, and we said we'd see them later.

We charged into what must have been one of the blandest and most uninteresting pubs on the south coast. I'm sure the landlord was delighted but we were simply glad to be off the ruddy bus. We were thinking we might just hold up in a pub before going to the game, but this place was horrible and we soon decided to head off down into the town centre. Although the locals said it was a mere stone's throw away, the sea wasn't on any horizon I could see. It looked like being a long and boring walk and I doubt we'd travelled 50 yards before we all decided that public transport might be the way to go. The woman standing at the bus stop was surely a good sign that transport was imminent and, indeed, upon questioning her she confirmed that a bus would be coming along in the next five minutes. And, so, we waited patiently, peacefully.

Now, one woman waiting at a bus stop to go into Torquay for the Saturday shopping with 30 or so Chesterfield supporters, all standing behind her in an orderly queue, has to be seen to be believed. If it had been a dream, Freud would have taken up knitting! 'Bizarre' doesn't even come close. But we did all stand in line and wait. The woman at the head of the queue was, perhaps, a little worried, especially when the bus didn't turn up after her promised five minutes.

"It won't be long," she continued to remind us, but we simply joked with her about how awful the public transport system was in this country and she laughed back and agreed, probably wondering what all the fuss was about with football supporters. After all, this lot seemed relatively nice.

The problem is, when you've already been on a bus for what seems like an eternity, then the idea of catching another one simply to get into the town seems warped at best. But you also have a lot less tolerance after such a lengthy drive than you might have had if you'd travelled for just an hour. And, so, after about ten minutes of hanging around waiting for the bus, we all started the long walk down the hill into the town. The woman kindly pointed us in the right direction and off we set, on a brisk November walk, into the town centre.

Half-way down the hill we crossed over the road behind a parked milk float, its driver reading his newspaper and eating that day's sandwiches. Someone nicked a bottle of milk from one of the crates, and then everyone else followed suit. Well, most did. I was among the boring bunch that just watched the whole thing unfurl in front of them. When I reached the front of the milk float, I turned and watched everyone still taking bottles. The chink of glass on crate was clearly audible and you could see the float bouncing gently up and down under its attack. The driver did nothing. He just lowered his paper slightly and said nothing, hoping that he was not about to be the victim of a ruthless football mob. But there was no chance of that since 'ruthless' was the last thing you would have called us. There were people who, if needs be, would have rolled up their sleeves and got stuck in but, unlike Wynnie's Tours, there was no one in our group who would have started any trouble on a large scale. The WTC didn't have a great capacity for violence. We wanted a good laugh more than anything else.

All *I* wanted was to find a decent pub and, as usual, I'd memorised the names of quite a few of the pubs in *The Good Beer Guide* – but I didn't find a single one of the buggers. I did enter several but always had the same problem. You see, to make sure my head stayed on my shoulders, I had started to do my drinking alone at away matches – or I tried to, anyway. One couldn't be too careful. I always thought that, while five or six youths entering a pub looked a bit suspicious, they were also less likely to get served. However, on your own you could get away with it. Trouble with this trip was that, after I'd broken away from the main group, I'd go into a pub and, bugger me, if five minutes later a dozen youths off our coach would come waltzing in, too.

"O'rate, Stan, what's beer like?"

Any anonymity I'd had was now well and truly smashed, so I supped up and tried to find the next alehouse. Five minutes later, ditto. It was as if they were attached to me by elastic!

Eventually, I gave up any hope of a quiet drink and went into the indoor shopping area. I lost them. In here, however, I ran into Nige and a few others. Now, I'm making 'Mr Big' out to sound like a right thief and he wasn't – well, not really. Nige was an opportunist; I never saw him miss one. We played for the same Sunday League side and the following day we had a big match and Nige needed some new boots. He was hoping to get a pair, not necessarily both of the same brand. He was just looking for two size 9 football boots. As long as one of them was left and the other right, he would be happy. But on this trip he was thwarted. If the service stations had sold football boots he would have been fine; in fact, he would probably have opened up a market stall! But security in the shops in Torquay was much better than in Chesterfield and, so, he had to leave bootless. He did try several shops. In fact, the last time I saw him, before entering the ground, he was being chased through the indoor shopping centre by a security guard!

The bus-load had split up considerably while we were in the centre but we regrouped at the ground and a large chunk of us, about 25, entered the away end. At that time you could transfer to the stand for about £1, I think, but we stormed the old geezer collecting the dosh and sat down. He tried to get us to pay up and we insisted we had "just lost our tickets." No one was listening to him and some were giving him a hard time because they couldn't see round him. In the end, he gave in and, like us, he sat down and watched the match.

Directly opposite us there were half a dozen Town fans mingling with the Torquay lot. We had no idea they were even there until Phil Brown scored from the spot and then you could see them jumping up and down. There was a moment of drama as that all-too-familiar circle appeared around them: the one where the home fans move away to size up the opposition, and then rush forward and kick the shit out of the intruders. Yes, the circle appeared; yes, the home fans threatened them; no, they didn't do anything about it. In fact, the half dozen Town fans were so pissed that they threatened them back, and the rest of the game was spent just exchanging songs with them! Pointless exercise really as there were so few of them that we couldn't hear a word.

It was a crap game, but it was great fun. I think I would have paid to go on the trip just for the laugh. The journey home was nothing like as much fun – or, at least, I don't remember it being. But, then, you can only put so much into one day and we *had* already gone way over the limit!

FA Cup Second Round

December 8ᵗʰ, 1984 Walsall 1 v 0 Chesterfield

Gosh, I'd travelled around a lot this season but we were doing well: up near the top of the league and promotion looking a distinct possibility. Mind you, I'd said the same an awful lot under Cox and Barlow, so there was no reason to get carried away. While the side Duncan had built was nothing like as spectacular as the one Cox had built, the opponents we played were nothing like as good. But you can only beat what is put in front of you and, today, we hoped like hell that it would be Walsall as there had never been a great deal of love lost between the two clubs and they also seemed to have some kind of jinx over us. But, perhaps the Cup would put paid to that.

Once again, the WTC sprang into action – or should I say it limped into action? I'm not quite sure why I'm even bothering to write this as it wasn't the greatest trip ever. In fact, the oddest thing about it was making the journey in a box van on hire from *Serpent Motors*. Three lucky people managed to get the cushy seats up front, while the rest of us were consigned to the dark, dingy and stuffy interior. It was roomy in the back but, as there were only six of us in there, we rattled around like the last few *Smarties* in a tube. Yes, it was a sizeable interior but, with the door rolled down and no fresh air getting in, then it gets very uncomfortable, very quickly. Also, we didn't have any seats, so we were more or less laid out in the back, trying to find comfort where none existed. We felt every single bump the driver went over – and some that he didn't!

On the way, we tried to converse with the guys in the front by pummelling on the wooden backboard and screaming for them to stop at a garage so we could relieve ourselves. I was slightly concerned that one of our number might actually decide he couldn't wait any longer and do one up the side of the van, which would only increase our discomfort, not to mention the smell! However, we managed to persuade him that it was actually in his best interest to try to hang on and, anyway, does anyone really mind a ruptured bladder?

I wasn't sure whether it was the screams coming from the back of the van or the fact that we needed petrol that made the driver pull into the garage, but we were all aware of what was happening and the back door was open before anyone could issue a warning of 'Be careful!' (Not that we would have.) The desperate youth, whose name escapes me – genuinely, it does, but he was a bit of a lad, in a funny sort of way – raced into the garage, raced out again, and then ran round the back, presumably to where the toilets were. The driver filled up with petrol and paid and had just started the engine when this lad reappeared from the back, ran back into the garage, snatched a few bags of crisps and started on his way back to the van. A young lad from the garage tried to stop him but, moving much more freely now that his bladder was empty, the youth chinned him with one swift movement and ran towards us. By this time the garage was emptying of staff and I could see that we were going to be in big trouble unless we got going pretty sharpish. But we managed to drag him aboard as the van picked up speed. In acknowledgement of his gratitude, he shared his crisps with us, bless him.

As for the game, well, we lost as always and, so, dreams of taking a bus-load to some Division 1 club evaporated.

The journey home was like coming back off holiday: six of us sitting in the back of the van with the door up and our legs dangling over the edge. It was quite dangerous because each time we went over a bump we were thrown about a foot in the air. But we never thought about falling or, rather, we did think about it but decided it would happen to someone else and not to us. We waved kindly at all the motorists coming up behind us and stuck our fingers up at anyone who didn't wave back. Childish, yes, but funny. As I said, it might not have been the most exciting trip ever but, for some reason, the frivolity of it stays with me to this day.

Every Day Is A Winding Road

December 21st, 1984 Rochdale 3 v 1 Chesterfield

I think it would be fair to say that over the previous few years I'd been a slightly fortunate football supporter. I'd never been arrested. (Amazing, when you consider that some of the company I kept on a Saturday afternoon went on to see the insides of prison cells!) Indeed, all I had to show for my years of slightly left-field football supporting was a smack in the mouth from some dickhead of a Forest fan and a truncheon round the skull from an even bigger dickhead from the Merseyside Constabulary. Believe me, I was more than happy to keep it that way.

I'm not quite sure who came up with the idea of going to Rochdale for a midweek game but I do remember putting my brother's name down on the sheet so that we had a full complement; and this time, rather than travel in the back of a horrible old van, we were in the relative opulence of a hired minibus. As my brother and I walked up the road, I remember seeing my mother's face peering through the window, watching as her youngest was being led astray by that idiot middle child she'd borne – ME, the one she'd managed (more by luck than judgement) to steer in the direction of Chesterfield Football Club. She carried the look of a worried woman; a look I'd seen just once before when I'd introduced our Chris to the delights of CFC away at Sheffield

United via special train. I can't imagine why she was worried, though. Had I ever been in trouble? Exactly! What could possibly go wrong when a bunch of friends decide to go to an away game? I'm sure my mother wished I had a life – and, in all fairness, you cannot imagine how many times over the years I've wished the same thing – but, like that stubborn piece of chewing gum stuck in the tread of your shoe, I was stuck with Chesterfield *and*, I suppose, they were stuck with me.

It would be wrong to suggest that the WTC operated on the same scale as Wynnie's Tours. That was never the case or, indeed, the intention. Describing the two modes of transport would be like trying to describe wine. Wynnie's Tours' outings were intense, full-blooded affairs (sometimes literally), whilst the WTC's were more light and subtle on the palate, much more jovial little numbers. In fact, all the Wingerworth Travel Club hoped for was to provide a relatively cheap mode of transport to away games that offered a little more freedom than the strait-jacket approach that seemed to exist with the supporters' club coach trips. The only similarity between Wynnie's Tours and the WTC was that they both operated out of Wingerworth which, let's face it, isn't really the hooligan capital of the north. However, although the two had very little in common, it would be wrong to suggest that what happened on the WTC tours wasn't worth committing to paper. Far from it. In fairness, I look back on these days as being some of the best I've ever encountered.

Now, Spotland has never really been my ground of choice, and certainly not back then, and on a wet, cold December night, it's even less appealing. At the best of times Rochdale has all the elegance of frozen snot on a tramp's nose. The place is an unfortunate hell-hole, regardless of the weather. About the only place I can think of that is equally as miserable is Bury. So, on a wintry Wednesday night any charm it might have possessed had been well and truly washed down the gutter. As I said earlier, why we even bothered with this game I can't imagine. There must have been something decent on TV, surely? But bother we did, and off we set.

There had been the usual democratic process of choosing a driver. It didn't take long. Someone would usually shout, *"Oh, for fuck's sake, Bondy, thee drive it!"* and, bereft of the power of argument, Bondy duly climbed aboard, let loose the clutch and, with rain slanting from the leaden skies of Wingerworth, we headed off into the evening for a 7.30 kick-off.

We entered the outskirts of Rochdale at around 6.00pm and were settled in a pub at 6.30. How we managed to make such cracking time is beyond me as we usually got lost before we even reached Chesterfield. But, on this occasion, there was a fair wind and the journey went smoothly. The landlord of our chosen hostelry looked somewhat bewildered to see a dozen people settle themselves in his pub at such an early hour. It appeared as if he only really opened mid-week on the off chance of catching a passing stray, so he was more than happy to see his coffers amply boosted by such a mob. There was much drinking done, although not by me personally, I hasten to add. I have neither the ability to consume copious amounts of beer nor, indeed, at that time, the wallet. Alas, at some point during the evening the barrel ran dry, and we laughed and joked and ribbed the poor unfortunate landlord about this sorry state of affairs. He was so eager to keep his customers happy that he told us not to go away as it would take him but five minutes to put a new one on and, with that, he disappeared into the cellar.

We were sitting, talking, noisily at first, when one of our members, Doggy, got up from his table and, being aware that no one was at the bar, he calmly placed himself behind it and for a few seconds played at being landlord. The pretence didn't last, though, because before long he was actually *practising* being one, not by actually dispensing drinks but by making sure that a few bottles of beer made their way into his pockets! There was a flurry of hands and gloves and soon his large, black crombie was clinking with bottles. The talking had suddenly become much quieter but we all agreed, in rather hushed tones, that maybe he should put some of them back. In the end, he settled on a full bottle of port. Now, I agree that on such a lousy night whisky would probably have been more appropriate, but port was the only full bottle there was – and, also, perhaps the only bottle not screwed to a shelf by an optic – therefore, it proved to be the easiest target. I am assured that other spirits *were* taken but can't remember what they were.

I don't care what anyone says and I don't care how wrong it was, it was bloody funny. Watching him standing behind the bar in his long, black crombie and blue and white bobble hat, searching, seemingly without a care in the world and certainly as if he had all the time in it, for the bottle of spirits that offered the best nicking value (ie, the one that was full) was an incredulous sight. Well, be reasonable, it is pretty pointless getting yourself into that position only to ruin it by nicking an empty bottle of gin!

Now, I know Doggy well. He's a tall, gangly youth and possesses all the malice of a coffee cream chocolate. But, for some strange reason, he didn't seem to give a fuck about anything. He had a sense of humour that was drier than a camel's arse hole in a sandstorm. What you might call, a great youth. If the landlord had come back and caught him, I'm sure he'd probably have shredded Doggy through his hand pump – but, fortunately, he didn't.

I expected we'd take the lead from this little bit of naughtiness by supping up and leaving, but we stayed put and had another drink and a laugh with the landlord; presumably, him laughing because he'd taken so much money, so early on, and us laughing because we knew he was a bottle of port lighter, not to mention a few bottles of beer and the odd free squirt of lager. Actually, I think the landlord finished down on the deal. But, having given us the directions to Spotland, he waved us goodbye and we waved back with the stuff we'd nicked. Talk about rubbing it in.

Spotland turned out to be the same miserable hole that I'd remembered but I have to admit to feeling slightly cheered at the money-saving ideas concealed up a certain Town fan's sleeve; that of Nige, the Everton fan, who had quite a famous magic trick involving smoke, mirrors, platform tickets and all manner of escapology tricks which enabled him to watch Everton each week for just £1. (He did offer to show me how it was done but I bottled it and, instead, another friend of mine went along and confirmed that it had happened just as the magician had said.) So, to prove to me that it could be done, Nige employed one of these tricks to get into Spotland. While we were walking towards the turnstiles, Nige whispered in my ear, "When you go through the turnstile, open your legs." (Having just typed that it sounds as if something vaguely erotic was in the offing but, trust me, it wasn't.) Anyway, I did what I was asked but can't say I was actually ready for what happened next. I'd no sooner opened my legs than Nige, quick as a flash, was on all fours, scrambling between my legs and through the turnstile, all while I was paying my gate money and about to give the turnstile a push. The bloke operating the turnstile knew something was amiss and spluttered out a shout of, "Stop!" without knowing who or what he was telling to stop. But it wouldn't have mattered because Nige was mingling with the Chesterfield fans before I could put my change in my pocket!

Some might say that I'm easily impressed and it's fair to say that on this occasion I was. Having said that, though, it wasn't so much the act itself that impressed me but him having the audacity to do it. He never boasted about these tricks, he just did them and then he would offer a wry grin back when questioned about them. For him, they were just second nature. I almost felt as if they were completely out of character for him, too, because he was one of the most down-to-earth youths you could ever wish to meet. His mum and dad were lovely and Nige himself was a pleasure to be with. I played football and cricket with him so I could say I knew him really well and, to be honest, you couldn't wish to meet a nicer youth.

Anyway, we were in; some of us by fair means, others by foul. However, one of our party was missing. We didn't realise it at first but Doggy, the guy who nicked the port, had gone astray. We knew he'd turn up at some point and I can't remember anyone being unduly worried by his disappearance. If truth be known, we were probably more worried about the weather than our missing passenger.

Now, back then, the away end was a shallow, open end behind one goal. The starless skies above Spotland looked as if they were about to let loose yet another deluge of rain but, despite the dark, foreboding skies, we did manage to raise a cheer when the teams ran out to commence play. It was at this point that we heard a lone cheer coming from the Rochdale kop. Some deranged idiot in the home end was singing, *"Chesterfield!"* and waving his arms around. A space appeared around him as the Rochdale fans made way for this lunatic. Suddenly, someone said, "That's Doggy," and we all started to laugh. The greedy sod had sneaked off and sunk the best part of the bottle of port (not to mention some Pernod he'd snaffled from a supermarket in town) and there he was, well and truly liquored, among the Rochdale fans, waving the nearly empty bottle of port around. It's debateable whether he actually knew where he was – in fact, it's debatable whether he knew *who* he was – but this didn't stop him from trying to extend the Christmas spirit to the Rochdale fans. For him, it was the season of goodwill and he was sharing a drink. For them, it was the season when a crazed psychopath charged them on the kop, armed with a bottle of port!

From their reactions we could tell that the Rochdale fans had mistaken this soft centre from the layer underneath for a nuttier combination from the layer on top. All his attempts at offering someone a drink went the same way. To us, a hundred yards away, he displayed all the actions of a pissed-up youth. But, then, to us, it was Doggy; we knew he wouldn't hurt anyone. Each time he staggered towards the home fans, they quickly ran away. It must have been soul-destroying for the youth. But it was funny. Eventually, the police moved in and stuck him on the running track. They didn't throw him out, which I thought was odd, and so the youth kept right on walking, past the Chesterfield fans and off towards the stands. Most of us were crying with laughter, it was so funny. And by the time he'd finished the port, he was just walking aimlessly around the ground. We did eventually manage to entice him into the away end but all hope was lost – he was as pissed as a fart!

From a football perspective, well, nothing really happened until just before half-time when Ernie powered home a diving header. Suddenly, we were all on the pitch. The joy of scoring such an important goal had me crossing that line and dancing in the goal-mouth. It wasn't the first time I'd been on the pitch to celebrate a goal but it was the first time I'd actually celebrated it with the scorer! About half a dozen of us surrounded Ernie, jumping up and down and singing. It was extremely muddy. Ernie turned to make his way back to the half-way line when some Chesterfield fan came hurtling over the wall to join in the celebrations. As I say, it was very, very muddy and after just three or four steps the fan's legs shot from under him and he slid on his arse further than I've ever seen anyone slide before. I think he was back at the half-way line before Ernie was! The cheers reserved for Ernie were now replaced with cheers of delight for our mudlark. When the lad did eventually come to a stop, the cheers for Ernie's goal had been overtaken by '*slide*-splitting' laughter! I'm pretty sure I've never seen anyone slide so far without the use of a sledge, some snow and a big hill!

When the half-time whistle went, my Everton colleague suggested a drink in the players' bar. I laughed. He didn't.

"They must have one," he said.

So, me, my brother and this lad jump up onto the track surrounding the pitch and walk towards the half-way line. It really was that simple, if you had the bottle – and I wasn't sure that I did.

"Look," he said, "we'll go down the tunnel and, if they won't let us through, we'll wait for someone. Just keep agreeing with me."

We had a quick look in the dug-outs, contemplated whether we needed a couple of footballs more than a drink – which we did but I couldn't see them letting us walk out with a ball under each arm – walked down the players' tunnel, which was lined with people, and on towards the door at the end. They wouldn't let us through. The idea now was to wait until the teams came out, say "Good luck" to the players as if we knew them and carry on through the door. We could then have a drink and watch the rest of the game from the directors' box.

Now, I never had any faith in this working. Maybe if my friend had gone alone he would have pulled it off but him issuing instructions to me and my brother just looked odd. So we stood against the wall and waited. I noticed a gentleman leave and I thought we should do the same. And I was right because he'd gone to fetch the police. The copper went to the other side of the tunnel and asked this guy what the problem was. He pointed at us. The defender of law and order then approached my friend and had a word in his shell-like, but I grabbed my brother's shoulder and marched him out of the tunnel. I could hear my friend saying things like, "Of course I should be here; I've played for them for years. I'm injured." We walked back to the away end, escaping punishment, but my friend was thrown out, along with another Town fan who'd seen us, followed and nearly made it through the door. Cobbing them out was an empty gesture, though: one of them climbed back in over the turnstile; while the other explained he'd been thrown out by mistake, so the man on the gate let him back in for 50p!

The second half was miserable. We lost 3–1.

Now, you'd hardly call our crew 'animals' – not even 'hooligans,' come to that – but, as I've mentioned elsewhere, a couple of them were more than happy to get stuck in. Let's just say they were lads with spirits higher than they should have been. They weren't serial hooligans who did it at every opportunity, but just when the mood took them, and being wet on the back of a 3–1 drubbing, well, the mood took them.

They charged out of the ground and smacked some Rochdale fans standing over the other side of the road. It was nothing horrific; just a case of picking on lads smaller than themselves. But we managed to get them back into the minibus and entered a line of slow-moving traffic. Two Rochdale fans, only young lads, gave the obvious 'V' sign and received more than they bargained for in return. Suddenly, the back doors flung open and this youth on our bus leapt out and chased them. The Rochdale lads darted up a garden path and banged heavily on someone's front door but, before the occupant had chance to open it, Martin (at least, I think that was his name) was on them. He swung the first lad round and hit him on the chin. You could hear his head go back and bang on the door and I could imagine some old woman struggling to the door shouting, *"I'm coming, I'm coming. Keep your hair on!"* The other lad tried to run past Martin, back down the path, but he wasn't quick enough. A firm hand on his shoulder turned him round and it was more of a shove than a punch that sent this Rochdale fan sprawling across the front garden where he made a right mess of a water feature.

The trouble now was two-fold: to start with, the traffic eased and we were beginning to pick up speed; secondly, the police down the road had seen the offence and were walking slowly but surely in their direction. We screamed a warning and Mart, who was standing there admiring his handiwork, looked round at the boys in blue who were now running towards him. I well remember the look of horror as he turned away from the job in hand to see us accelerating away.

Half the bus was shouting, "Slow down, Bondy, you wanker!" while the other half, who obviously thought, *'Fuck him,'* were shouting, "Get yer toe down!" I was with the first lot. How on earth could you leave your supporters behind? I don't care what they've done. But, boy, did this youth run! At what seemed like sixty miles an hour, he flung himself desperately at the back end of the minibus. Half of him landed inside the bus, the other half dragged along the ground, but with a few hefty tugs he was on board, the back doors were shut and we were off, sticking two fingers up at the police in manic jubilation.

There was much laughter on the way home, not to mention 12 different ways of how to get there. Some, me included, were shouting, "Take that road," just for the hell of it, while others were screaming out the right directions. As for Bondy, the driver, well, he was laughing crazily and listening to no one in particular. This was probably why, an hour later, we were driving through the deserted streets of a cobbled Manchester outback. We knew we weren't far away from the city centre, as there were plenty of signs informing us of that fact, but as for where we were exactly, well, that was another matter. It was like pre-war Britain where all the relevant road signs had been removed – although, on this occasion, they'd more than likely been vandalised. Wherever we were, it was deserted. So we trailed around those streets, with our heads hanging out of the windows, singing, *"CHES-TER-FIELD!"*

Now, that really was good fun. There were a lot of 'We hate Man United' chants, too, and that was equally brilliant and just as funny. It was like we owned the place. It was a ghost town and our songs echoed wonderfully down the sodden streets. I dare say that if those streets had been full of slavering Manure fans, then we might well have kept our gobs shut and pretended we were on our way home from the bingo. It was particularly poignant for me as I really, really hate Man United, especially after one of their fans threatened to kill me on a train. Well, you'd hate them after that, wouldn't you? Wouldn't you!?

But, eventually, we settled down. What with the defeat, wet clothes, and with hunger setting in, we were now on the look-out for a chip shop. The first place we tried was on the verge of closing but if you had the chance of getting rid of your stock you'd be a fool not to take it. There was a small room at the back of this shop where you could sit and eat your purchase and, so, with 12 rounds of chips and various accompaniments ordered, we walked into the back. Just because they were there, more than anything else, several bottles of pop were lifted on the way. Sitting around three or four little tables waiting for your chips is one thing, but doing so while drinking the pop you'd nicked from the same shop is overdoing it slightly! I'm not sure whether I actually believed we'd end up with our fish and chips or not, but I do know I wasn't surprised when the woman came through saying they wouldn't be serving us. Someone had the gall to ask her why and she even felt the need to explain about the nicked pop. In a last ditch attempt to salvage our supper, those still holding on to bottles of fizzy stuff agreed to put them back and, suddenly, there was not only an assortment of flavours in the crate but also bottles with an assortment of fluid ounces in them, too! She threw us out.

We tried every chip shop we came to but, by now, it was getting extremely late and they were all shut. Some still boasted light from the windows and, when we came across such a building, a few selected people would leap from the bus, bang heartily on the window and demand to be served. It sounds pathetic, I suppose, but I think it was one of those jokes where you just have to be there to appreciate it. Needless to say, we ended up chipless – but managed to scare the shit out of many a late night fryer!

Bad Backs And Englishmen

March 23rd, 1985 Darlington 1 v 3 Chesterfield

I hate gardening! I know that many of you out there think there's nothing better than taking the hover for a spin around the lawn on a sunny Sunday and pottering about in your pristine and weedless flowerbeds. And it is understandable. I know from personal experience that gardening can give one immense pleasure, as it did my dad who cultivated award-winning chrysanthemums – occasionally. However, I also know from personal experience that it can be one of the most soul-destroying, physically demanding jobs on the planet and I wouldn't do it again if someone paid me properly! You see, for many years I was, indeed, a gardener; my correct title being 'Nurseryman,' which means fuck all in the grand scheme of things. What it does mean is that you get paid a pittance for slaving over a hot spade for eight hours a day. You may, no doubt, be wondering what this has got to do with football or Chesterfield, or anything for that matter, but it has – in a very spurious kind of way. You see, I hated my job as a gardener and just about the only thing that got me through each dead-end day was the thought of having my hopes dashed by Chesterfield FC! (Boy, I sound like some kind of masochist extra!) However, coming off the back of a three-match unbeaten run, I was looking forward to thrashing Halifax at home and then getting on the bus down to Hereford to see *us* sort *them* out.

Unfortunately, Monday before we entertained Halifax the following Saturday, I was at work and handed the not so charming task of digging up about 75 horse chestnut trees, all about 12ft high. These particular trees were notorious. We usually shifted stuff around so it didn't get too comfortable and was easier to lift come winter. But these trees had been overlooked and the bloody things almost smiled at us as we attempted to dig them out of what was nothing more than a bog. How many we'd managed to get out I can't remember but it was a cold day at the top of Tansley and we were all very hot and sweaty. I remember feeling my back go. It was nothing much, just a sharp pain at the bottom of my back, and although I grimaced and straightened up slowly I really didn't think it would amount to very much. However, by 4 o'clock, when we were winding down, it had started to feel a little stiff and it was becoming uncomfortable to walk. That night I got into the back of the van to come home and half an hour later, when it was my turn to be dropped off, I literally could not stand. I don't think I've ever experienced pain like it. The closest I can recall was a particularly bad case of toothache when I was a kid, but this felt worse. Everything was an effort and the next morning, on realising I couldn't walk, I made an appointment to see the doctor. He examined me, didn't say much, but did say that, considering my job, it was to be expected at some point. He signed me off for two weeks and told me to get some rest.

"Just go to bed for two weeks and don't move," were his final parting words.

I wanted to say something about the match on Saturday but decided it would be best to keep that under my hat.

So I spent the rest of the week in bed, as the doctor had instructed, hardly daring to move, save for the obvious ablutions. I certainly wasn't going to spend any time shaving and, so, come Saturday dinner, I was sporting what could be described as over-zealous designer stubble. Despite my mother urging me not to go to the home match against Halifax, I just had to. Well, I had a season ticket. Didn't that mean you had to attend every game? I stood away from my usual place in the Kop and watched as we won 3–0. I can't say I leapt up and down when we scored but I clapped and cheered without moving a muscle whatsoever in my torso. It's a good trick, if you can master it. After the game I made my way home rather gingerly and went straight to bed, deciding that the stubble would remain until Chesterfield lost!

By Tuesday it was a baby beard. I lay in bed, feeling more than a little scruffy, and listened as the reports came in from Hereford. I knew I should have been there but when we scored my smile broadened and I cheered from my recumbent position (not that you could tell I was smiling as the beard hid all). That was another 3 points towards the holy grail of promotion.

By Thursday I was bored shitless but could sense that my back was easing a little. Friday I phoned John Day and asked him to book me a place on the bus to Darlington and, although I was still sore and a little fragile, on Saturday I took my place as we headed through the rain to Darlo.

There was a great atmosphere when we arrived there and everyone seemed to be relaxed and more than a little confident that we could beat our promotion rivals in their own backyard. I remember thinking that it was a pivotal game and, should we win, promotion would, indeed, be ours. Not quite sure why I was so confident. After years of being let down by the club I ought to know better than to make bold statements like that. It was, however, a really good game and to say we trounced them would be a fair reflection of the match. Kendal was in sublime form and took them apart from midfield, and Newton slotted home the obligatory couple of goals. It was a masterful performance all round.

But something else went on inside the ground, apart from the football. In one corner, an almighty ruck broke out. I wasn't sure if it was their fans trying to get over what constituted a fence (but was, in fact, little more than a stile) to get at the Town fans or if it was us trying to do likewise to them. Perhaps it was a bit of both but, either way, they were at it for some time and the police appeared powerless to stop them – either that or they didn't particularly want to. It seemed to go on for ages and I can't remember anyone getting cobbed out of the ground by the police. Rumour had it that the ones fighting weren't Darlington fans but Middlesbrough; but, then, I'd heard stories like that before and, as far as I was aware, it was just a story. To be honest, I didn't care. As I boarded the coach to go home, my back and my beard were still intact and that was the main thing.

On the Tuesday morning after the game I went to see an osteopath, who cracked every bone in my back and had me walking pain-free in no time. My doctor wasn't very happy when I told him about it but, as I pointed out, she *had* actually got me walking, which was more than he'd managed to do.

On April 3rd we lost away at Blackpool and, as promised, the beard disappeared; just in time for Mansfield away.

I Like Driving In My Car...Well, Dean's Actually
April 6th, 1985 Mansfield 0 v 0 Chesterfield

Dean Newman seems to feature quite a lot this season, but then that's probably because he was more than happy, most of the time, to take us to away games. And so it was that on Saturday, April 6th Dean picked me, Higgy, John Day and Pete Chappell up from town. Some of us had partaken of a few beverages before Dean got there and it would be wrong to say that we weren't in good spirits as we sped towards that hole in the universe they named Mansfield.

The traffic started to crawl as we made our way through the busy sprawl. There were gangs of lads everywhere, all closely marshalled by gangs of police. Dean was starting to get anxious and was asking us where he ought to park. Why he was asking or, indeed, expecting any sense out of the four of us is anyone's guess. You couldn't get much sense out of us sober, but tipsy... And, most of all, together, we were just an uncaring bunch of would-be companions.

"Look! There's somewhere!" I shouted excitedly as we passed a car park, and I probably sounded more like some three-year-old who had just discovered the art of pointing and shouting at the same time than I did a 29-year-old adult.

"I've missed the entrance!" Dean replied in exasperation. He had that tone of voice of someone who really wanted to say, *"YES, I CAN SEE IT'S A FUCKIN' CAR PARK, YOU IDIOT. HOW DO I GET IN?"*

It was as if we were reading his mind because, to a man, we all answered him: "Look! Turn left! There's another entrance." This time we were all pointing and shouting excitedly.

"No, that's an *exit*," Dean said.

"Oh, who gives a fuck? No one'll care if you go in through there to park yer car. Look! There's no one coming out. Come on, Dean! We might not get a better chance."

Obviously, I'm paraphrasing here and I don't want you to think it was that simple. Dean had four people, all urging him to do roughly the same thing and all saying it at once. At that point, I think the poor man was so flustered that if we'd asked him to give us his wife to sell on the black market he might well have agreed. You might think this is harsh but the power of persuasion is immense, even if it comes from four dickheads who neither know nor care what you actually do. And this was proved true when Dean suddenly grabbed the steering wheel hard and swung the car down the side street, making for the car park exit that would provide us with an entrance.

Within minutes, no, let me rephrase that, within a matter of seconds, the car was halted by hoards of Mansfield yobs standing in the middle of the road and pressing their ugly, demented faces against the windscreen. They knew we were Chesterfield fans: we'd washed! That and the fact that we were the ones driving the wrong way down a one-way street in their town. I suppose that does kind of give it away a little, doesn't it? I can't begin to describe the vile things they were saying. A lot of it wasn't even speech; it was just a series of grunts punctuated by a swear-word they'd obviously heard more educated football fans use. It was slightly scary – or, indeed, very scary – but it was scary in a ridiculous way. Sitting in this tin box, I felt quite safe (perhaps that was still the effects of the alcohol) and I couldn't help but snigger as some of the Mansfield lot climbed up onto Dean's bonnet while others aimed kicks towards various side panels. I dare say Dean wasn't laughing, though. He looked out in horror as their acidic spit started to eat away at his fine paint job. The thumps on top of the car and on the windscreen were getting louder and our smiles were just starting to turn to frowns when... they'd gone, replaced by the reflective glow of half a dozen coppers. Dean wound his window down and explained that we'd taken a wrong turn, and the coppers helped by stopping the traffic on the main road and letting us reverse out. We really were laughing now – in fact, I think even Dean was sniggering – but we all admitted to getting more than a tad nervous back there.

Eventually, Dean parked the car but we were miles from the ground, or appeared to be. We could see the floodlights in the distance but didn't really have time to discuss the way to the ground as no sooner had we got out of the car than we found ourselves running, hotly pursued by another bunch of Scabs. I couldn't believe they were the same ones. These looked a bit younger; not that I saw that much of them as I was always making sure there was as much distance as possible between me and them. All I remember is vaulting a fence and running off across a field in the general direction of the ground. I was pretty fit back then (not 'Corrrrrr, he's a bit of alright' fit but more

'Blimey, he can run fast for a short arse' kind of fit) so I had no problem keeping ahead of my assailants and up with my mates. Well, not until I turned my ankle in a pot-hole. That slowed me down, I can tell you. However, not wanting to get caught and hammered, I carried on running. Then we were jumping over another fence and, suddenly, lo and behold, we were on the road behind the away end. I'm not quite sure how it happened – those fields have probably long since been turned into a housing estate or something – but that was what I vaguely remembered. As for my ankle, well, that really hurt and the next day at the hospital they told me I'd torn my ankle ligaments. (That was my Sunday football season over!)

Back at Field Mill, well, the game was a nightmare. There were over 2,000 Chesterfield supporters among the crowd of 6,000, and this was the biggest attendance at Feel Ill since we'd played there on Boxing Day of 1983. I wonder if all Mansfield's biggest crowds were when they were playing us?

It wasn't long before trouble erupted on the terraces and the police had to work really hard as the fighting spilled over onto the edge of the pitch. In all, the police made over 16 arrests that day and both Chesterfield and Mansfield fans were charged with public order offences, criminal damage and carrying offensive weapons. On top of that, over £1,000 worth of damage was caused to a toilet in the ground, although that does seem rather excessive for the time. I think we could probably have demolished and rebuilt it for that price! It must have been one hell of a fancy toilet to do that amount of damage, that's all I can say. This is Field Mill, for God's sake, not Buckingham Palace! Also, one poor policeman was detained in hospital with concussion and bruising and a Chesterfield fan was bailed until May 8th for this assault.

Despite fighting on the pitch and fans being ejected throughout the game, play was not affected, which was a shame really as it wasn't the greatest ever game. It had 0–0 written all over it right from the first whistle and I can't remember if it was a result that suited anyone or not but, with nine games to go, it would take the mother of all fuck-ups to blow this one. But this was Chesterfield; anything was still possible.

Inching Ever Closer

Wins at home to Swindon (1–0) and then away at Tranmere (1–0) edged us ever closer to that glorious promised land of promotion, only for a dire 2–0 defeat at Wrexham to bring us all back down to earth with a bump. However, three successive 1–0 wins (at home to Torquay, away at Southend and then, the most famous one, away at Stockport) guaranteed us promotion. All we had to fight for now was the right to be the Champions. A 3–1 home victory over Crewe meant that a solitary point at Peterborough would be enough for us to be crowned Champions.

Someone said to me that night: "We ought to take a coach to Peterborough. That'll be a great day!"

I agreed. A day out at Peterborough watching us win the league was just what we needed and, after all, we *had* to be there, after everything we'd been through this season. And, somehow, despite me only having agreed with the original statement, it was decreed that *I* would be running that coach. To be honest, I seem to think that most of the passengers knew I was running it even before I did but, with it seemingly being cast in stone, I couldn't let them down, could I? Trust me, I wanted to, as my record in running coaches hadn't been great thus far. And, as I set the wheels in motion, the fact that my one previous attempt to run a coach to a game had failed, due to a distinct lack of numbers, was playing on my mind ever so slightly. But I shouldn't have worried; the whole thing went like clockwork. Well, almost.

This Will Be The Last Time

May 6th, 1985 Peterborough Utd 0 v 0 Chesterfield

I wanted this trip to be different. I didn't want it to be marred by violence or yobbish behaviour. I wanted to see 52 youths (or however many the coach held) behave impeccably and then see all those youths come home again after we'd won the Division 4 Championship.

When I looked at my charges that morning I knew I was asking for a little too much. Don't get me wrong, I didn't have any problems at all with anyone on the bus. As far as I can remember, I knew them all and I got on with them all, to a degree. I also knew, though, that while most of them were absolutely no trouble whatsoever, some of them, if pushed, would react; and, so, with this thought in mind, I had to assume that I wouldn't be coming back with a full load.

Now, apart from my one sojourn into the travel market when I tried to take over a Wynnie's Tours trip to Hereford, I had absolutely no idea about organising a coach to anywhere and expected lots of problems. However, I was surprised at how easily this trip came together. In fact, at one point I was even thinking that I might be able to run two coaches because, unlike my last fruitless venture, getting people signed up for this one was like shooting fish in a barrel. People were actually phoning *me*, asking if I had any places left! A very privileged position to be in, I can tell you. Okay, I wasn't *Thomas Cook* just yet – but, then, everyone has to start somewhere. With only days to go before the off, I had the money in (well, most of it), the deposit paid to *Slack's* of Tansley, and I was busy working out the best route to Peterborough that incorporated calling in at a proper hostelry. Now, without the aid of an atlas and a Good Beer Guide from that time, I'm afraid I'm not in a position to tell you which village I'd chosen just outside Peterborough for this stop or, for that matter, the name of the pub. All I can remember is that we turned right at the last major roundabout and ambled into a sleepy little village. I know the pub was a *Bateman's* pub as I'd chosen it specifically. I'd figured that as I was running the bus, then it was only fair that I got to say where we enjoyed our pre-match booze-up – which would, hopefully, be our pre-Championship booze-up!

As the bus pulled alongside the pub and into the car park, I stood up to lead the way. Again, I didn't see why I should have to wait behind 50 youths to get served. And, then, the driver double-sixed me. As I was stepping down towards the door, he said, "You *have* contacted them to see if they'll accept a coach party, haven't you?"

I looked at him aghast! Of course I fuckin' hadn't! Who did he think I was: *Thomas Cook*?! I didn't really need to answer him back because the shocked, blank look on my face told him all he needed to know.

"Well, perhaps you'd better go and see them, then, and see if they will."

I really hadn't reckoned on this and contacting the pub beforehand had never crossed my mind for a second. Obviously, the driver had more experience in this area than I had but, then, that goes without saying really. My problem was how to approach the landlord of a sleepy village pub and get him to see the advantages of 50-odd youths trampling all over his property.

Slowly, I walked inside and faced a deserted pub. Literally deserted. There wasn't even anyone behind the bar! I looked around and coughed and made as much noise as one person could make whilst standing still, leaning on a bar, and, eventually, was presented with a chubby, ruddy-faced man who was obviously the landlord. He smiled. It was a bemused smile because I don't think he was that used to seeing people in his pub at dinner-time.

"Hello!" he beamed. "And what can we be doing for you?"

"Errrrrrrrrr," I began, nervously. "I was just wondering if you'd accept a coach party?"

I must admit, I did omit the bit about it being a coach party of Chesterfield fans but, then, I figured that once we were in he would work that out for himself. Mind you, I think he'd stopped thinking when I said the words 'coach' and 'party.' I swear to God, you could hear 'KERCHING' echoing around behind those wonderful, smiling eyes.

He carried on staring at me for what seemed like an eternity. I did think he was mulling it over at first but, now, I realise he was just unable to speak. He simply couldn't believe his luck and was about to make as much money in an afternoon as he usually made in a week!

"Coach party? Ehm, yes. Why, yes, that's no problem! That's great! Yes, of course!" At this point he turned away from me and shouted, "Jeeeeeaaaaannnnn, I'm going to need some help in the bar... and bring our Sam!"

I walked out of the bar and stood outside, beside the bar door, and in my most nonchalant fashion beckoned everyone to join me. I felt like I'd just brokered the Treaty of Versailles! The driver had done a wonderful job of keeping everyone corralled in the bus; a little bit like the dog controlling the sheep on *One Man and His Dog* while I, the shepherd, went and opened the gates.

To say we had a terrific time in that pub would be something of an understatement. People were literally dancing on the tables, and the landlord seemed perfectly happy with it and even positively encouraged it! All the bar staff were exceptionally pleasant and, in fact, the landlord's daughter was gorgeous, so much so that I kept away from the rowdiness of the other bar and kept her talking in the quiet snug. I say I kept her talking but that's not strictly true. For a great deal of the time she was in the other room thrashing the crap out of everyone at pool. She was nothing if not a hustler: standing there, looking all gorgeous and batting her eyelids whilst pretending she'd never heard of this game before with the pointy stick and balls. With her pockets full of change, it soon became apparent that she knew more about the game of pool than our lot put together! It was only after she'd robbed everyone that she came and talked to me. Nothing happened, of course – well, not unless you count getting a free steak sandwich and chips as a happening – as I was way too shy for anything like that. On the beer front, quite a few of us were drinking the exceptionally quaffable *Bateman's* while most of the younger element were drinking bottled lagers, so much so that, as we wandered out to get on the coach, the landlord was stacking the empty crates beside the door!

"Surely we didn't drink all that!" I laughed, and he smiled the 'Oh-yes-you-did-smile' back.

To be honest, if it hadn't been for the driver we might still have been in there now as it was he who alerted us to the fact that we really ought to be getting going. So, we waved goodbye to our host of the last couple of hours and he wished us well on our quest for the solitary point and said that if we got it we might like to come back that night and celebrate. Wow! That was some offer – although I'm not sure what his regulars would have made of it.

We were a happy bunch as we entered Peterborough. The beer had seduced most of us but, when the driver opened the door, there were a couple of lads who obviously hadn't been seduced enough as their first words on seeing a couple of Borough fans were along the lines of, "Oi, you fuckin' wankers!" They were, I believe, going to make merry with fans of said club but, to be honest, their feet never actually touched the tarmac as two police officers came up alongside, grabbed the more vocal of the two and slung him in a police van. I was going to be one short for the journey home and the game hadn't even started! Not the perfect opening – but, then, that was their fault, not mine.

We knew Peterborough's ground well and we were aware that the away end had a huge fence around it; something which would no doubt impede our celebrations should the solitary point be gained. Some of us had considered standing on the open side of the ground with the less vocal Borough fans and keeping our mouths shut for 90 minutes. Then, come the final whistle, we could invade the pitch and celebrate with our heroes. However, in the end, perhaps because of the police presence, we all trooped into that away end for one of the most important games we'd ever seen in our Chesterfield FC supporting days.

As we stood there, craning our necks in a vain attempt to see what was happening on the pitch, I noticed Simon from off our bus who had sneaked into the home end, unnoticed. The crafty pillock had obviously realised that while ever he was with 20 or so youths he was always going to attract attention, so he waited till we were in the ground and did a U-turn. We did our best to blow his cover but he didn't even look at us or acknowledge us or show any sign of emotion throughout the entire game. Now, that in itself wasn't particularly difficult as it was quite a dull affair. But we did get the point we were after and we were the Champions!

As soon as the final whistle blew, Simon was over the small wall, celebrating with the team, and I envied him so much. He wasn't the only one; others had done a similar thing. But, for most of us, we just tried to cheer the lads for securing the title. Oh, life can, occasionally, be sweet.

Eventually, we boarded the bus and headed home. There was a lot of talk about staying in Peterborough and making sure we got our friend out of the police station. The driver was given more than one set of instructions but he didn't seem to mind whether we turned around and went back or carried on home. I think, in the end, we realised it was fruitless going back and, so, we pointed the bus towards Chesterfield and headed home as Champions. There was some discussion about celebrating with our new friend in the pub but the general consensus was to get back to town and celebrate, which was a shame because no one was celebrating in town. Honestly, it was really very strange. The moment we stepped off the bus we realised that we should have been back in the pub near Peterborough but, hey-ho, it had been one epic day.

In truth, it had been one hell of a season. The team's strength had been its ability not to lose and we had, in fact, lost only six league games throughout the entire season. The final act was played out at Saltergate in front of a crowd of 7,006 who witnessed a drab 0–0 draw with Rochdale but, more importantly, witnessed the presentation of the Championship trophy.

But it wasn't all sweetness and light on the footballing front. On the national scene, 38 people died during the European Cup Final and suddenly football violence was high on the agenda again. There were talks about ID cards, clubs being responsible for their fans (which is like asking me to be responsible for next door's cats – ludicrous!) and all manner of injunctions. The *Daily Mail* would have had every football supporter hanging from lampposts, regardless of whether they'd committed a crime or not. It generally all went a bit bonkers. It just gave a little more ammunition to those who wanted to continue to treat football supporters like cattle and, so, shoving us into pens was acceptable behaviour for many a year – and we all know what that led to, don't we?

But, for now, we were promoted. We could drink from the fountain of success at last. It had been the best possible high. Well, it had until the club received notification from the Football League that it would need a safety certificate for the following year and this would cost upwards of £250,000 in improvements – money the club didn't have. The following week the Chesterfield Supporters Club launched SOS: 'Save Our Saltergate.'

Happy days, eh? As if you'd get anything like that happening in this day and age...

Town fans making their presence felt at Stockport 84/85

Another view of the town fans at Stockport in 84/85

Another view of the town fans at Stockport in 84/85

The celebrations started before we even kicked of at Peterborough in 84/85 with Chesterfield fans in fancy dress having a great time on the pitch

Some Chesterfield players were blessed before the Peterborough game... although I'm not sure if it counts for much when it's a priest accompanied by a gorilla and assorted clowns

Ernie celebrates with the crowd after we won the championship title in 84/85

Ferguson celebrates our 0-0 draw at Peterborough in 84/85 with the Chesterfield fans. The league title is ours!

Some Kind Of Back Pass
A CAUTIONARY TALE
November 21st, 1987 Chesterfield 1 v 1 Sunderland

As I have constantly said in these tales, I'm no hooligan. I have a very low pain threshold. Basically, I'm a coward and the thought of fighting with a bunch of rival fans is something that's about as far away from my mind as Mansfield is to being called 'home.' But – ah yes, sadly, there is a but – I *have* strayed, just the once, from underneath the halo of being 'Mr Perfect Supporter.' Who knows? Perhaps we all have in some small way. The difference here, of course, is that I'm about to tell you of my indiscretion whereas *you*, no doubt, will keep your bloody mouths shut. (Well, you will if you have any sense.) Having spent the last hundred thousand words or so trying to impress upon you what a thoroughly decent sort of fellow I am, this memory comes with a health warning – not for anyone reading, but for me! The embarrassment accompanying this confession makes me squirm even now, sitting here, typing it up. I want nothing more than to leave it be and go and make a cup of tea. Yet, I'm about to spill my guts out on these pages, all for my art. What a twat! But, less of *Les Miserables* and on with the Panto!

The reason I call this part 'A Cautionary Tale' is because, hopefully, it will show you that anyone can get involved in football violence. Really, it's easy! By this, I don't mean they can be seduced by it; I just mean they can find they're in a little deeper than they ever thought possible.

Now the incident I'm going to tell you about happened back in 1987/88 (so much more recent than anything else I've written) but, even so, back then I was the same amicable, friendly, smiling, young man you'll find today – except that I had more hair! Football violence hadn't gone away completely but it certainly wasn't the tabloid, headline-grabbing phenomenon it had been some four or five years earlier. That could have been down to better policing, as well as the fact that the emphasis had seemingly shifted from club to country. It would be wrong to suggest that football violence never happened, just as it would be wrong to suggest that it doesn't go on today. However, whatever the reason, football crowds were controlled and policed in a much better way than they had ever been before, so how I managed to let myself get dragged into the goings on after this particular game is anyone's guess.

Thinking back to 1987/88 is like recalling a particular tooth extraction without anaesthetic. We managed to stay in Division 3 but, to this day, I don't know how. Excitement on the football field wasn't exactly at a premium; in fact, it would be fair to say that the bowel movements I had that season were far more exciting than anything being passed off as entertainment at Chesterfield. Yes, this was the season of that humiliating 10–0 thrashing at Gillingham!

The Sunderland game was an important game for both sides. We desperately needed the points to haul our arses out of the relegation zone, while Sunderland were just as eager to snatch the points and push their noses ever closer to the Championship and promotion. It was a typical November day, wet and cool(ish), and Saltergate was muddy – what you might call a perfect day for football. Now me, being the saintly little person that I am, I was in the ground at half past two, soaking up the atmosphere, adrenalin pumping, on the Kop, no problem. Sunderland had brought a fair few fans and turned our average 2,200 gate into a 5,700 best-home-gate-of-the-season job. I think Sunderland were top of the table at the time but were being pushed hard by Brighton. (Sunderland won the league by 9 clear points in the end.) To be fair, though, the side we put out that day should have been thumped into the tail end of next week. I'm sure they won't thank me for saying that, especially as Muggleton, Rogers, Bloomer, Waller and Arnott were nothing short of gods in their own way, but they were having to make up for a lot of deficiencies in other areas.

The massed ranks of Chesterfield supporters on the Kop gave it their all. Please correct me if I'm mistaken but, with about 20 minutes to go, Mr Hewitt stepped up from his right back berth, pounced on a loose ball and lashed one past the keeper from about 20 yards. A truly stunning goal. To be honest, if it had gone in off his arse I would have thought it was a stunning goal! Any goal against a team that is riding high at the top of the league and turns up acting as if they're playing below themselves will always be treated as stunning in my book. Whether we deserved to be in front is anyone's guess and, to be honest, who bloody cares! It was marvellous, magic, brill. And, boy, did we need those points? My God, how we needed those points. Sunderland, however, were made of sterner stuff and they pushed hard for the equaliser. We whistled for full-time. Even with 15 minutes to go, we were whistling!

And then it happened – that moment that, as football fans, we all hate: some twonker in a red and white shirt fell over and, for the thirteenth time that afternoon, the massed ranks of Mackems[6] screamed yet again for a penalty. It wasn't, of course; not in my blue and white world. It never looked like a penalty, but the referee was under immense pressure. It was at the Cross Street end of the ground. Their fans were baying for it, their players were surrounding him and, like the yellow-livered shit we all knew he was, he caved in under the pressure and gave it.

Needless to say, they scored. Needless to say, I was pissed off. I felt like a schoolboy unfairly chastised, robbed of my points. There is nothing worse than watching away supporters dance in delight at a goal, especially when there's a lot of them. It feels almost personal. At such times, I half expect a banner to be shoved into the air saying, "YAH-BOO, RADFORD." Crazy, I know, but that's how it is. They were happy with the point they'd gained during injury time; and we were like parrots... sick as, of course.

As soon as the penalty hit the net some Chesterfield fans left the ground, not because they were fed up but because they wanted to see if there were any stray Sunderland fans hanging around on any street corners waiting for lifts. As my brother, a few of his mates and I dragged our weary feet down to the bus stop, we could hear the commotion as rival gangs met up somewhere behind us. We didn't care. When we got down as far as *Boots* a big but quite ordinary lad came up to us. I wouldn't have classed him as being particularly thuggish but he did seem to know me. As I've travelled with just about every hooligan known to Chesterfield Constabulary over the years, then it's quite possible that he did recognise me. I can't say I knew him and, indeed, I can't say I've ever seen him again to this day – and even if I had I wouldn't tell you. It never crossed my mind that he might be looking for Sunderland fans, not even when he looked at me and said, "Loads of 'em abaat?"

"Yes, I suppose there will be," I replied.

---

[6] Derogatory term for Sunderland and its inhabitants; most probably first coined by the folk of Newcastle.

Now, it could be that he asked me this question to ascertain my accent, I really don't know, but I do think he genuinely clocked us as Chesterfield fans. Perhaps it was the slumped shoulders and dragging feet that gave us away. In the end, it doesn't really matter. There was a little bit of a conversation about what a bunch of jammy toe-rags they were, or words to that effect, and we were just about to carry on walking down to the library steps and on to the bus station when our friendly thug spotted four Sunderland fans walking towards us.

"Here's some," he said, convinced in his ability to spot away fans at 100 paces.

They weren't covered in red and white scarves or singing jubilant Sunderland songs but they did stick out like four sore thumbs. They were walking along, heads straight forward, and weren't saying a word. That was the give-away, really. If they'd been talking to each other, or pointing at things, or pushing one another, they may have got away with it; although, when you think about the accent, I doubt it very much.

Anyway, they were only young lads but they were big and tall. As they silently passed us, our friendly thug walked up to one of them and said, "Have you got the time, mate?" and, rather than answer, the lad just held up his wrist and showed him his watch. If he was deaf, then the sign language he gave was that of someone saying, *'I'm from Sunderland, smack me!'* Of course, the silence was all the Town fan needed and, so, without any further analysis of the situation, he larruped the guy in the chops. And I mean, larruped! It was a real stinger. I think we were all a bit shocked and we all just stood there, looking at this Sunderland fan grovelling around on the floor, when the Chesterfield fan shouted, "Gerrum!"

Now, the rest happened very quickly, but I can hardly offer that as my defence. The fact of the matter is that, once the Chesterfield fan had shouted 'Gerrum,' three of the Sunderland fans, including the lad who'd been punched, were off and running down Low Pavements, while the other lad bolted the other way and ran down between *Boots* and *McDonalds* towards the library steps. Everyone seemed to be going in different directions and, basically, it was just general confusion. (Well, that's my excuse and I'm sticking to it.) Without really realising it, I found myself chasing the three Sunderland fans down Low Pavements. Alone! I also felt sure I'd seen my brother disappearing down past *Boots* after the other Sunderland fan, and this in itself was a shock to me. However, it wasn't as big a shock as *me* chasing someone, I can tell you!

Now, back then, as I've mentioned before, I was a bit nippy with the old running malarkey – and before I knew what was happening I was gaining on them! Me! Chasing three Sunderland fans. If they'd stopped and turned and confronted me, they would have kicked the living crap out of me. But fortune favours the brave or, in this case, the stupid. When it finally dawned on me that I was actually gaining on them, I started to get worried. What happens if I actually catch them? What do I do then? I really hadn't considered these options at all. One thing was definite: if I wanted to walk back into town with some sort of credibility (not to mention a face that my mother would recognise – intact) then I had to make sure I didn't catch them. However, I couldn't just stop. 'Why?' you may well ask, and I think you would have every right to ask that very sane and normal question. Well, here's the really stupid bit: I couldn't stop because people were watching! Market traders packing up their stalls had all taken time out to watch this chase and I'm thinking, *"Blimey, what will they say?"* They would probably have said that it was a wise move, but I didn't think that at the time. So I kept running, rather than lose face, and, heaven knows, that was surely what was going to happen if I caught up with them.

So, instead of stopping and giving in like the coward that I was, I started to slow down. It was hardly noticeable at first. It was like a really fast version of the moon walk: my legs were going like the clappers but I wasn't covering half as much ground as I should have been. (Michael Jackson, eat your heart out!) Eventually, I got slower... and slower... and slower. I was like a mime artist pretending to run against the wind through really thick mud. And before you could say, 'Look at that yellow-bellied bastard!' there was absolutely no chance of me catching them and, more importantly, of them catching me. As far as I was concerned, I was really subtle but, then, that's just in my mind. If someone had told me I'd screeched to a halt and done a swift about turn, I wouldn't be at all surprised. I gradually gave up the chase and, like someone who'd just watched his bus disappear up the road after running 50 yards to catch it, I sort of swatted the air with my fist in mock aggravation as if I was really disappointed that they'd managed to slip away from me. And I felt a right pillock, I can tell you. It must have been the single most stupid gesture ever, by anyone, at any time. I walked back to where I'd left my brother and tried to hide my embarrassment under a cloak of bravado – but I think I failed miserably.

As for Mr Thug, well, he seems to have dropped one punch and then scarpered. No one had any idea where he went or what he did after belting the youth in the kisser. Where did he disappear to? Was he the ghost of violence past? Or did he just have a happy knack of kicking-off brawls and then melting into the background? I suppose by doing that you can be assured of an arrest-free evening from the police.

For Chesterfield FC's newest 'never-would-be' hooligans, it was a quiet bus ride home. No one really spoke of the incident at all and I know *I* was far too embarrassed to bring it up as a conversation piece. And, despite seeing my brother chase a Sunderland fan down towards the library, I decided I wouldn't even ask what had happened down there as *he* might have been ashamed of that fact, too. If anything had happened, then that would be something he would have to live with. However, years later I did ask him and, trust me, it was years. He smiled impishly as he replayed the night in his head and told me that he had, indeed, pursued the youth round by *Boots* and down towards the library but it seems the Sunderland fan had taken the corner so hard that he'd slipped and fallen over. My brother Chris rounded the corner to find the lad grovelling on the floor and he looked up at my brother, resigning himself to a good kicking. It just so happens that our Chris was made of the same backbone as me, and so he stuttered to a halt, looked at the fan on the floor, shrugged his shoulders, and then turned round and walked back to join his mates. The Sunderland fan got back up onto his feet and, presumably, made his way back to his fellow travellers.

You can just imagine the conversation when they all joined up at their car, can't you? One would be sporting a bruised jaw, while another would be telling of the fan whose idea of giving you a good kicking was to shrug his shoulders and walk off, while the rest would be either telling their own tales or laughing about the Chesterfield fan who ran like Michael Jackson in mud.

In all seriousness, if you had to pick someone to chase a load of football supporters down the street, then I wouldn't make your top 1,000. I'm really not the man for the job. I'm not now and I certainly wasn't back then. And, yet, for some strange reason, I bloody did it! In fact, as soon as the youth shouted 'Gerrum,' I bet we all moved; it's just that the others had a bit more about them. Common sense clicked in at the right time. My common sense was still reeling on the terraces from the cruel injury-time penalty. I could have stopped running earlier, I admit, but I guess I was just too bloody stupid. And that, dear readers, is my one and only indiscretion. HONEST! Ask anyone!

The incident did change my views on violence, though. I mean, if some dick can shout 'Gerrum' and get a mummy's boy like me to charge down the road, then perhaps we are all capable of it in some form. Or perhaps I'm just trying to make excuses again. Yes, we might all be capable; but it's bloody worrying when you realise that you actually did it!

So, there you have it: my one brief moment as a football hooligan. But one memory from that day haunts me more than any other. I will never, ever, forget the look on the face of one old dear I ran past in my fake pursuit. She gave me that 'bloody hooligans' look and I desperately wanted to stop and tell her that I wasn't a hooligan. I wanted more than anything to stop and explain what had actually happened and, if she'd looked carefully, she would have seen that I was, indeed, slowing down. But she would never have believed me and would probably have worked me over with her brolly into the bargain!

Now, this tale might not mean much to you. You may well have been involved in much greater skirmishes or, indeed, you may now feel like looking down your nose at me for being so gullible. But for someone who had spent his life trying to avoid any confrontation whatsoever, this was, and still is, agonisingly painful.

Where It All Began

Or

Ejection Night Special

Football League Cup First Round First Leg

August 30th, 1988 Port Vale 3 v 2 Chesterfield

The reason for writing these articles in the first place is because of what happened on this infamous night. Because I felt I had been wronged and because I was so stroppy about the whole affair, I decided to write to

Stuart Basson at the *Crooked Spireite*.[7] Yes, that would see justice prevail and no mistake. Well, it would get it off my chest and make me feel a bit better about the whole thing. You see, we all have our Achilles heel, and mine is that I've never been able to handle taking the blame for something I haven't done. Even to this day, blame me for something that is someone else's fault at your peril because, before you know what's happening, I'll have the League of Nations, the UN, Batman and the A Team all fighting for my just cause. If I've done something wrong, then I'll admit it. I'll hold up my hands and say, "Sorry, guv, that's my fault." Admittedly, this latter trait is one that has come about through age and some vague sort of wisdom. I'll be the first to admit that when I was a kid I was a right dishonest little twat, as I'm sure my mother, God bless her, would vouch for (only not in those words exactly).

So, yes, these stories all started in Burslem, home of Port Vale FC. There I was, standing on the open terrace in the drizzle (why does it always drizzle or rain when I go to Burslem?), having just spent the last of my dole money to gain entry to the stadium and taken out a mortgage on what can only loosely be described as a meat pie, when one of the boys in blue ushered me to one side. He explained that he was going to eject me from the ground for, apparently, "flicking a wank." After mopping away the tears of mirth, I enquired what exactly that entailed – and he showed me. He flicked one at me! I must admit that, whilst I did know the universal gesture for the five-fingered shuffle, I can't say I'd ever thought of giving it a name. Yes, I'd given that gesture to people in the past, usually as part of a joke or during a Sunday football match, but I'd never gone into the changing rooms and said to my team mates, "I've just flicked a wank at their right back!" So, when I asked the constable what he meant by that saying, I was being completely honest. I had absolutely no idea what he was talking about and when he circled his fingers and moved them up and down in a masturbatory motion in front of my face I was more than a little shocked!

The reason for my apparent misdemeanour was because of a shot from a Port Vale player that went so wide of the target he nearly missed the country. Such was the mirth of every Chesterfield supporter there that night that we all parted our arms wide, in time-honoured fashion,

---

[7] Chesterfield Fanzine, first published January 1988. Ran for a good six years, if memory serves – ah, happy days indeed.

just to show how much he'd missed by. I, on the other hand, decided to wave the ball goodbye, too, as it was the last we would see of the thing that evening. I must admit, I didn't realise I was contravening some ancient Burslem by-law: *'Thou must not remindeth yon home fans of how shite their team's shooting is, unless thou wanteth to be charged by ye Olde Bill!'* So, perhaps you can understand me when I say I wasn't exactly quaking in my boots and looking around thinking, *"Have they seen me? Oh, my God, what will I do if they've seen me?"* I admit that one or two people had flicked wanks, although, personally, I don't like the gesture. Well, not over a distance of about 150 yards anyway. It's far more subtle when done to someone close to you (that would be 'close' as in 'in the vicinity,' not as in someone you're emotionally tied to). However, I'm pretty sure it was the waving that did me. Perhaps in Burslem waving is akin to flicking a wank? I will never know and I really don't care. I only know that I was innocent. Thinking back, I suppose I was just asking for trouble; after all, the police had been down earlier to tell us to stop singing and not to get too excited if we scored. Honestly, what a ridiculous thing to say! I went to football matches for that very reason: to get excited. Telling me not to is like the wife or girlfriend looking up at you and mentioning that the ceiling needs painting just as you start to do a reasonable impression of Goofy.

However, the policeman was very sure of my guilt and gave me a long lecture on how it was "not very nice" to make gestures like that. I spluttered and pointed and pleaded my innocence but he was convinced I'd done wrong. In the end, I just thought I'd let him get on with it and then I could get back to watching the game instead of trying to stare over his shoulder at the action. And this, my friends, is where it all went a bit pear-shaped. I never, not in a zillion years, thought he would do any more than tell me off. I've been bollocked before, and by far more frightening people than him, so a telling-off by a twelve-year-old policeman was nothing. (I was even told off once by the Old Bill at Chester for excessive swearing.) Away to my left, I could hear my friends laughing, although I use the word 'friends' lightly as they have all been cut from my social circle now and never receive Christmas cards. (Yes, Lee Richards. Yes, Richard Wort. You know who you are.) I was about to turn around and rejoin them when said constable grabbed my shoulder and started to pull me along with him.

"What are you doing?" I enquired.

He looked at me as if I was some kind of imbecile who had never been thrown out of a football ground before. (Well, he certainly got the last bit right.)

"Are you throwing me out?" I said.

He just carried on walking me towards what I thought was the exit.

"But I haven't done anything. I didn't do anything. You can't throw me out for no reason."

And I still couldn't quite believe what was happening. Half of me was thinking, *"Go away, I want to watch the match,"* while the other half was still trying to get to grips with the situation. But he didn't go away or, rather, he did but I had to go with him!

As the policeman led me away, my pleas of innocence became more frantic and I offered him everything from money to sheep. Even my last ditch cries of, "I'm a mason, I'm a mason," fell upon deaf ears. Suddenly, it wasn't funny anymore. My so-called friends may have had tears rolling down their cheeks but I was apoplectic with rage! This was it, the big one, the red card. After 20 years of football supporting, I was getting my first 'premature ejaculation' from a football ground.

The actual process of being thrown out was quite humiliating. If I'd been taken to a side door and cobbed out onto the street, then fair enough. It would have been unpleasant and I would felt hard done by; so much so that, once home, I would have written letters to Port Vale FC and Staffordshire Constabulary complaining about blind policemen and the need for investing in training on gesticulatory techniques. But, no. Just chucking me out would have been too easy. Instead, I was taken to some grotty portakabin tucked away in a far corner of the ground where an exceptionally unpleasant police sergeant was waiting. He just looked angry. He just looked as if he didn't want to be there and dealing with people like me didn't make his life any easier. To say he treated me like something he'd brought into the room on his shoe would be a massive understatement. I don't know. Perhaps his wife was having an affair with his dog (hope so); or perhaps he just didn't like football or the supporters of said game. Either way, he was thoroughly unpleasant.

The sergeant sat me down and he took photographs of me from the front and from the side. He growled at me a lot and then returned to his desk and started writing out some kind of report. At first, I thought I was going to be there all night — it certainly took a lot longer than I'd anticipated — but, in the end, the sergeant, who had a face like a gnarled-up old testicle, shoved a piece of paper in my hand and then shouted for the other bobby to come and get me. The piece of paper turned out to be an eviction notice and it stated quite clearly that if I was ever thrown out at Port Vale or Stoke City again, then I would be banned from their grounds for life! I thought that was a tad heavy-handed considering I hadn't done anything wrong. To be fair, it would have been a tad heavy-handed if you *had* committed the offence. I could have imagined being handed such a document if I'd run amok with a brick and given a single finger salute to every copper in the ground, but for waving…? Oh, boy, don't get me started.

When PC Nice Bobby (the one who arrested me in the first place) arrived back in the hut he took my arm and escorted me to a side door. He opened it and let me out onto the street.

"Goodnight, Mr Radford," he said very cheerfully.

I looked at him with my mouth wide open and completely unable to speak. Mr Radford! Mr fuckin' Radford! *'Oh, we're all sweetness and light now, aren't we, you sycophantic twat!'* was what I wanted to say. Instead, I just dribbled on my jacket, as he closed the door with a wave. (Or was *he* flicking a wank!?) In the end, I managed to say goodnight back, only it started with an 'F' and ended with 'off!' But I was angry. I was innocent. I hadn't actually done anything wrong. I hadn't actually done anything! Okay, so I was being thrown out of a football league ground. Big deal! Thousands more have had similar experiences. But it was as if I'd been charged with grievous bodily harm when all I'd actually done was help an old lady onto a bus.

I trooped around the ground for ten minutes or so until I found a suitably placed wall to sit on where I could see half of the pitch, so I did get to see some action. I was eventually joined by a Port Vale fan who had been thrown out for fighting his own fans. I was a bit worried at first but he was okay; just a silly bugger. However, when I showed him my eviction notice he couldn't believe it.

"I get chucked out most weeks," he boasted. "Never had one of them."

After the match I returned to the car where my brother and his mate Mark were waiting for me. They had huge smiles on their faces but I was really pissed off. I was annoyed, more than anything, and wanted them to be annoyed as well. But they weren't; they just laughed. To be fair, had I been in their shoes I would have laughed, too – but I wasn't and I didn't. As my innocence seemed to be such a huge joke, I told my brother that I'd been done for making rude and obscene gestures and was to appear in court on the Friday. That knocked a few smiles sideways, I can tell you, and I don't think my brother was that pleased either when I told him I was winding him up – although, to be fair, he did say he'd take the day off work and drive me down for the hearing. Bless!

The following Saturday, Mark gave me a cartoon he'd drawn of the whole incident (which, I confess, I still have and I still find funny, despite the fact that he draws like a 4-year-old). I've got to say, I did think the whole idea of an eviction notice was a bit stupid, really. I mean, how on earth are they going to remember my face among all the other football supporters they see week in, week out? So I wasn't particularly worried when I went back to Vale a few weeks later for the league game. But, as I left the ground on that occasion, the copper who'd thrown me out walked up to me and said, "You were much better behaved tonight," or words to that effect. 'Stunned' is one word to describe my reaction. Just a shame he hadn't noticed how well behaved I was the previous visit!

I still have my ejection notice, somewhere, but I bet they wouldn't remember me now; not that I intend to test this theory by going back to Vale Park and flicking a wank, that is.

What really hurt, though, was that a couple of seasons later I was watching the FA Cup highlights on the BBC and they were showing Port Vale v Everton. As I write, I cringe with injustice. The Everton fans were congregated behind one of the goals – a goodly number of them, too. As Port Vale attacked that goal in the first half, some white-shirted valiant sliced the ball horribly wide when he really should have done better. Almost to a man, it seemed, the Everton fans stood and jeered and flicked wanks. And they held their arms wide denoting the mileage by which the ball had missed the goal. Then they sat back down again and the game continued. The moment I saw them gesticulating, I pulled myself to the edge of my seat and waited for the police to wade in and throw them out for making rude and obscene gestures. *"They have to, surely,"* I thought. They threw *me* out when I was innocent. How could this bunch of Merseyside nob-heads be left to wantonly flick wanks without the slightest protestation from the police? Justice? Huh!

So there you have it: an inglorious end to a not-so-glorious decade and a bit of watching Town. It would be nice to say that football violence went quietly away but it didn't; it continued, in its own fashion. I've had hairy moments at several grounds around the country but, despite all this, I've continued to keep my nose *very, very clean!*

KEEP THE FAITH!

ND - #0020 - 101121 - C0 - 234/156/27 - PB - 9781780354187 - Gloss Lamination